Clinical Practice Guideline

Treating Tobacco Use and Dependence: 2008 Update

Guideline Panel

Michael C. Fiore, MD, MPH
  (Panel Chair)
Carlos Roberto Jaén, MD, PhD, FAAFP
  (Panel Vice Chair)
Timothy B. Baker, PhD
  (Senior Scientist)
William C. Bailey, MD, FACP, FCCP
Neal L. Benowitz, MD
Susan J. Curry, PhD
Sally Faith Dorfman, MD, MSHSA
Erika S. Froelicher, PhD, RN, MA, MPH
Michael G. Goldstein, MD
Cheryl G. Healton, DrPH
Patricia Nez Henderson, MD, MPH

Richard B. Heyman, MD
Howard K. Koh, MD, MPH, FACP
Thomas E. Kottke, MD, MSPH
Harry A. Lando, PhD
Robert E. Mecklenburg, DDS, MPH
Robin J. Mermelstein, PhD
Patricia Dolan Mullen, DrPH
C. Tracy Orleans, PhD
Lawrence Robinson, MD, MPH
Maxine L. Stitzer, PhD
Anthony C. Tommasello, PhD, MS
Louise Villejo, MPH, CHES
Mary Ellen Wewers, PhD, MPH, RN

Guideline Liaisons

Ernestine W. Murray, RN, BSN, MAS, (Project Officer), Agency for Healthcare Research
  and Quality
Glenn Bennett, MPH, CHES, National Heart, Lung, and Blood Institute
Stephen Heishman, PhD, National Institute on Drug Abuse
Corinne Husten, MD, MPH, Centers for Disease Control and Prevention
Glen Morgan, PhD, National Cancer Institute
Christine Williams, MEd, Agency for Healthcare Research and Quality

Guideline Staff

Bruce A. Christiansen, PhD (Project Director)
Megan E. Piper, PhD (Project Scientist)
Victor Hasselblad, PhD (Project Statistician)
David Fraser, MS (Project Coordinator)
Wendy Theobald, PhD (Editorial Associate)
Michael Connell, BS (Database Manager)
Cathlyn Leitzke, MSN, RN-C (Project Researcher)

D0179869

U.S. Department of Health and Human Services
Public Health Service
May 2008

Guideline Update Development and Use

The 2008 update to *Treating Tobacco Use and Dependence*, a Public Health Service-sponsored Clinical Practice Guideline, is the result of an extraordinary partnership among Federal Government and nonprofit organizations comprised of the Agency for Healthcare Research and Quality; Centers for Disease Control and Prevention; National Cancer Institute; National Heart, Lung, and Blood Institute; National Institute on Drug Abuse; Robert Wood Johnson Foundation; American Legacy Foundation; and University of Wisconsin School of Medicine and Public Health's Center for Tobacco Research and Intervention. Each member of this consortium is dedicated to improving the Nation's public health, and their participation in this collaboration clearly demonstrates a strong commitment to tobacco cessation.

This Guideline is an updated version of the 2000 *Treating Tobacco Use and Dependence* Guideline. It is the product of a private-sector panel of experts ("the Panel"), consortium representatives, and staff. The update was written to include new, effective clinical treatments for tobacco dependence that have become available since the 2000 Guideline was published. *Treating Tobacco Use and Dependence: 2008 Update* will make an important contribution to the quality of care in the United States and the health of the American people.

The Panel employed an explicit, science-based methodology and expert clinical judgment to develop recommendations on the treatment of tobacco use and dependence. Extensive literature searches were conducted, and critical reviews and syntheses were used to evaluate empirical evidence and significant outcomes. Peer reviews were undertaken and public comment invited to evaluate the validity, reliability, and utility of the Guideline for clinical practice. The Panel's recommendations primarily are based on published, evidence-based research. When the evidence was incomplete or inconsistent in a particular area, the recommendations reflect the professional judgment of Panel members.

The recommendations herein may not be appropriate for use in all circumstances and are designed particularly for clinical settings. Decisions to adopt any particular recommendation must be made by clinicians in light of available resources and circumstances presented by individual patients and in light of new clinical information such as that provided by the U.S. Food and Drug Administration (FDA).

This Public Health Service-sponsored Clinical Practice Guideline update gives hope to the 7 out of 10 smokers who visit a clinician each year. This Guideline urges every clinician, health plan, and health care institution to make treating tobacco dependence a top priority during these visits. Please ask your patients two key questions: "Do you smoke?" and "Do you want to quit?" followed by use of the recommendations in this Guideline.

Abstract

Treating Tobacco Use and Dependence: 2008 Update, a Public Health Service-sponsored Clinical Practice Guideline, is a product of the Tobacco Use and Dependence Guideline Panel ("the Panel"), consortium representatives, consultants, and staff. These 37 individuals were charged with the responsibility of identifying effective, experimentally validated tobacco dependence treatments and practices. The updated Guideline was sponsored by a consortium of eight Federal Government and nonprofit organizations: the Agency for Healthcare Research and Quality (AHRQ); Centers for Disease Control and Prevention (CDC); National Cancer Institute (NCI); National Heart, Lung, and Blood Institute (NHLBI); National Institute on Drug Abuse (NIDA); American Legacy Foundation; Robert Wood Johnson Foundation (RWJF); and University of Wisconsin School of Medicine and Public Health's Center for Tobacco Research and Intervention (UW-CTRI). This Guideline is an updated version of the 2000 *Treating Tobacco Use and Dependence: Clinical Practice Guideline* that was sponsored by the U.S. Public Health Service, U. S. Department of Health and Human Services.

An impetus for this Guideline update was the expanding literature on tobacco dependence and its treatment. The original 1996 Guideline was based on some 3,000 articles on tobacco treatment published between 1975 and 1994. The 2000 Guideline entailed the collection and screening of an additional 3,000 articles published between 1995 and 1999. The 2008 Guideline update screened an additional 2,700 articles; thus, the present Guideline update reflects the distillation of a literature base of more than 8,700 research articles. Of course, this body of research was further reviewed to identify a much smaller group of articles that served as the basis for focused Guideline data analyses and review.

This Guideline contains strategies and recommendations designed to assist clinicians; tobacco dependence treatment specialists; and health care administrators, insurers, and purchasers in delivering and supporting effective treatments for tobacco use and dependence. The recommendations were made as a result of a systematic review and meta-analysis of 11 specific topics identified by the Panel (proactive quitlines; combining counseling and medication relative to either counseling or medication alone; varenicline; various medication combinations; long-term medications; cessation interventions for individuals with low socioeconomic status/limited formal education; cessation interventions for adolescent smokers; cessation interventions for pregnant smokers; cessation interventions for individuals with psychiatric disorders, including substance use disorders; providing cessation interventions as a health benefit; and systems interventions, including provider training and the combination of training and systems interventions). The strength of evidence that served as the basis for each recommendation is indicated clearly in the Guideline update. A draft of the Guideline update was peer reviewed prior to publication, and the input of 81 external reviewers was considered by the Panel prior to preparing the final document. In addition, the public had an opportunity to comment through a *Federal Register* review process. The key recommendations of the updated Guideline, *Treating Tobacco Use and Dependence: 2008 Update,* based on the literature review and expert Panel opinion, are as follows:

■ Ten Key Guideline Recommendations

The overarching goal of these recommendations is that clinicians strongly recommend the use of effective tobacco dependence counseling and medication treatments to their patients who use tobacco, and that health systems, insurers, and purchasers assist clinicians in making such effective treatments available.

1. Tobacco dependence is a chronic disease that often requires repeated intervention and multiple attempts to quit. Effective treatments exist, however, that can significantly increase rates of long-term abstinence.

2. It is essential that clinicians and health care delivery systems consistently identify and document tobacco use status and treat every tobacco user seen in a health care setting.

3. Tobacco dependence treatments are effective across a broad range of populations. Clinicians should encourage every patient willing to make a quit attempt to use the counseling treatments and medications recommended in this Guideline.

4. Brief tobacco dependence treatment is effective. Clinicians should offer every patient who uses tobacco at least the brief treatments shown to be effective in this Guideline.

5. Individual, group, and telephone counseling are effective, and their effectiveness increases with treatment intensity. Two components of counseling are especially effective, and clinicians should use these when counseling patients making a quit attempt:

- Practical counseling (problemsolving/skills training)

- Social support delivered as part of treatment

6. Numerous effective medications are available for tobacco dependence, and clinicians should encourage their use by all patients attempting to quit smoking—except when medically contraindicated or with specific populations for which there is insufficient evidence of effectiveness (i.e., pregnant women, smokeless tobacco users, light smokers, and adolescents).

- Seven first-line medications (5 nicotine and 2 non-nicotine) reliably increase long-term smoking abstinence rates:
  – Bupropion SR
  – Nicotine gum
  – Nicotine inhaler
  – Nicotine lozenge
  – Nicotine nasal spray
  – Nicotine patch
  – Varenicline

- Clinicians also should consider the use of certain combinations of medications identified as effective in this Guideline.

7. Counseling and medication are effective when used by themselves for treating tobacco dependence. The combination of counseling and medication, however, is more effective than either alone. Thus, clinicians should encourage all individuals making a quit attempt to use both counseling and medication.

8. Telephone quitline counseling is effective with diverse populations and has broad reach. Therefore, both clinicians and health care delivery systems should ensure patient access to quitlines and promote quitline use.

9. If a tobacco user currently is unwilling to make a quit attempt, clinicians should use the motivational treatments shown in this Guideline to be effective in increasing future quit attempts.

10. Tobacco dependence treatments are both clinically effective and highly cost-effective relative to interventions for other clinical disorders. Providing coverage for these treatments increases quit rates. Insurers and purchasers should ensure that all insurance plans include the counseling and medication identified as effective in this Guideline as covered benefits.

The updated Guideline is divided into seven chapters that provide an overview, including methods (Chapter 1); information on the assessment of tobacco use (Chapter 2); clinical interventions, both for patients willing and unwilling to make a quit attempt at this time (Chapter 3); intensive interventions (Chapter 4); systems interventions for health care administrators, insurers, and purchasers (Chapter 5); the scientific evidence supporting the Guideline recommendations (Chapter 6); and information relevant to specific populations and other topics (Chapter 7).

A comparison of the findings of the updated Guideline with the 2000 Guideline reveals the considerable progress made in tobacco research over the brief period separating these two publications. Tobacco dependence increasingly is recognized as a chronic disease, one that typically requires ongoing assessment and repeated intervention. In addition, the updated Guideline offers the clinician many more effective treatment strategies than were identified in the original Guideline. There now are seven different first-line effective agents in the smoking cessation pharmacopoeia, allowing the clinician and patient many different medication options. In addition, recent evidence provides even stronger support for counseling (both when used alone and with other treatments) as an effective tobacco cessation strategy; counseling adds to the effectiveness of tobacco cessation medications, quitline counseling is an effective intervention with a broad reach, and counseling increases tobacco cessation among adolescent smokers.

Finally, there is increasing evidence that the success of any tobacco dependence treatment strategy cannot be divorced from the health care system in which it is embedded. The updated Guideline contains new evidence that health care policies significantly affect the likelihood that smokers will receive effective tobacco dependence treatment and successfully stop tobacco use. For instance, making tobacco dependence treatment a covered benefit of insurance plans increases the likelihood that a tobacco user will receive treatment and quit successfully. Data strongly indicate that effective tobacco interventions require *coordinated interventions*. Just as the clinician must intervene with his or her patient, so must the health care administrator, insurer, and purchaser foster and support tobacco intervention as an integral element of health care delivery. Health care administrators and insurers should ensure that clinicians have the training and support to deliver consistent, effective intervention to tobacco users.

One important conclusion of this Guideline update is that the most effective way to move clinicians to intervene is to provide them with information regarding multiple effective treatment options and to ensure that they have ample institutional support to use these options. Joint actions by clinicians, administrators, insurers, and purchasers can encourage a culture of health care in which failure to intervene with a tobacco user is inconsistent with standards of care.

This document is in the public domain and may be used and reprinted without special permission. The Public Health Service appreciates citation as to source, and the suggested format is provided below:

Fiore MC, Jaén CR, Baker TB, et al. *Treating Tobacco Use and Dependence: 2008 Update.* Clinical Practice Guideline. Rockville, MD: U.S. Department of Health and Human Services. Public Health Service. May 2008.

The complete Guideline author list can be found on the title page.

Acknowledgments

This Guideline would not have been possible without the collaborative efforts of many individuals and organizations. Each made significant contributions throughout the process of updating this document. Although too numerous to list here, the Contributors section of this publication provides a listing of support staff, individual peer reviewers, and others. Some individuals and organizations, however, deserve special mention.

The Panel wishes to acknowledge the support and guidance provided by the consortium partners in general and their dedicated, hard-working representatives in particular. In addition to the Guideline Liaisons, the Panel gratefully acknowledges the extraordinarily supportive efforts and substantial contributions of Jean Slutsky, Director, Center for Outcomes and Evidence, AHRQ, and the staff at the Office of Communications and Knowledge Transfer, AHRQ; Sandra Cummings, Deputy Director of Operations, Publishing Team; Harriett Bennett, Public Affairs and Marketing Specialist; and Julius Patterson, Guideline Managing Editor.

The Panel also wishes to thank Victor Hasselblad, PhD, who served the project as statistical consultant.

Contents

Tables

Strategies

Figures

Executive Summary

Context

The 1996 *Smoking Cessation Clinical Practice Guideline*[1] emphasized the dire health consequences of tobacco use and dependence, the existence of effective treatments, and the importance of inducing more smokers to use such treatments. It also called for newer, even more effective tobacco dependence treatments. All of these points still are germane. Nevertheless, heartening progress has been made in tobacco control since that time, and this progress is part of a larger pattern of change that stretches back over the past 40 years. This progress reflects the achievements of clinicians, the public health community, scientists, government agencies, health care organizations, insurers, purchasers, and smokers who have successfully quit. As a result, the current prevalence of tobacco use among adults in the United States (about 20.8%) is less than half the rate observed in the 1960s (about 44%).[2,3]

This Guideline concludes that tobacco use presents a rare confluence of circumstances: (1) a highly significant health threat;[4] (2) a disinclination among clinicians to intervene consistently;[5] and (3) the presence of effective interventions. This last point is buttressed by evidence that tobacco dependence interventions, if delivered in a timely and effective manner, significantly reduce the smoker's risk of suffering from smoking-related disease.[6-13] Indeed, it is difficult to identify any other condition that presents such a mix of lethality, prevalence, and neglect, despite effective and readily available interventions.

Although tobacco use still is an enormous threat, the story of tobacco control efforts during the last half century is one of remarkable progress and promise. In 1965, current smokers outnumbered former smokers three to one.[14] During the past 40 years, the rate of quitting has so outstripped the rate of initiation that, today, there are more former smokers than current smokers.[15] Moreover, 40 years ago smoking was viewed as a habit rather than a chronic disease. No scientifically validated treatments were available for the treatment of tobacco use and dependence, and it had little place in health care delivery. Today, numerous effective treatments exist, and tobacco use assessment and intervention are considered to be requisite duties

1

of clinicians and health care delivery entities. Finally, every state now has a telephone quitline, increasing access to effective treatment.

The scant dozen years following the publication of the first Guideline have ushered in similarly impressive changes. In 1997, only 25 percent of managed health care plans covered any tobacco dependence treatment; this figure approached 90 percent by 2003,[16] although this increased coverage often includes barriers to use. Numerous states added Medicaid coverage for tobacco dependence treatment since the publication of the first Guideline so that, by 2005, 72 percent offered coverage for at least one Guideline-recommended treatment.[16-18] In 2002, The Joint Commission (formerly JCAHO), which accredits some 15,000 hospitals and health care programs, instituted an accreditation requirement for the delivery of evidence-based tobacco dependence interventions for patients with diagnoses of acute myocardial infarction, congestive heart failure, or pneumonia (*www. coreoptions.com/new_site/jcahocore.html*; hospital-specific results: *www. hospitalcompare.hhs.gov*). Finally, Medicare, the Veterans Health Administration, and the United States Military now provide coverage for tobacco dependence treatment. Such policies and systems changes are paying off in terms of increased rates of assessment and treatment of tobacco use.

Data show that the rate at which smokers report being advised to quit smoking has approximately doubled since the early 1990s.[19-22] Recent data also suggest a substantial increase in the proportion of smokers receiving more intensive cessation interventions.[23,24] The National Committee for Quality Assurance (NCQA) reports steady increases for both commercial insurers and Medicaid in the discussion of both medications and strategies for smoking cessation.[25] Finally, since the first Guideline was published in 1996, smoking prevalence among adults in the United States has declined from about 25 percent to about 21 percent.[26]

An inspection of the 2008 Guideline update shows that substantial progress also has been made in treatment development and delivery. Telephone quitlines have been shown to be effective in providing wide access to evidence-based cessation counseling.[27,28] Seven U.S. Food and Drug Administration (FDA)-approved medications for treating tobacco dependence are now available, and new evidence has revealed that particular medications or combinations of medications are especially effective.

This Guideline update also casts into stark relief those areas in which more progress is needed. There is a need for innovative and more effective counseling strategies. In addition, although adolescents appear to benefit from counseling, more consistent and effective interventions and options for use with children, adolescents, and young adults clearly are needed. Smoking prevalence remains discouragingly high in certain populations, such as in those with low socioeconomic status (SES)/low educational attainment, some American Indian populations, and individuals with psychiatric disorders, including substance use disorders.[3] New techniques and treatment delivery strategies may be required before the needs of these groups are adequately addressed. Moreover, although much of the available data come from randomized clinical trials occurring in research settings, it is imperative that new research examine implementation of effective treatments in real-world clinical settings. Finally, new strategies are needed to create consumer demand for effective treatments among tobacco users; there has been little increase in the proportion of smokers who make quit attempts, and too few smokers who do try to quit take advantage of evidence-based treatment that can double or triple their odds of success.[29] New research and communication efforts must impart greater hope, confidence, and increased access to treatments so that tobacco users in ever greater numbers attempt tobacco cessation and achieve abstinence. To succeed, all of these areas require adequate funding.

Thus, this 2008 Guideline update serves as a benchmark of the progress made. It should reassure clinicians, policymakers, funding agencies, and the public that tobacco use is amenable to both scientific analysis and clinical interventions. This history of remarkable progress should encourage renewed efforts by clinicians, policymakers, and researchers to help those who remain dependent on tobacco.

Guideline Origins

This Guideline, *Treating Tobacco Use and Dependence: 2008 Update,* a Public Health Service-sponsored Clinical Practice Guideline, is the product of the Treating Tobacco Use and Dependence Guideline Panel ("the Panel"), government liaisons, consultants, and staff. These individuals were charged with the responsibility of identifying effective, experimentally validated tobacco dependence clinical treatments and practices. This Guideline update is the third Public Health Service Clinical Practice Guideline published on tobacco use. The first Guideline, the 1996 *Smoking Cessation Clinical Practice Guideline No. 18,* was sponsored by the Agency for Healthcare Policy and Research (AHCPR, now the Agency for Healthcare Research and Quality [AHRQ]), U.S. Department of Health and Human Services (HHS). That Guideline reflected scientific literature published between 1975 and 1994. The second Guideline, published in 2000, *Treating Tobacco Use and Dependence*, was sponsored by a consortium of U. S. Public Health Service (PHS) agencies (AHRQ; Centers for Disease Control and Prevention [CDC]; National Cancer Institute [NCI]; National Heart, Lung, and Blood Institute [NHLBI]; National Institute on Drug Abuse [NIDA]) as well as the Robert Wood Johnson Foundation (RWJF) and the University of Wisconsin Center for Tobacco Research and Intervention (UW-CTRI). That Guideline reflected the scientific literature published from 1975 to 1999. The current 2008 update addresses literature published from 1975 to 2007.

The updated Guideline was written in response to new, effective clinical treatments for tobacco dependence that have been identified since 1999. These treatments promise to enhance the rates of successful tobacco cessation. The original 1996 Guideline was based on some 3,000 articles on tobacco treatment published between 1975 and 1994. The 2000 Guideline required the collection and screening of an additional 3,000 articles published between 1995 and 1999. The 2008 Guideline update screened an additional 2,700 articles; thus, the present Guideline update reflects the distillation of a literature base of more than 8,700 research articles. This body of research of course was further reviewed to identify a much smaller group of articles, based on rigorous inclusion criteria, which served as the basis for focused Guideline data analyses and review.

The 2008 updated Guideline was sponsored by a consortium of eight Federal Government and private nonprofit organizations: AHRQ, CDC, NCI, NHLBI, NIDA, American Legacy Foundation, RWJF, and UW-CTRI. All of these organizations have as their mission reducing the human costs of tobacco use. Given the importance of this issue to the health of all Americans, the updated Guideline is published by the PHS, HHS.

Guideline Style and Structure

This Guideline update was written to be applicable to all tobacco users—those using cigarettes as well as other forms of tobacco. Therefore, the terms "tobacco user" and "tobacco dependence" will be used in preference to "smoker" and "cigarette dependence." In some cases, however, the evidence for a particular recommendation consists entirely of studies using cigarette smokers as participants. In these instances, the recommendation and evidence refers to "smoking" to communicate the parochial nature of the evidence. In most cases, though, Guideline recommendations are relevant to all types of tobacco users. Finally, most data reviewed in this Guideline update are based on adult smokers, although data relevant to adolescent smokers are presented in Chapter 7.

The updated Guideline is divided into seven chapters that integrate prior and updated findings:

Chapter 1, Overview and Methods, provides the clinical practice and scientific context of the Guideline update project and describes the methodology used to generate the Guideline findings.

Chapter 2, Assessment of Tobacco Use, describes how each patient presenting at a health care setting should have his or her tobacco use status determined and how tobacco users should be assessed for willingness to make a quit attempt.

Chapter 3, Clinical Interventions for Tobacco Use and Dependence, summarizes effective brief interventions that can easily be delivered in a primary care setting. In this chapter, separate interventions are described for the patient who is *willing* to try to quit at this time, for the patient who is *not yet willing* to try to quit, and for the patient who has recently quit.

Chapter 4, Intensive Interventions for Tobacco Use and Dependence, outlines a prototype of an intensive tobacco cessation treatment that comprises strategies shown to be effective in this Guideline. Because intensive treatments produce the highest success rates, they are an important element in tobacco intervention strategies.

Chapter 5, Systems Interventions, targets health care administrators, insurers, and purchasers, and offers a blueprint to changes in health care delivery and coverage such that tobacco assessment and intervention become a standard of care in health care delivery.

Chapter 6, Evidence and Recommendations, presents the results of Guideline literature reviews and statistical analyses and the recommendations that emanate from them. Guideline analyses address topics such as the effectiveness of different counseling strategies and medications; the relation between treatment intensities and treatment success; whether screening for tobacco use in the clinic setting enhances tobacco user identification; and whether systems changes can increase provision of effective interventions, quit attempts, and actual cessation rates. The Guideline Panel also made specific recommendations regarding future research needs.

Chapter 7, Specific Populations and Other Topics, evaluates evidence on tobacco intervention strategies and effectiveness with specific populations (e.g., HIV-positive smokers; hospitalized smokers; lesbian/gay/bisexual/transgender smokers; smokers with low SES/limited educational attainment; smokers with medical comorbidities; older smokers; smokers with psychiatric disorders, including substance use disorders; racial and ethnic minorities; women smokers; children and adolescents; light smokers; pregnant smokers; and noncigarette tobacco users). The Guideline Panel made specific recommendations for future research on topics relevant to these populations. This chapter also presents information and recommendations relevant to weight gain after smoking cessation, with specific recommendations regarding future research on this topic.

Findings and Recommendations

The key recommendations of the updated Guideline, *Treating Tobacco Use and Dependence: 2008 Update*, based on the literature review and expert Panel opinion, are as follows:

▪ Ten Key Guideline Recommendations

The overarching goal of these recommendations is that clinicians strongly recommend the use of effective tobacco dependence counseling and medication treatments to their patients who use tobacco, and that health care systems, insurers, and purchasers assist clinicians in making such effective treatments available.

1. Tobacco dependence is a chronic disease that often requires repeated intervention and multiple attempts to quit. Effective treatments exist, however, that can significantly increase rates of long-term abstinence.

2. It is essential that clinicians and health care delivery systems consistently identify and document tobacco use status and treat every tobacco user seen in a health care setting.

3. Tobacco dependence treatments are effective across a broad range of populations. Clinicians should encourage every patient willing to make a quit attempt to use the counseling treatments and medications recommended in this Guideline.

4. Brief tobacco dependence treatment is effective. Clinicians should offer every patient who uses tobacco at least the brief treatments shown to be effective in this Guideline.

5. Individual, group, and telephone counseling are effective, and their effectiveness increases with treatment intensity. Two components of counseling are especially effective, and clinicians should use these when counseling patients making a quit attempt:

   • Practical counseling (problemsolving/skills training)

   • Social support delivered as part of treatment

6. Numerous effective medications are available for tobacco dependence, and clinicians should encourage their use by all patients attempting to quit smoking—except when medically contraindicated or with specific populations for which there is insufficient evidence of effectiveness (i.e., pregnant women, smokeless tobacco users, light smokers, and adolescents).

   • Seven first-line medications (5 nicotine and 2 non-nicotine) reliably increase long-term smoking abstinence rates:

      – Bupropion SR
      – Nicotine gum
      – Nicotine inhaler
      – Nicotine lozenge
      – Nicotine nasal spray
      – Nicotine patch
      – Varenicline

- Clinicians also should consider the use of certain combinations of medications identified as effective in this Guideline.

7. Counseling and medication are effective when used by themselves for treating tobacco dependence. The combination of counseling and medication, however, is more effective than either alone. Thus, clinicians should encourage all individuals making a quit attempt to use both counseling and medication.

8. Telephone quitline counseling is effective with diverse populations and has broad reach. Therefore, clinicians and health care delivery systems should both ensure patient access to quitlines and promote quitline use.

9. If a tobacco user currently is unwilling to make a quit attempt, clinicians should use the motivational treatments shown in this Guideline to be effective in increasing future quit attempts.

10. Tobacco dependence treatments are both clinically effective and highly cost-effective relative to interventions for other clinical disorders. Providing coverage for these treatments increases quit rates. Insurers and purchasers should ensure that all insurance plans include the counseling and medication identified as effective in this Guideline as covered benefits.

Guideline Update: Advances

A comparison of the findings of the 2008 Guideline update with the 2000 Guideline reveals the considerable progress made in tobacco research over the brief period separating these two works. Among many important differences between the two documents, the following deserve special note:

- The updated Guideline has produced even stronger evidence that counseling is an effective tobacco use treatment strategy. Of particular note are findings that counseling adds significantly to the effectiveness of tobacco cessation medications, quitline counseling is an effective intervention with a broad reach, and counseling increases abstinence among adolescent smokers.

- The updated Guideline offers the clinician a greater number of effective medications than were identified in the previous Guideline. Seven different effective first-line smoking cessation medications are now approved by the FDA for treating tobacco use and dependence. In addition, multiple combinations of medications have been shown to be effective. Thus, the clinician and patient have many more medication options than in the past. The Guideline also now provides evidence regarding the effectiveness of medications relative to one another.

- The updated Guideline contains new evidence that health care policies significantly affect the likelihood that smokers will receive effective tobacco dependence treatment and successfully stop tobacco use. For instance, making tobacco dependence a benefit covered by insurance plans increases the likelihood that a tobacco user will receive treatment and quit successfully.

Future Promise

The research reviewed for this 2008 Guideline update suggests a bright future for treating tobacco use and dependence. Since the first AHCPR Clinical Practice Guideline was published in 1996, encouraging progress has been made in tobacco dependence treatment. An expanding body of research has produced a marked increase in the number and types of effective treatments and has led to multiple new treatment delivery strategies. These new strategies are enhancing the delivery of tobacco interventions both inside and outside health care delivery systems. This means that an unprecedented number of smokers have access to an unprecedented number of effective treatments.

Although the data reviewed in this Guideline update are encouraging and portend even greater advances through future research, for many smokers, the progress has been an undelivered promissory note. Most smokers attempting to quit today still make unaided quit attempts,[29-32] although the proportion using evidence-based treatments has increased since the publication of the 1996 AHCPR Guideline.[33-35] Because of the prevalence of such unaided attempts (those that occur without evidence-based counseling or medication), many smokers have successfully quit through this approach.[6,36] It is clear from the data presented in this Guideline, however, that smokers are significantly more likely to quit successfully if they use an evidence-based counseling or medication treatment than if they try to quit without such aids. Thus, a future challenge for the field is to ensure that smokers, clinicians, and health systems have accurate information on the effectiveness of clinical interventions for tobacco use, and that the 70 percent of smokers who visit a primary care setting each year have greater access to effective treatments. This is of vital public health importance because the costs of failure are so high. Relapse results in continuing lifetime exposure to tobacco, which leads to increased risk of death and disease. Additional progress must be made in educating clinicians and the public about the effectiveness of clinical treatments for tobacco dependence and in making such treatments available and attractive to smokers.

Continued progress is needed in the treatment of tobacco use and dependence. Treatments should be even more effective and available, new counseling strategies should be developed, and research should focus on the development of effective interventions and delivery strategies for populations that carry a disproportionate burden from tobacco (e.g., adolescents; pregnant smokers; American Indians and Alaska Natives; individuals with low SES/limited educational attainment; individuals with psychiatric disorders, including substance use disorders). The decrease in the prevalence of tobacco use in the United States during the past 40 years, however, has been a seminal public health achievement. Treatment of tobacco use and dependence has played an important role in realizing that outcome.

Chapter 1 Overview and Methods

Introduction

Tobacco use has been cited as the chief avoidable cause of illness and death in our society and accounts for more than 435,000 deaths each year in the United States.[37,38] Smoking is a known cause of multiple cancers, heart disease, stroke, complications of pregnancy, chronic obstructive pulmonary disease (COPD), and many other diseases.[4] In addition, recent research has documented the substantial health dangers of involuntary exposure to tobacco smoke.[4] Despite these health dangers and the public's awareness of those dangers, tobacco use remains surprisingly prevalent. Recent estimates are that about 21 percent of adult Americans smoke,[3] representing approximately 45 million current adult smokers.[3,39] Moreover, tobacco use remains a pediatric disease.[40-42] Each day, about 4,000 youth ages 12 to 17 years smoke their first cigarette, and about 1,200 children and adolescents become daily cigarette smokers.[43-44] As a result, new generations of Americans are at risk for the extraordinarily harmful consequences of tobacco use.

Tobacco use exacts a heavy cost to society as well as to individuals. Smoking-attributable health care expenditures are estimated at $96 billion per year in direct medical expenses and $97 billion in lost productivity.[28] It has been estimated that the per pack additional cost of smoking to society is approximately $7.18 per pack,[45] and the combined cost of each pack to society and the individual smoker and family is nearly $40.[46] If all smokers covered by state Medicaid programs quit, the annual savings to Medicaid would be $9.7 billion after 5 years.[47]

Despite the tragic consequences of tobacco use, clinicians and health care systems often fail to treat it consistently and effectively. For instance, in 1995, about the time of the release of the first clinical practice guideline, smoking status was identified in only about 65 percent of clinic visits, and smoking cessation counseling was provided in only 22 percent of smokers' clinic visits.[48,49] Moreover, treatment typically was offered only to patients already suffering from tobacco-related diseases.[48] This pattern gradually began to improve as of 2005, with up to 90 percent of smokers reporting they had been asked about smoking status and more than 70 percent reporting having received some counseling to quit.[23,50,51] However, the failure to assess and intervene consistently with all tobacco users continues despite substantial evidence that even brief interventions can be effective among many different populations of smokers.[52-58] Also, the use of effective medications is low. Among current smokers who attempted to stop for at least 1 day in the past year, only 21.7 percent used cessation medication.[33]

This Guideline concludes that tobacco use presents a rare confluence of circumstances: (1) a highly significant health threat;[4] (2) a lack of consistent intervention by clinicians; and (3) the presence of effective interventions. This last point is buttressed by evidence that tobacco use interventions, if delivered in a timely and effective manner, can rapidly reduce the risk of suffering from smoking-related disease.[6-13] Indeed, it is difficult to identify any other condition that presents such a mix of lethality, prevalence, and neglect, despite effective and readily available interventions.

Significant barriers interfere with clinicians' assessment and treatment of smokers. Many clinicians lack knowledge about how to identify smokers quickly and easily, which treatments are effective, how such treatments can be delivered, and the relative effectiveness of different treatments.[59-62] Additionally, clinicians may fail to intervene because of inadequate clinic or institutional support for routine assessment and treatment of tobacco use[48,60,63] and for other reasons such as time constraints, limited training in tobacco cessation interventions, a lack of insurance coverage for tobacco use treatment, or inadequate payment for treatment.[64-67]

Rationale for Guideline Development and Periodic Updates

In the early 1990s, the Agency for Healthcare Policy and Research ([AHCPR] now the Agency for Healthcare Research and Quality [AHRQ]) convened an expert panel to develop the *Smoking Cessation Clinical Practice Guideline* (the "Guideline"), Number 18 in the AHCPR series of Clinical Practice Guidelines. The need for this Guideline was based on several factors, including tobacco use prevalence, related morbidity and mortality, the economic burden imposed by tobacco use, variation in clinical practice, availability of methods for improvement of care, and availability of data on which to base recommendations for care. More than 1 million copies of the 1996 Guideline and its affiliated products were disseminated. The original Guideline recommendations inspired changes in diverse health care settings such as managed care organizations and the Veterans Health Administration. The original Guideline also provided a framework for educating clinicians, administrators, and policymakers about the importance of tobacco dependence and its treatment. It stimulated discussions that addressed the development of tobacco dependence treatment programs at the Federal and State levels and by professional medical organizations.

Significant new research findings regarding tobacco use and its treatment led to the 2000 Guideline update, which was authored by the expert panel that developed the 1996 Guideline. The 2000 Guideline update was a product of the U. S. Public Health Service (PHS), sponsored by a consortium of private and public partners, including AHRQ; National Cancer Institute (NCI); National Heart, Lung, and Blood Institute (NHLBI); National Institute on Drug Abuse (NIDA); Centers for Disease Control and Prevention (CDC); Robert Wood Johnson Foundation (RWJF); and University of Wisconsin School of Medicine and Public Health Center for Tobacco Research and Intervention (UW-CTRI).

The 2000 Guideline, titled *Treating Tobacco Use and Dependence,* comprised specific evidence-based recommendations to guide clinicians, tobacco treatment specialists, insurers, purchasers, and health care administrators in their efforts to develop and implement clinical and institutional changes that support the reliable identification, assessment, and treatment of patients who use tobacco. This title underscores three truths about tobacco use.[68] First, all tobacco products—not just cigarettes—exact devastating costs on the Nation's health and welfare. Second, for most users, tobacco use results in true drug dependence, comparable to the dependence caused by opiates, amphetamines, and cocaine.[69-72] Third, both chronic tobacco use and dependence warrant clinical intervention and, as with other chronic disorders, these interventions may need to be repeated over time.[73,74]

The 2000 *Treating Tobacco Use and Dependence* document was the most widely disseminated Guideline ever released by AHRQ, with more than 5 million copies of the Guideline and related products distributed. Moreover, it has had an enormous influence on tobacco use treatment and policy worldwide, serving as the basis for Guidelines in Australia, Canada, Chile, Japan, Portugal, and Switzerland, among other countries.

The continued expansion of new scientific findings on the effective treatment of tobacco use led to calls for the current update, *Treating Tobacco Use and Dependence: 2008 Update.* The 2008 update reviewed scientific evidence from 1975 to 2007 on selected topics and in total reviewed more than 8,700 scientific publications. The result of this methodologically rigorous review is an updated set of recommendations on effective counseling and medication treatments and institutional policies that can guide clinicians, specialists, and health systems in intervening with tobacco users. Appendix D summarizes new recommendations and changes to the 2000 Guideline.

The clinician audience for this Guideline update is all professionals who provide health care to tobacco users. This includes: physicians, nurses, physician assistants, medical assistants, dentists, hygienists, respiratory therapists, psychologists, mental health counselors, pharmacists, and others. The ultimate beneficiaries of the Guideline are tobacco users and their families.

Most tobacco users in the United States are cigarette smokers. As a result, the majority of clinician attention and research in the field has focused on the treatment and assessment of smoking. Clinicians, however, should intervene with all tobacco users, not just with those who smoke cigarettes. To foster a broad implementation of this Guideline update, every effort has been made to describe interventions so that they are relevant to all forms of tobacco use. In some sections of this Guideline, the term "smoker" is used instead of "tobacco user." The use of the term "smoker" means that all relevant evidence for a recommendation arises from studies of cigarette smokers. Additional discussion of noncigarette forms of tobacco use is found in Chapter 7.

The 2008 Guideline update generally is consistent with the findings of the 2000 Guideline (see Appendix D). It also is important to note that other Guidelines and analyses on the treatment of tobacco dependence have been published with essentially consistent findings, including those from the American Psychiatric Association,[75,76] the American Medical Association,[77] the American Dental Association,[78] the American Nurses Association,[79] the American College of Obstetricians and Gynecologists, the Institute of Medicine,[80] the United Kingdom Guideline,[81] and the Cochrane Collaboration (*www.cochrane.org/index.htm*). Finally, throughout the Guideline update, the terms "tobacco use treatment" and "tobacco dependence treatment" will be used interchangeably to emphasize the fact that both chronic use and dependence merit clinical intervention.

Tobacco Dependence as a Chronic Disease

Tobacco dependence displays many features of a chronic disease. Only a minority of tobacco users achieve permanent abstinence in an initial quit attempt. The majority of users persist in tobacco use for many years and typically cycle through multiple periods of remission and relapse. A failure to appreciate the chronic nature of tobacco dependence may impede clinicians' consistent assessment and treatment of the tobacco user over time.

Epidemiologic data suggest that more than 70 percent of the 45 million smokers in the United States today report that they want to quit, and approximately 44 percent report that they try to quit each year.[3] Unfortunately, most of these efforts are both unaided and unsuccessful. For example, among the 19 million adults who attempted to quit in 2005,[39] only 4 to 7 percent were likely successful.[82,83] These statistics may discourage both smokers and clinicians.

Modern approaches to treating tobacco use and dependence should reflect the chronicity of tobacco dependence. A chronic disease model recognizes the long-term nature of the disorder with an expectation that patients may have periods of relapse and remission. If tobacco dependence is recognized as a chronic disease, clinicians will better understand the relapsing nature of the condition and the requirement for ongoing, rather than just acute, care. The existence of numerous effective treatments gives the clinician and patient many options should repeated quit attempts be needed.

A chronic disease model emphasizes for clinicians the importance of continued patient education, counseling, and advice over time. Although most clinicians are comfortable in counseling their patients about other chronic diseases such as diabetes, hypertension, or hyperlipidemia, many believe that they are less effective in providing counseling to patients who use tobacco.[84,85] As with these other chronic disorders, clinicians should be encouraged to provide tobacco-dependent patients with brief advice, counseling, and appropriate medication. It is important for clinicians to know that assessing and treating tobacco use generally leads to greater patient satisfaction with health care.[23,50,86-88] Moreover, policy changes (e.g., tax increases, smoke-free ordinances) often lead smokers to seek treatment for this chronic disease.

In updating the Guideline, the Panel has presented evidence-based analytic findings in a format accessible and familiar to practicing clinicians. Although this should aid clinicians in the assessment and treatment of tobacco users, clinicians should remain cognizant that relapse is likely and that it reflects the chronic nature of dependence. Most smokers who ultimately quit smoking experience episodes of relapse on the way to success. Relapse should not discourage the clinician or the tobacco user from renewed quit attempts.

Coordination of Care: Institutionalizing the Treatment of Tobacco Dependence

Increasing evidence shows that the success of any tobacco dependence treatment strategy cannot be divorced from the health care system in which it is embedded. Data strongly indicate that the consistent and effective delivery of tobacco interventions requires *coordinated interventions*. Just as a clinician must intervene with his or her patient, so must the health care administrator, insurer, and purchaser ensure the provision of tobacco dependence treatment as an integral element of health care delivery. Health care purchasers and insurers should ensure that evidence-based tobacco dependence counseling and medications are a covered and available health insurance benefit for all enrollees and that enrollees are aware of such benefits. Health care administrators also should provide clinicians with the training and institutional support and systems to ensure consistent identification of and intervention with patients who use tobacco. Therefore, insurers, purchasers, and health care organizations should promote the utilization of covered treatments and assess usage and outcomes in performance measurement systems.[89] Finally, increasing evidence shows that, for maximum public health benefit, access to effective treatments should be increased during and following the implementation of population-level tobacco control policies (i.e., tobacco tax increases and clean indoor air laws), which boost motivation and support for quitting efforts.[90]

Guideline Development Methodology

▪ Introduction

Panel recommendations are intended to provide clinicians with effective strategies for treating patients who use tobacco. Fundamentally, this document is a clinical practice guideline. Recommendations were influenced by two goals. The first was to identify effective treatment strategies. The second was to formulate and present recommendations that can be implemented easily across diverse clinical settings (e.g., primary care and specialty clinics; pharmacies; hospitals, including emergency departments; worksites; and school-based clinics) and patient populations.

The Guideline update is based on three systematic reviews of the available scientific literature. The first review occurred during the creation of the original Guideline published in 1996 and included literature published from 1975 through 1994. The second review was conducted for the 2000 Guideline and included literature from 1995 through January 1999. The third review was conducted on literature published from 1999 to June 2007. The three data sets were combined into a single database that was used for the 2008 analyses.

The Panel identified randomized placebo/comparison controlled trials as the strongest level of evidence for the evaluation of treatment effectiveness. Thus, evidence derived from randomized controlled trials serves as the basis for meta-analyses and for almost all of the recommendations contained in this Guideline. Questions have been raised about medication placebo controls because individuals sometimes guess their actual medication condition at greater than chance levels.[91] It is possible, therefore, that the typical randomized control trial does not control completely for placebo effects. This should be borne in mind when appraising the results of the medication meta-analyses. Further, in studies of counseling, it often is not possible to control for a nonspecific placebo effect.

The Panel occasionally made recommendations in the absence of randomized controlled trials when faced with an important clinical practice issue for which other types of evidence existed. This Guideline clearly identifies the level or strength of evidence that serves as the basis for each of its recommendations.

▓ Topics Included in the Guideline

The Panel identified tobacco use as the targeted behavior and tobacco users as the clinical population of interest. Tobacco dependence treatments were evaluated for effectiveness, as were interventions aimed at modifying both clinician and health care delivery system behavior. At the start of the 2008 update process, Guideline Panel members, outside experts, and consortium representatives were consulted to determine those aspects of the 2000 Guideline that required updating. These consultations resulted in the following chief recommendations that guided the update efforts: (1) to conduct new literature reviews and meta-analyses on topics distinguished by their public health importance and for which significant new evidence is available; (2) to review previous recommendations and to identify a subset of recommendations for which to review new data; special attention was paid to clinical situations for which the Panel had previously achieved consensus in the absence of relevant controlled trials ("C"-level recommendations) to ensure that these still warranted Guideline Panel support; (3) to consider anew the strategies that might be used in clinical settings to deliver brief tobacco dependence interventions (see Chapter 3); and (4) to identify important topics for future research. Eleven topics out of 64 considered were chosen by the Panel for updated meta-analysis (see Table 1.1).

Table 1.1. Topics chosen by the 2008 Guideline Panel for updated meta-analysis

Effectiveness of proactive quitlines
Effectiveness of combining counseling and medication relative to either counseling or medication alone
Effectiveness of varenicline
Effectiveness of various medication combinations
Effectiveness of long-term medication use
Effectiveness of tobacco use interventions for individuals with low SES/limited formal education
Effectiveness of tobacco use interventions for adolescent smokers
Effectiveness of tobacco use interventions for pregnant smokers
Effectiveness of tobacco use interventions for individuals with psychiatric disorders, including substance use disorders
Effectiveness of providing tobacco use interventions as a health benefit
Effectiveness of systems interventions, including provider training and the combination of training and systems interventions

This Guideline update was specifically intended to review the evidence regarding clinical treatment of tobacco dependence. Interventions for the primary prevention of tobacco use were not examined in detail, with the exception of interventions directly relevant to clinical practice. Readers also may refer to the 1994 Surgeon General's Report, *Preventing Tobacco Use Among Young People*[41] and the 2000 Surgeon General's Report, *Reducing Tobacco Use*,[6] for information on the primary prevention of tobacco use. Community-level interventions (e.g., mass media campaigns) that are not usually implemented in primary care practice settings were not addressed. For more information on community-based tobacco use prevention, refer to the Centers for Disease Control and Prevention *Guide to Community Preventive Services.*[92] The Guideline update did not examine evidence regarding unaided quit attempts as this Guideline focused on clinical interventions. Finally, the use of exposure reduction strategies[93] (strategies in which tobacco users alter, rather than eliminate, their use of nicotine or tobacco in an attempt to reduce or avoid its harmful consequences) were not considered due to a lack of data and the fact that they are beyond the scope of a clinical practice guideline focused on treating tobacco use and dependence. Current research does not offer answers to key questions regarding exposure reduction strategies: their population-wide impact on cessation and initiation of smoking, their long-term benefits as compared with those of a strategy focused on tobacco abstinence, and their success in reducing long-term exposure to tobacco toxins.

This Guideline update is designed for two main audiences: first, clinicians; and second, health care administrators, insurers, and purchasers. It is designed to be used in a wide variety of clinical practice settings, including private medical practices; dental offices; pharmacies; academic health centers; mental health and substance abuse treatment clinics; telephone quitlines; managed care organizations; public health department clinics; hospitals, including emergency departments; and school or worksite clinics. The ultimate beneficiaries of the Guideline are tobacco users and their families.

■ Guideline Development Process

The 2008 Guideline update development process (see Figure 1.1) was initiated in mid-2006. The methodology was consistent with that followed by the 2000 Guideline except where specifically identified below.

■ Selection of Evidence

Published, peer-reviewed, randomized controlled studies were considered to constitute the strongest level of evidence in support of Guideline recommendations. This decision was based on the judgment that randomized controlled trials provide the clearest scientifically sound basis for judging

Figure 1.1. 2008 Guideline development process

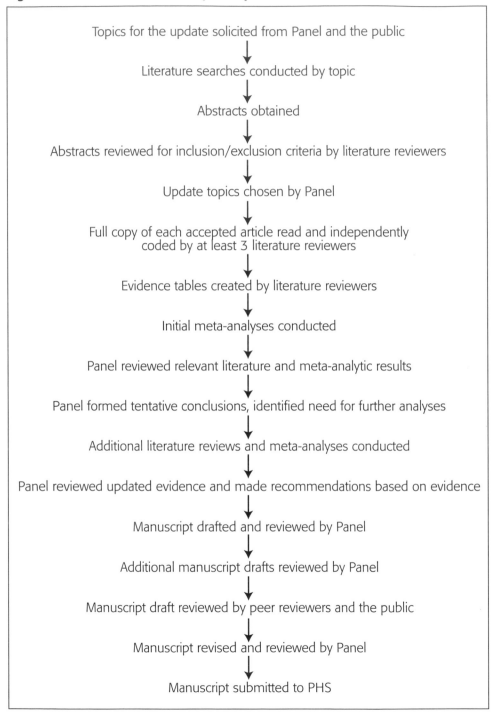

Topics for the update solicited from Panel and the public

↓

Literature searches conducted by topic

↓

Abstracts obtained

↓

Abstracts reviewed for inclusion/exclusion criteria by literature reviewers

↓

Update topics chosen by Panel

↓

Full copy of each accepted article read and independently
coded by at least 3 literature reviewers

↓

Evidence tables created by literature reviewers

↓

Initial meta-analyses conducted

↓

Panel reviewed relevant literature and meta-analytic results

↓

Panel formed tentative conclusions, identified need for further analyses

↓

Additional literature reviews and meta-analyses conducted

↓

Panel reviewed updated evidence and made recommendations based on evidence

↓

Manuscript drafted and reviewed by Panel

↓

Additional manuscript drafts reviewed by Panel

↓

Manuscript draft reviewed by peer reviewers and the public

↓

Manuscript revised and reviewed by Panel

↓

Manuscript submitted to PHS

comparative effectiveness. Most of these randomized trials, however, were conducted with individuals who proactively sought treatment and who volunteered to fulfill various research requirements. It is possible that these individuals were more highly motivated to quit smoking than the typical smoker encountered in a clinical practice setting. Thus, the percentage abstinent estimates supplied with the meta-analyses may overestimate the actual level of abstinence produced by some of the treatments in real-world settings. Analyses conducted for the previous Guideline editions, though, suggest that the treatment effect sizes (odds ratios or ORs) are relatively stable across individuals seeking treatment ("treatment seekers") and those recruited via inclusive recruitment strategies ("all-comers"). Randomized controlled trials were exclusively used in meta-analyses. However, the Panel recognized that variations in study inclusion criteria sometimes were warranted. For instance, research on tobacco interventions in adolescents frequently assigns interventions on the basis of larger units, such as schools. These units, rather than individuals, were allowed to serve as units of analysis when analyzing interventions for adolescents. In such cases, studies were combined for inclusion in meta-analyses if the study satisfied other review criteria. A similar strategy was followed in the review of health systems research.

In certain areas, research other than randomized clinical trials was evaluated and considered to inform Panel opinion and judgment, though not submitted to meta-analysis. This occurred with topics such as tobacco dependence treatment in specific populations, tailoring interventions, and cost-effectiveness of tobacco dependence treatment.

■ Literature Review and Inclusion Criteria

Approximately 8,700 articles were screened to identify evaluable literature. This figure includes approximately 2,700 articles added to the literature since publication of the 2000 Guideline. These articles were obtained through searches of 11 electronic databases and reviews of published abstracts and bibliographies. An article was deemed appropriate for meta-analysis if it met the criteria for inclusion established *a priori* by the Panel. These criteria were that the article: (a) reported the results of a randomized, placebo/comparison controlled trial of a tobacco use treatment intervention randomized on the patient level (except as noted above); (b) provided followup results at least 5 months after the quit date (except in the case of studies evaluating tobacco dependence treatments for pregnant smokers); (c) was published in a peer-reviewed journal; (d) was published between January 1975 and June 2007; (e) was published in English; and (f) was one of the 11 topics chosen to be included in the 2008 update (see Table 1.1). It is important to note that the article-screening criteria were updated for the 2008 Guideline update. Additionally, articles were screened for relevance to safety, economic, or health systems issues. As a result of the original and update literature reviews, more than 300 articles were identified for possible inclusion in a meta-analysis, and more than 600 additional articles were examined in detail by the Panel. These latter articles were used in the formulation of Panel recommendations that were not supported by meta-analyses. The literature search for the update project was validated by comparing the results against a search conducted by the CDC and through review by the expert Panel.

When individual authors published multiple articles meeting the meta-analytic inclusion criteria, the articles were screened to determine whether they contained unique data. When two articles reported data from the same group of subjects, both articles were reviewed to ensure that complete data were obtained. The data were treated as arising from a single study in meta-analyses.

■ Preparation of Evidence Tables

Two Guideline staff reviewers independently read and coded each article that met inclusion criteria. The reviewers coded the treatment characteristics that were used in data analyses (see Tables 6.1 and 6.2 in Chapter 6). The same general coding procedure employed during the 2000 Guideline process was employed during the update. When adjustments to the coding process were made, articles coded with the original process were re-coded to reflect the changed coding (e.g., more refined coding criteria were used for the coding of treatment intensity).

A third reviewer then examined the coding of both reviewers and adjudicated any differences. Discrepancies that could not be resolved through this process were adjudicated by the project manager, Panel chair, and/or the Panel's senior scientist. Finally, each article accepted for a meta-analysis had key fields reviewed by the project manager as a final quality check. The data then were compiled and used in relevant analyses and/or Panel deliberations. Analyses done for the 2000 Guideline revealed that intervention coding categories could be used reliably by independent raters.[94]

Outcome Data

Six-month followup after the quit date is a standard followup duration for reporting data from clinical trials. Therefore, focusing on a 6-month timepoint in meta-analyses allowed the investigators to capture the greatest number of studies for analysis. Also, research indicates that a high percentage of those who ultimately return to smoking will do so by 6 months.[95-98] Because a strict adherence to a 6-month timepoint would have eliminated a significant number of studies, a 1-month window was permitted such that studies with 5 months of followup data were included, but 6-month data were used if both 5- and 6-month data were available. When quit rates were provided for longer endpoints, outcome data from the endpoint closest to 6 months were used, so long as they did not exceed 3 years. Outcome data beyond 3 years rarely were available and were not included in the Guideline analyses. In the area of medication treatment, the inclusive meta-analysis reported in Table 6.26 was repeated with longer term outcome data (10–14 month postquit). This additional meta-analysis largely replicated the results of the meta-analysis based on a 6-month followup time frame. This suggested that the shorter, more inclusive, followup timepoint captured effect sizes that were similar to those yielded by the use of longer followup timepoints. There was one exception to the selection of followup data described above. In the case of pregnancy studies, both predelivery and postdelivery (5 months) outcomes were analyzed.

Panel staff also coded biochemical confirmation of self-reported tobacco use abstinence. Previous Guideline analyses show that studies with and without biochemical confirmation yield similar meta-analysis results. Therefore, meta-analyses presented in the Guideline reflect a pooling of these studies. If both biochemically confirmed and nonconfirmed data were available from the same study, however, the confirmed data were used in analyses. As in the 2000 Guideline, only studies that used biochemical verification were used in the meta-analyses of pregnant smokers because of the under-reporting of smoking status by pregnant women.

All of the new meta-analyses conducted for the 2008 Guideline were based exclusively on intent-to-treat data, in which the denominator was the number of participants randomized to treatment and the numerator was the number of abstinent participants contacted at followup. Some meta-analyses conducted for the 1996 and 2000 Guideline comprised a small number of studies in which the denominator consisted only of participants who completed treatment. The vast majority of studies across all analyses reported intent-to-treat data and these data were used if both types of data were available.

Studies were coded for how the outcome measures were reported—"point prevalence," "continuous," or "unknown/other." If abstinence data were based on tobacco use occurrence within a set time period (usually 7 days) prior to a followup assessment, the outcome measure was coded as "point prevalence." "Continuous" was used when a study reported abstinence based on whether study subjects were continuously abstinent from to-bacco use since their quit day. "Unknown/other" was used when it was not possible to discern from the study report whether the authors used a point prevalence or continuous measure for abstinence or if abstinence was measured from some point other than the quit day.

As in the 1996 and 2000 Guidelines, a point prevalence outcome mea-sure (7-day point prevalence, when available), rather than continuous abstinence, was used as the chief outcome variable. Point prevalence was preferred for several reasons. First, this was the modal reporting method among the analyzable studies. Second, continuous abstinence data may underestimate the percentage of individuals who are abstinent at par-ticular followup timepoints, although some data suggest that these rates are similar.[99] Finally, most relapse begins early in a quit attempt and per-sists.[95-97,100-102] A point prevalence measure taken at 6 months certainly would capture the great majority of those relapse events. Therefore, when-ever possible, 7-day point prevalence abstinence data were used. If point prevalence data were not available, the preferred alternative was continu-ous abstinence data.

■ Meta-Analytic Techniques

The principal analytic technique used in this Guideline update was meta-analysis. This statistical technique estimates the impact of a treatment or variable across a set of related investigations. The primary meta-analytic model used in this and the previous two Guidelines was logistic regression using random effects modeling. The modeling was performed at the level of the treatment arm, and study effects were treated as fixed. The panel methodologist chose to employ random effects modeling, assuming that both the subject populations and the treatment elements analyzed would vary from study to study (e.g., counseling might be done somewhat differently at two different sites). Random effects modeling is well suited to accommodate such variation among studies.[103] The statistician used the EGRET Logistic Normal Model.[104] A complete and detailed review of the meta-analytic methods used in the Guideline can be found in the *Smoking Cessation Guideline Technical Report No. 18,* available from AHRQ as AHCPR Publication No. 97-N004. The specific articles used in each meta-analysis included in the 2008 Guideline can be found at *www.surgeon general.gov/tobacco/gdlnrefs.htm.*

In general, meta-analysis was used only with studies with randomization at the level of subject. In some areas (health systems changes, adolescents), however, studies often involved randomization at another level (e.g., clinician, clinic, etc.). Such studies were used in meta-analyses of a small number of topics when such studies occurred in sufficient numbers to permit inferences. Screening of such articles considered factors such as data nonindependence, the evaluation of pre-intervention or baseline status, and the number and types of higher level units.

The initial step in meta-analysis was the selection of studies that were relevant to the treatment characteristic being evaluated. After relevant studies were identified (i.e., those that contained a self-help intervention if self-help treatments were being evaluated), Panel staff reviewed the studies to ensure that they passed screening criteria. Some screening criteria were general (e.g., study presents greater than 5 months of followup data), whereas other criteria were specific to the type of treatment characteristic evaluated (i.e., in the analysis of quit lines, screening ensured that treatment arms were not confounded with differing intensities of in-person counseling).

The separate arms (treatment or control groups) in each study then were inspected to identify confounders that could compromise interpretation. Seriously confounded arms were excluded from analysis. Relevant characteristics of each arm were then coded to produce meaningful analytic comparisons. Criteria for performing a meta-analysis included: (1) the Guideline Panel judged the topic to be addressed in the meta-analysis as having substantial clinical significance; (2) at least two studies meeting selection criteria existed on the topic and the studies contained suitable within-study control or comparison conditions (e.g., each study had to contribute at least two arms that would permit the estimation of within-study effects); and (3) there was an acceptable level of interstudy homogeneity in the analyzed variable or treatment so as to permit meaningful inference (e.g., an analyzed treatment was sufficiently similar across various studies so that combining studies was meaningful).

Limitations of Meta-Analytic Techniques. Several factors can compromise the internal validity of meta-analyses. For example, publication biases (particularly the tendency to publish only those studies with positive findings) may result in biased summary statistics. The complement to publication bias is the "file-drawer effect," in which negative or neutral findings are not submitted for publication. In addition, either the magnitude or the significance of the effects of meta-analyses may be influenced by factors such as the frequency with which treatments occurred in the data set and by the extent to which treatments co-occurred with other treatments. All else being equal, a treatment that occurs infrequently in the data set is less likely to be found significant than a more frequently occurring treatment. Also, when two treatments co-occur frequently in the same groups of subjects, it is difficult to apportion statistically the impact of each. In addition, comparability biases can exist when substantially different groups or treatments are coded as being the same (e.g., when treatments are similar only on a superficial attribute).

The generalizability of meta-analytic findings was evaluated for previous Guideline editions with respect to whether patients sought cessation treatment ("self-selected") or whether treatment was delivered without the patient seeking it ("all-comers," as when cessation treatment occurred as an integral part of health care). Conducting separate meta-analyses in these different subject populations yielded very similar findings across a variety of treatment dimensions (e.g., treatment format, treatment intensity). No other population characteristic (e.g., years smoked, severity of dependence) was explored in meta-analyses.

Interpretation of Meta-Analysis Results. The meta-analyses yielded logistic regression coefficients that were converted to odds ratios. The meaning or interpretation of an odds ratio can be seen most easily by means of an example depicted in a 2 x 2 table. Table 1.2 contains data showing the relation between maternal smoking and low birth-weight in infants. Data are extracted from Hosmer and Lemeshow, 2000.[105] The odds of a low birth-weight infant if the mother smokes are 30:44, or 0.68 to 1. The odds of a low birth-weight infant if the mother does not smoke are 29:86, or 0.34 to 1. The odds ratio may be estimated as (30/44)/(29/86) = 2.02 to 1. Therefore, the odds ratio can be seen roughly as the odds of an outcome on one variable, given a certain status on another variable(s). In the case above, the odds of a low birth-weight infant are about double for women who smoke compared with those who do not.

Table 1.2. Relation between maternal smoking and low birth-weight in infants

		Maternal smoking		
		Yes	No	
Low birth-weight	Yes	30	29	59
	No	44	86	130
		74	115	189

Once odds ratios were obtained from the meta-analyses, 95 percent confidence intervals (C.I.) were estimated around the odds ratios. An odds ratio is only an estimate of a relation between variables. The 95 percent confidence interval presents an estimate of the precision of the particular odds ratio obtained. If the 95 percent confidence interval for a given odds ratio does not include "1," then the odds ratio represents a statistically significant difference between the evaluated treatment and the reference or control condition at the 0.05 level. The confidence intervals generally will not be perfectly symmetrical around an odds ratio because of the distributional properties of the odds ratio. The confidence intervals do not reveal whether active treatments differ significantly from one another, only whether they differ from the comparison condition (e.g., placebo medication, no contact). In the inclusive meta-analysis on medications, comparisons of an active medication versus the nicotine patch were accomplished via *a posteriori* contrasts, not on the basis of nonoverlapping confidence intervals.

After computing the odds ratios and their confidence intervals, the odds ratios were converted to abstinence percentages and their 95 percent confidence intervals (based on reference category abstinence rates). Abstinence percentages indicate the estimated long-term abstinence rate achieved under the tested treatment or treatment characteristic. The abstinence percentage results are approximate estimates derived from the odds ratio data. Therefore, they essentially duplicate the odds ratio results but are presented because their meaning may be clearer for some readers. Because the placebo/control abstinence percentage for a particular analysis is calculated exclusively from the studies included within that meta-analysis, these abstinence percentages vary across the different analyses. Therefore, the odds ratios and abstinence rates presented across the different tables are estimated relative to different placebo or control conditions.

■ How To Read the Data Tables

Table 1.3 depicts results from one of the meta-analyses reported in this Guideline update. This table presents results from the analysis of the effects of proactive telephone counseling (see Formats of Psychosocial Treatments in Chapter 6). In this table, the comparison condition, or "reference group," for determining the impact of different treatment options was smokers who received minimal or no counseling or self-help. The "Estimated odds ratio" column reveals that treatment conditions receiving proactive telephone counseling had an odds ratio of 1.6. The odds ratio indicates a statistically significant effect because the lower boundary of the confidence interval did not include "1." This odds ratio means that when smokers receive proactive telephone counseling, they are more than one and one-half times more likely to remain abstinent than if they had received minimal or no counseling or self-help.

Table 1.3. Meta-analysis (2008): Effectiveness of and estimated abstinence rates for proactive telephone counseling compared to minimal interventions, self-help, or no counseling (n = 9 studies)

Intervention	Number of arms	Estimated odds ratio (95% C.I.)	Estimated abstinence rate (95% C.I.)
Minimal or no counseling or self-help	11	1.0	10.5
Quitline counseling	11	1.6 (1.4–1.8)	15.5 (13.8–17.3)

The column labeled "Estimated abstinence rate" shows the abstinence percentages for the two treatment conditions. For instance, the reference condition (minimal or no counseling) in the analyzed data set was associated with an abstinence rate of 10.5 percent. Consistent with the odds ratio data reviewed above, proactive telephone counseling produced modest increases in abstinence rates (15.5%).

The total number of studies included in each meta-analysis is provided within the title of the corresponding table. A list of published articles used in each meta-analysis can be found at: *www.surgeongeneral.gov/tobacco/gdlnrefs.htm.* Finally, the 2008 Guideline update includes meta-analyses completed for the 1996, 2000, and 2008 Guidelines. In the title of each meta-analysis, the year in which it was first published is provided.

The column labeled "Number of arms" specifies the number of treatment groups across all analyzed studies that contributed data to the various treatment conditions (e.g., Quitline counseling was provided in 11 treatment arms). Therefore, this column depicts the number of treatment groups relevant to each analyzed category. Because a study may have multiple treatment groups, the number of treatment arms may exceed the number of studies included in a meta-analysis.

The outcome data in the tables may include findings from both studies with "all-comers" (individuals who did not seek a treatment intervention) and "self-selected" populations, studies using point-prevalence and continuous abstinence endpoints, and studies with and without biochemical confirmation, except where otherwise described. Some meta-analyses (such as those evaluating medications) included predominantly studies with "self-selected" populations who volunteered for intensive treatment. In addition, in medication studies, both experimental and control subjects typically received substantial counseling. Both of these factors might have produced higher abstinence rates in reference or placebo subjects than typically are observed among self-quitters. Finally, although there is an important scientific distinction between "efficacy" and "effectiveness,"[106] this 2008 clinical update uses the term "effectiveness" exclusively, recognizing that the majority of the studies summarized here reflect efficacy research, which requires random assignment and a high degree of experimental control. This was done for purposes of clarity for the intended clinical audience.

■ Strength of Evidence

Every recommendation made by the Panel bears a strength-of-evidence rating that indicates the quality and quantity of empirical support for the recommendation. Each recommendation and its strength of evidence reflects consensus of the Guideline Panel.

The three strength-of-evidence ratings are described below:

A. Multiple well-designed randomized clinical trials, directly relevant to the recommendation, yielded a consistent pattern of findings.

B. Some evidence from randomized clinical trials supported the recommendation, but the scientific support was not optimal. For instance, few randomized trials existed, the trials that did exist were somewhat inconsistent, or the trials were not directly relevant to the recommendation.

C. Reserved for important clinical situations in which the Panel achieved consensus on the recommendation in the absence of relevant randomized controlled trials.

As noted previously, the Panel evaluated evidence from nonrandomized trials to inform members' understanding of certain topics (e.g., policy issues). If treatment recommendations were based primarily on such evidence, they were of the "C" level and depended on the consistency of findings across different studies. In some areas, the highest quality evidence does not depend on randomized trials (e.g., cost-effectiveness). In these areas, the strength-of-evidence rating depended on the number, quality, and consistency of the studies and evidence. Finally, the Panel declined to make recommendations when there was no relevant evidence or the evidence was too weak or inconsistent to support a recommendation.

■ Caveats Regarding Recommendations

The reader should note some caveats regarding Guideline recommendations. First, an absence of studies should not be confused with a proven lack of effectiveness. In certain situations, there was little direct evidence regarding the effectiveness of some treatments, and in these cases the Panel usually rendered no opinion. Second, even when there were enough studies to perform a meta-analysis, a nonsignificant result does not prove ineffectiveness. Rather, nonsignificance merely indicates that effectiveness was not demonstrated given the data available.

The primary emphasis of this Guideline update is to identify effective interventions, not to rank-order interventions in terms of effectiveness. The most important goal of the analytic process is to identify effective interventions. Selection or use of particular intervention techniques or strategies usually is a function of practical factors: patient preference, time available, training of the clinician, cost, and so on. The Panel believes clinicians should choose the most appropriate intervention from among the effective interventions identified in this Guideline update, given clinical circumstances. An excessive emphasis on relative effectiveness might discourage clinicians from using interventions that have a small but reliable impact on quit rates. One meta-analysis that is new to this update does provide focused tests of the relative effectiveness of different interventions. Specifically, the inclusive meta-analysis of the tobacco use medications involved *a posteriori* tests of medication effectiveness versus the nicotine patch (Table 6.28). These tests of relative effectiveness were conducted on this topic because: (1) numerous treatments were available for comparison; (2) selection from among the various tobacco use medications has been noted as an important clinical concern;[107-109] and (3) the various interventions are somewhat interchangeable and widely available so that the clinician or patient might be able to select a medication based on effectiveness. Finally, the panel occasionally identified an intervention as superior to another in the absence of formal statistical contrasts; some interventions were so superior to control or no-treatment conditions that the Panel clearly identified them as superior to another intervention. For instance, although minimal person-to-person contact can increase smoking abstinence rates over no-treatment conditions, there is little doubt that longer person-to-person interventions have greater impact (see Chapter 6).

■ External Review of the Guideline

For the present update, the Panel and consortium members invited 106 reviewers to make comments. In addition, a draft of the Guideline was published in the *Federal Register* in September 2007 for public comment. A total of 81 invited reviewers and 15 members of the public supplied written comments. Peer reviewers included clinicians, health care administrators, social workers, counselors, health educators, researchers, consumers, key personnel at selected Federal agencies and State tobacco control programs, and others. All peer reviewers made financial disclosure statements, which were provided to the Panel. Reviewers were asked to evaluate the Guideline based on five criteria: validity, reliability, clarity, clinical applicability, and utility. Comments from the peer reviewers and public were incorporated into the Guideline when appropriate. Two individuals made oral presentations to the Guideline Panel during an advertised open presentation period.

Organization of the Guideline Update

This updated Guideline is divided into seven chapters that reflect the major components of tobacco dependence treatment (see Figure 1.2 for the treatment model):

Chapter 1, Overview and Methods, provides an overview and rationale for the updated Guideline, as well as a detailed description of the methodology used to review the scientific literature and develop the original and updated Guidelines.

Chapter 2, Assessment of Tobacco Use, establishes the importance of determining the tobacco use status of every patient at every visit.

Chapter 3, Clinical Interventions for Tobacco Use and Dependence, is intended to provide clinicians with guidance as they use brief interventions to treat tobacco users willing to quit, tobacco users unwilling to make a quit attempt at this time, and tobacco users who have recently quit.

   A. For the Patient Willing To Quit, provides brief clinical approaches to assist patients in quit attempts.

   B. For the Patient Unwilling To Quit, provides brief clinical approaches designed to motivate the patient to make a quit attempt.

   C. For the Patient Who Has Recently Quit, provides clinicians with strategies designed to reinforce a former tobacco user's commitment to stay tobacco-free and assist patients who have relapsed.

Chapter 4, Intensive Interventions for Tobacco Use and Dependence, provides clinicians with more intensive strategies to treat tobacco users.

Chapter 5, Systems Interventions, targets health care administrators, insurers, purchasers, and other decisionmakers who can affect health care systems. This chapter provides these decisionmakers with strategies to modify health care systems to improve the delivery of tobacco treatment services.

Chapter 6, Evidence and Recommendations, presents the evidentiary basis for the updated Guideline recommendations.

A. Counseling and Psychosocial Evidence: Provides recommendations and analysis results regarding screening for tobacco use and specialized assessment, advice, intensity of clinical interventions, type of clinician, format, followup procedures, types of counseling and behavioral therapies, and the combination of counseling and medication.

B. Medication Evidence: Provides recommendations and analysis results regarding the seven first-line medications, combination medications, second-line medications, and other medication issues.

C. Systems Evidence: Provides recommendations and analysis results regarding systems changes, including provider training, cost-effectiveness, and health insurance coverage for tobacco use treatments.

Chapter 7, Specific Populations and Other Topics, provides information on specific populations, including HIV-positive smokers; hospitalized smokers; lesbian/gay/bisexual/transgender smokers; smokers with low SES/limited formal education; smokers with medical comorbidities; older smokers; smokers with psychiatric disorders, including substance use disorders; racial and ethnic minorities; women smokers; children and adolescents; light smokers; and noncigarette tobacco users. This chapter also presents information and recommendations relevant to weight gain after quitting smoking, with specific recommendations regarding future research on this topic.

▌References

Given the volume of literature referenced in this Guideline, references are listed at *www.surgeongeneral.gov/tobacco/gdlnrefs.htm*, rather than in this document. This was done to manage the length of this Clinical Guideline update and to facilitate electronic searches and manipulation of the references. Within this Web site, text references are numbered to match the numbers in this Guideline update. References to randomized control trials used in all of the meta-analyses (1996, 2000, 2008) are listed separately and by table number and title. The entire Guideline update, with and without references, can be downloaded from the site.

Figure 1.2. Model for treatment of tobacco use and dependence

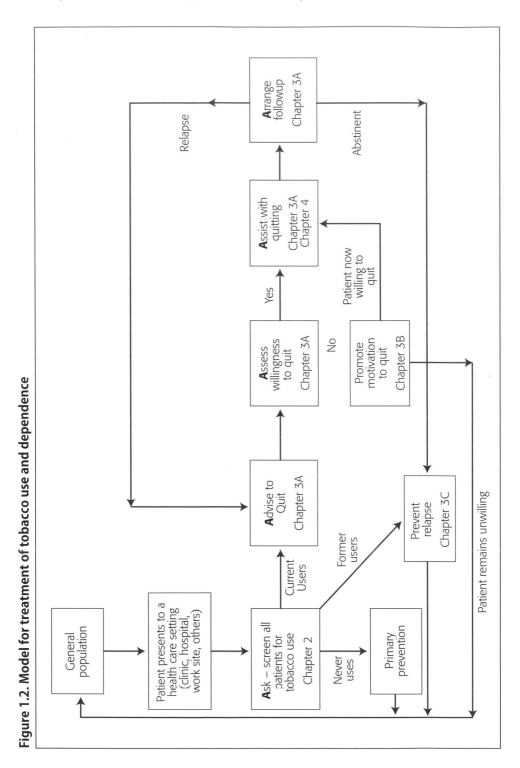

Chapter 2 | Assessment of Tobacco Use

At least 70 percent of smokers see a physician each year, and almost one-third see a dentist.[19,110] Other smokers see physician assistants, nurse practitioners, nurses, physical and occupational therapists, pharmacists, counselors, and other clinicians. Therefore, virtually all clinicians are in a position to intervene with patients who use tobacco. Moreover, 70 percent of smokers report wanting to quit,[111] and almost two-thirds of smokers who relapse want to try quitting again within 30 days.[112] Finally, smokers cite a physician's advice to quit as an important motivator for attempting to stop smoking.[113-118] These data suggest that most smokers are interested in quitting, clinicians and health systems are in frequent contact with smokers, and clinicians have high credibility with smokers.

Unfortunately, clinicians and health systems do not capitalize on this opportunity consistently. According to the National Committee for Quality Assurance's (NCQA) *State of Health Care Quality Report*,[119] there has been some improvement in tobacco dependence clinical intervention for the insured population. In 2005, 71.2 percent of commercially insured smokers received cessation advice (up slightly from 69.6% in 2004); and 75.5 percent of Medicare smokers received advice to quit, up 11 percentage points from 2004 for this group. Despite this progress, there is a clear need for additional improvement. Only 25 percent of Medicaid patients reported any practical assistance with quitting or any ensuing followup of their progress.[22] Only one-third of adolescents who visited a physician or dentist report receiving counseling about the dangers of tobacco use, according to the 2000 National Youth Tobacco Survey.[120] Pregnant women who smoke were identified at 81 percent of physician visits but received counseling at only 23 percent of these visits.[121] In addition, few smokers get specific help with quitting. Recent Healthcare Effectiveness Data and Information Set (HEDIS) data showed that only 39 percent of smokers reported that their clinician discussed either medications or counseling strategies to quit (*www.web.ncqa. org/tabid/59/Default.aspx*). To capitalize on this opportunity, the 2008 Guideline update provides empirically validated tobacco treatment strategies designed to spur clinicians, tobacco treatment specialists, and health systems to intervene effectively with patients who use tobacco.

The first step in treating tobacco use and dependence is to identify tobacco users. As the data analysis in Chapter 6 shows, the identification of smokers itself increases rates of clinician intervention. Effective identification of tobacco use status not only opens the door for successful interventions (e.g., clinician advice and treatment), but also guides clinicians to identify appropriate interventions based on patients' tobacco use status and willingness to quit. Based on these findings, the Guideline update recommends that clinicians and health care systems seize the office visit for universal assessment and intervention. Specifically, ask every patient who presents to a health care facility if s/he uses tobacco (Ask), advise all tobacco users to quit (Advise), and assess the willingness of all tobacco users to make a quit attempt at this time (Assess) (the first 3 of the 5 A's; see Chapter 3).

Screening for current or past tobacco use will result in four possible responses: (1) the patient uses tobacco and is willing to make a quit attempt at this time; (2) the patient uses tobacco but is not willing to make a quit attempt at this time; (3) the patient once used tobacco but has since quit; and (4) the patient never regularly used tobacco. This Clinical Practice Guideline is organized to provide the clinician with simple but effective interventions for all of these patient groups (see Figure 2.1).

Figure 2.1. Algorithm for treating tobacco use

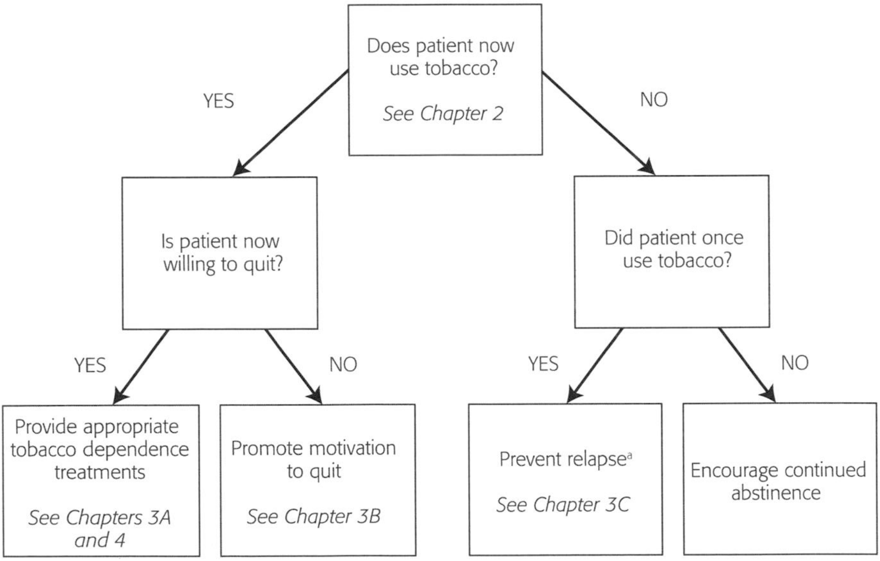

^aRelapse prevention interventions are not necessary in the case of the adult who has not used tobacco for many years.

Chapter 3 | Clinical Interventions for Tobacco Use and Dependence

Background

This section of the Guideline presents specific strategies to guide clinicians providing brief interventions (less than 10 minutes). These brief interventions can be provided by all clinicians but are most relevant to clinicians who see a wide variety of patients and are bound by time constraints (e.g., physicians, nurses, physician assistants, nurse practitioners, medical assistants, dentists, hygienists, respiratory therapists, mental health counselors, pharmacists, etc.). The strategies in this chapter are based on the evidence described in Chapters 6 and 7, as well as on Panel opinion. Guideline analysis suggests that a wide variety of clinicians can implement these strategies effectively.

Why should members of a busy clinical team consider making the treatment of tobacco use a priority? The evidence is compelling: (1) clinicians can make a difference with even a minimal (less than 3 minutes) intervention (see Chapter 6); (2) a relation exists between the intensity of intervention and tobacco cessation outcome (see Chapter 6); (3) even when patients are not willing to make a quit attempt at this time, clinician-delivered brief interventions enhance motivation and increase the likelihood of future quit attempts[122] (see Chapter 6); (4) tobacco users are being primed to consider quitting by a wide range of societal and environmental factors (e.g., public health messages, policy changes, cessation marketing messages, family members); (5) there is growing evidence that smokers who receive clinician advice and assistance with quitting report greater satisfaction with their health care than those who do not;[23,87,88] (6) tobacco use interventions are highly cost effective (see Chapter 6); and (7) tobacco use has a high case fatality rate (up to 50% of long-term smokers will die of a smoking-caused disease[123]).

The goal of these strategies is clear: to change clinical culture and practice patterns to ensure that every patient who uses tobacco is identified, advised to quit, and offered scientifically sound treatments. The strategies underscore a central theme: it is essential to provide at least a brief intervention to every tobacco user at each health care visit. Responsibility lies with both the clinician and the health care system to ensure that this occurs. Several observations are relevant to this theme. First, although many smokers are reluctant to seek intensive treatments,[124,125] they nevertheless can receive a brief intervention every time they visit a clinician.[66,126] Second, institutional support is necessary to ensure that all patients who use tobacco are identified and offered appropriate treatment (see Chapter 5, Systems Interventions: Importance to Health Care Administrators, Insurers, and Purchasers). Third, the time limits on primary care physicians in the United States today (median visit = 12–16 minutes),[127,128] as well as reimbursement restrictions, often limit providers to brief interventions, although more intensive interventions would produce greater success. Finally, given the growing use of electronic patient databases, smoker registries, and real-time clinical care prompts, brief interventions may be easier to fit into a busy practice and may be implemented in a variety of ways.

This chapter is divided into three sections to guide brief clinician interventions with three types of patients: (A) current tobacco users willing to make a quit attempt at this time; (B) current tobacco users unwilling to make a quit attempt at this time; and (C) former tobacco users who have recently quit. Patients who have never used tobacco or who have been abstinent for an extended period should be congratulated on their status and encouraged to maintain their tobacco-free lifestyle.

Given that more than 70 percent of tobacco users visit a physician and more than 50 percent visit a dentist each year,[129] it is essential that these clinicians be prepared to intervene with all tobacco users. The five major components (the "5 A's") of a brief intervention in the primary care setting are listed in Table 3.1. It is important for a clinician to *ask* the patient if he or she uses tobacco (Strategy A1), *advise* him or her to quit (Strategy A2), and *assess* willingness to make a quit attempt (Strategy A3). Strategies A1 to A3 need to be delivered to each tobacco user, regardless of his or her willingness to quit.

If the patient is willing to quit, the clinician should *assist* him or her in making a quit attempt by offering medication and providing or referring for counseling or additional treatment (Strategy A4), and *arrange* for fol-

Table 3.1. The "5 A's" model for treating tobacco use and dependence

Ask about tobacco use.	Identify and document tobacco use status for every patient at every visit. (Strategy A1)
Advise to quit.	In a clear, strong, and personalized manner, urge every tobacco user to quit. (Strategy A2)
Assess willingness to make a quit attempt.	Is the tobacco user willing to make a quit attempt at this time? (Strategy A3)
Assist in quit attempt.	For the patient willing to make a quit attempt, offer medication and provide or refer for counseling or additional treatment to help the patient quit. (Strategy A4) For patients unwilling to quit at the time, provide interventions designed to increase future quit attempts. (Strategies B1 and B2)
Arrange followup.	For the patient willing to make a quit attempt, arrange for followup contacts, beginning within the first week after the quit date. (Strategy A5) For patients unwilling to make a quit attempt at the time, address tobacco dependence and willingness to quit at next clinic visit.

lowup contacts to prevent relapse (Strategy A5). If the patient is unwilling to make a quit attempt, the clinician should provide a motivational intervention (Strategies B1 and B2) and *arrange* to address tobacco dependence at the next clinic visit. The Strategy tables below (A1–A5) comprise suggestions for the content and delivery of the 5 A's. The strategies are designed to be brief and require 3 minutes or less of direct clinician time. These intervention components constitute the core elements of a tobacco intervention, but they need not be applied in a rigid, invariant manner. For instance, the clinician need not deliver all elements personally. One clinician (e.g., a medical assistant) may ask about tobacco use status; and a prescribing clinician (e.g., physician, dentist, physician assistant, nurse practitioner) may deliver personal advice to quit, assess willingness to quit, and assist with medications, but then refer the patient to a tobacco intervention resource (e.g., a tobacco cessation quitline, health educator) that would deliver additional treatment to the patient. The clinician would remain responsible for the patient receiving appropriate care and subsequent followup, but, as with other sorts of health care, an individual clinician would not need to deliver all care personally.[130] Evidence indicates that full implementation of the 5 A's in clinical settings may yield results that are superior to partial implementation.[131]

The effectiveness of tobacco intervention may reflect not only the contributions of the individual clinician, but also the systems and other clinical resources available to him or her. For instance, office systems that institutionalize tobacco use assessment and intervention will greatly foster the likelihood that the 5 A's will be delivered (see Chapter 5). The 5 A's, as described in Table 3.1, are consistent with those recommended by the NCI[132,133] and the American Medical Association,[77] as well as others.[75,134-137] The clinical situation may suggest delivering these intervention components in an order or format different from that presented, however. For example, clinical interventions such as: Ask/Assess, Advise, Agree on a goal, Assist, Arrange followup; Ask and Act; and Ask, Advise, and Refer have been proposed.[116,130,138-140]

When "Assisting" smokers, in addition to counseling, all smokers making a quit attempt should be offered medication, except when contraindicated or with specific populations for which there is insufficient evidence of effectiveness (i.e., pregnant women, smokeless tobacco users, light smokers, and adolescents). See Tables 3.2 to 3.11 for guidelines for prescribing medication for treating tobacco use and dependence.

A. For the Patient Willing To Quit

Strategy A1. *Ask*—Systematically identify all tobacco users at every visit

Action	Strategies for implementation
Implement an officewide system that ensures that, for *every* patient at *every* clinic visit, tobacco use status is queried and documented.[a]	Expand the vital signs to include tobacco use, or use an alternative universal identification system.[b] **VITAL SIGNS** Blood Pressure: _____ Pulse: _____ Weight: _____ Temperature: _____ Respiratory Rate: _____ Tobacco Use (circle one): Current Former Never

[a] Repeated assessment is *not* necessary in the case of the adult who has never used tobacco or has not used tobacco for many years and for whom this information is clearly documented in the medical record.

[b] Alternatives to expanding the vital signs include using tobacco use status stickers on all patient charts or indicating tobacco use status via electronic medical records or computerized reminder systems.

Strategy A2. *Advise*—**Strongly urge all tobacco users to quit**

Action	Strategies for implementation
In a *clear, strong, and personalized* manner, urge every tobacco user to quit.	Advice should be: • *Clear*—"It is important that you quit smoking (or using chewing tobacco) now, and I can help you." "Cutting down while you are ill is not enough." "Occasional or light smoking is still dangerous." • *Strong*—"As your clinician, I need you to know that quitting smoking is the most important thing you can do to protect your health now and in the future. The clinic staff and I will help you." • *Personalized*—Tie tobacco use to current symptoms and health concerns, and/or its social and economic costs, and/or the impact of tobacco use on children and others in the household. "Continuing to smoke makes your asthma worse, and quitting may dramatically improve your health." "Quitting smoking may reduce the number of ear infections your child has."

Strategy A3. *Assess*—**Determine willingness to make a quit attempt**

Action	Strategies for implementation
Assess every tobacco user's willingness to make a quit attempt at the time.	Assess patient's willingness to quit: "Are you willing to give quitting a try?" • If the patient is willing to make a quit attempt at the time, provide assistance (see Chapter 3A, Strategy A4). – If the patient will participate in an intensive treatment, deliver such a treatment or link/refer to an intensive intervention (see Chapter 4). – If the patient is a member of a special population (e.g., adolescent, pregnant smoker, racial/ethnic minority), consider providing additional information (see Chapter 7). • If the patient clearly states that he or she is unwilling to make a quit attempt at the time, provide an intervention shown to increase future quit attempts (see Chapter 3B).

Strategy A4. *Assist*—**Aid the patient in quitting (provide counseling and medication)**

Action	Strategies for implementation
Help the patient with a quit plan.	*A patient's preparations for quitting:* • *Set a quit date.* Ideally, the quit date should be within 2 weeks. • *Tell* family, friends, and coworkers about quitting, and request understanding and support. • *Anticipate* challenges to the upcoming quit attempt, particularly during the critical first few weeks. These include nicotine withdrawal symptoms. • *Remove* tobacco products from your environment. Prior to quitting, avoid smoking in places where you spend a lot of time (e.g., work, home, car). Make your home smoke-free.
Recommend the use of approved medication, except when contraindicated or with specific populations for which there is insufficient evidence of effectiveness (i.e., pregnant women, smokeless tobacco users, light smokers, and adolescents).	Recommend the use of medications found to be effective in this Guideline (see Table 3.2 for clinical guidelines and Tables 3.3–3.11 for specific instructions and precautions). Explain how these medications increase quitting success and reduce withdrawal symptoms. The first-line medications include: bupropion SR, nicotine gum, nicotine inhaler, nicotine lozenge, nicotine nasal spray, nicotine patch, and varenicline; second-line medications include: clonidine and nortriptyline. There is insufficient evidence to recommend medications for certain populations (e.g., pregnant women, smokeless tobacco users, light smokers, adolescents).
Provide practical counseling (problemsolving/skills training).	*Abstinence.* Striving for total abstinence is essential. Not even a single puff after the quit date.[141] *Past quit experience.* Identify what helped and what hurt in previous quit attempts. Build on past success. *Anticipate triggers or challenges in the upcoming attempt.* Discuss challenges/triggers and how the patient will successfully overcome them (e.g., avoid triggers, alter routines). *Alcohol.* Because alcohol is associated with relapse, the patient should consider limiting/abstaining from alcohol while quitting. (Note that reducing alcohol intake could precipitate withdrawal in alcohol-dependent persons.) *Other smokers in the household.* Quitting is more difficult when there is another smoker in the household. Patients should encourage housemates to quit with them or to not smoke in their presence. For further description of practical counseling, see Table 6.19.

Strategy A4. *Assist*—**Aid the patient in quitting (provide counseling and medication) (continued)**

Action	Strategies for implementation
Provide intratreatment social support.	Provide a supportive clinical environment while encouraging the patient in his or her quit attempt. *"My office staff and I are available to assist you." "I'm recommending treatment that can provide ongoing support."* For further description of intratreatment social support, see Table 6.20.
Provide supplementary materials, including information on quitlines.	*Sources:* Federal agencies, nonprofit agencies, national quitline network (1-800-QUIT-NOW), or local/state/tribal health departments/quitlines (see Appendix B for Web site addresses). *Type:* Culturally/racially/educationally/age-appropriate for the patient. *Location:* Readily available at every clinician's workstation.
For the smoker unwilling to quit at the time	See Section 3B.

Strategy A5. *Arrange*—**Ensure followup contact**

Action	Strategies for implementation
Arrange for followup contacts, either in person or via telephone.	*Timing:* Followup contact should begin soon after the quit date, preferably during the first week. A second followup contact is recommended within the first month. Schedule further followup contacts as indicated. *Actions during followup contact:* For all patients, identify problems already encountered and anticipate challenges in the immediate future. Assess medication use and problems. Remind patients of quitline support (1-800-QUIT-NOW). Address tobacco use at next clinical visit (treat tobacco use as a chronic disease). For patients who are abstinent, congratulate them on their success. If tobacco use has occurred, review circumstances and elicit recommitment to total abstinence. Consider use of or link to more intensive treatment (see Chapter 4).
For smokers unwilling to quit at the time	See Section 3B.

Table 3.2. Clinical guidelines for prescribing medication for treating tobacco use and dependence

Who should receive medication for tobacco use? Are there groups of smokers for whom medication has not been shown to be effective?	All smokers trying to quit should be offered medication, except when contraindicated or for specific populations for which there is insufficient evidence of effectiveness (i.e., pregnant women, smokeless tobacco users, light smokers, and adolescents; see Chapter 7).
What are the first-line medications recommended in this Guideline update?	All seven of the FDA-approved medications for treating tobacco use are recommended: bupropion SR, nicotine gum, nicotine inhaler, nicotine lozenge, nicotine nasal spray, nicotine patch, and varenicline. The clinician should consider the first-line medications shown to be more effective than the nicotine patch alone: 2 mg/day varenicline or the combination of long-term nicotine patch use + *ad libitum* nicotine replacement therapy (NRT). Unfortunately, there are no well-accepted algorithms to guide optimal selection among the first-line medications.
Are there contraindications, warnings, precautions, other concerns, and side effects regarding the first-line medications recommended in this Guideline update?	All seven FDA-approved medications have specific contraindications, warnings, precautions, other concerns, and side effects. Refer to FDA package inserts for this complete information and FDA updates to the individual drug tables in this document (Tables 3.3–3.9). (See information below regarding second-line medications.)
What other factors may influence medication selection?	Pragmatic factors also may influence selection, such as insurance coverage, out-of-pocket patient costs, likelihood of adherence, dentures when considering the gum, or dermatitis when considering the patch.
Is a patient's prior experience with a medication relevant?	Prior successful experience (sustained abstinence with the medication) suggests that the medication may be helpful to the patient in a subsequent quit attempt, especially if the patient found the medication to be tolerable and/or easy to use. However, it is difficult to draw firm conclusions from prior failure with a medication. Some evidence suggests that re-treating relapsed smokers with the same medication produces small or no benefit,[142,143] whereas other evidence suggests that it may be of substantial benefit.[144]

Table 3.2. Clinical guidelines for prescribing medication for treating tobacco use and dependence (continued)

What medications should a clinician use with a patient who is highly nicotine dependent?	The higher-dose preparations of nicotine gum, patch, and lozenge have been shown to be effective in highly dependent smokers.[145-147] Also, there is evidence that combination NRT therapy may be particularly effective in suppressing tobacco withdrawal symptoms.[148,149] Thus, it may be that NRT combinations are especially helpful for highly dependent smokers or those with a history of severe withdrawal.
Is gender a consideration in selecting a medication?	There is evidence that NRT can be effective with both sexes;[150-152] however, evidence is mixed as to whether NRT is less effective in women than men.[153-157] This may encourage the clinician to consider use of another type of medication with women, such as bupropion SR or varenicline.
Are cessation medications appropriate for light smokers (i.e., < 10 cigarettes/day)?	As noted above, cessation medications have not been shown to be beneficial to light smokers. However, if NRT is used with light smokers, clinicians may consider reducing the dose of the medication. No adjustments are necessary when using bupropion SR or varenicline.
When should second-line agents be used for treating tobacco dependence?	Consider prescribing second-line agents (clonidine and nortriptyline) for patients unable to use first-line medications because of contraindications or for patients for whom the group of first-line medications has not been helpful. Assess patients for the specific contraindications, precautions, other concerns, and side effects of the second-line agents. Refer to FDA package inserts for this information and to the individual drug tables in this document (Tables 3.10 and 3.11).
Which medications should be considered with patients particularly concerned about weight gain?	Data show that bupropion SR and nicotine replacement therapies, in particular 4-mg nicotine gum and 4-mg nicotine lozenge, delay— but do not prevent—weight gain.
Are there medications that should especially be considered for patients with a past history of depression?	Bupropion SR and nortriptyline appear to be effective with this population[158-162] (see Chapter 7), but nicotine replacement medications also appear to help individuals with a past history of depression.

Table 3.2. Clinical guidelines for prescribing medication for treating tobacco use and dependence (continued)

Should nicotine replacement therapies be avoided in patients with a history of cardiovascular disease?	No. The nicotine patch in particular has been demonstrated as safe for cardiovascular patients. See Tables 3.3–3.9 and FDA package inserts for more complete information.
May tobacco dependence medications be used long-term (e.g., up to 6 months)?	Yes. This approach may be helpful with smokers who report persistent withdrawal symptoms during the course of medications, who have relapsed in the past after stopping medication, or who desire long-term therapy. A minority of individuals who successfully quit smoking use *ad libitum* NRT medications (gum, nasal spray, inhaler) long-term. The use of these medications for up to 6 months does not present a known health risk, and developing dependence on medications is uncommon. Additionally, the FDA has approved the use of bupropion SR, varenicline, and some NRT medications for 6-month use.
Is medication adherence important?	Yes. Patients frequently do not use cessation medications as recommended (e.g., they do not use them at recommended doses or for recommended durations); this may reduce their effectiveness.
May medications ever be combined?	Yes. Among first-line medications, evidence exists that combining the nicotine patch long-term (> 14 weeks) with either nicotine gum or nicotine nasal spray, the nicotine patch with the nicotine inhaler, or the nicotine patch with bupropion SR, increases long-term abstinence rates relative to placebo treatments. Combining varenicline with NRT agents has been associated with higher rates of side effects (e.g., nausea, headaches).

Table 3.3. Clinical use of bupropion SR (See FDA package insert for more complete information.)

	Clinical use of bupropion SR 150 (FDA approved)
Patient selection	Appropriate as a first-line medication for treating tobacco use
Precautions, warnings, contraindications, and side effects (see FDA package insert for complete list)	*Pregnancy* – Pregnant smokers should be encouraged to quit without medication. Bupropion has not been shown to be effective for tobacco dependence treatment in pregnant smokers. (Bupropion is an FDA pregnancy Class C agent.) Bupropion has not been evaluated in breastfeeding patients._ *Cardiovascular diseases* – Generally well-tolerated; occasional reports of hypertension.

Table 3.3. Clinical use of bupropion SR (See FDA package insert for more complete information.) (continued)

	Clinical use of bupropion SR 150 (FDA approved)
Precautions, contraindications, and side effects *(continued)*	*Side effects* – The most common reported side effects were insomnia (35–40%) and dry mouth (10%). *Contraindications* – Bupropion SR is contraindicated in individuals who have a history of seizures or eating disorders, who are taking another form of bupropion, or who have used an MAO inhibitor in the past 14 days.
Dosage	Patients should begin bupropion SR treatment 1–2 weeks before they quit smoking. Patients should begin with a dose of 150 mg every morning for 3 days, then increase to 150 mg twice daily. Dosage should not exceed 300 mg per day. Dosing at 150 mg twice daily should continue for 7–12 weeks. For long-term therapy, consider use of bupropion SR 150 mg for up to 6 months postquit.
Availability	Prescription only
Prescribing instructions	*Stopping smoking prior to quit date* – Recognize that some patients may lose their desire to smoke prior to their quit date or will spontaneously reduce the amount they smoke. *Dosing information* – If insomnia is marked, taking the PM dose earlier (in the afternoon, at least 8 hours after the first dose) may provide some relief. *Alcohol* – Use alcohol only in moderation.
Cost[a]	1 box of 60 tablets, 150 mg = $97 per month (generic); $197 to $210 (Brand name)

[a] Cost data were established by averaging the retail price of the medication at national chain pharmacies in Atlanta, GA, Los Angeles, CA, Milwaukee, WI, Sunnyside, NY, and listed online during January 2008 and may not reflect discounts available to health plans and others.

Table 3.4. Clinical use of nicotine gum (See FDA package insert for more complete information.)

	Clinical use of nicotine gum (FDA approved)
Patient selection	Appropriate as a first-line medication for treating tobacco use
Precautions, warnings, contraindications, and side effects (see FDA package insert for complete list)	*Pregnancy* – Pregnant smokers should be encouraged to quit without medication. Nicotine gum has not been shown to be effective for treating tobacco dependence in pregnant smokers. (Nicotine gum is an FDA pregnancy Class D agent.) Nicotine gum has not been evaluated in breastfeeding patients.

Table 3.4. Clinical use of nicotine gum (See FDA package insert for more complete information.) (continued)

	Clinical use of nicotine gum (FDA approved)
Precautions, warnings, contraindications, and side effects (see FDA package insert for complete list) (continued)	*Cardiovascular diseases* – NRT is not an independent risk factor for acute myocardial events. NRT should be used with caution among particular cardiovascular patient groups: those in the immediate (within 2 weeks) postmyocardial infarction period, those with serious arrhythmias, and those with unstable angina pectoris. *Side effects* – Common side effects of nicotine gum include mouth soreness, hiccups, dyspepsia, and jaw ache. These effects are generally mild and transient and often can be alleviated by correcting the patient's chewing technique (see *prescribing instructions,* below).
Dosage	Nicotine gum (both regular and flavored) is available in 2-mg and 4-mg (per piece) doses. The 2-mg gum is recommended for patients smoking less than 25 cigarettes per day; the 4-mg gum is recommended for patients smoking 25 or more cigarettes per day. Smokers should use at least one piece every 1 to 2 hours for the first 6 weeks; the gum should be used for up to 12 weeks with no more than 24 pieces to be used per day.
Availability	OTC only
Prescribing instructions	*Chewing technique* – Gum should be chewed slowly until a "peppery" or "flavored" taste emerges, then "parked" between cheek and gum to facilitate nicotine absorption through the oral mucosa. Gum should be slowly and intermittently "chewed and parked" for about 30 minutes or until the taste dissipates. *Absorption* – Acidic beverages (e.g., coffee, juices, soft drinks) interfere with the buccal absorption of nicotine, so eating and drinking anything except water should be avoided for 15 minutes before or during chewing. *Dosing information* – Patients often do not use enough *prn* NRT medicines to obtain optimal clinical effects. Instructions to chew the gum on a fixed schedule (at least one piece every 1–2 hours) for at least 1–3 months may be more beneficial than *ad libitum* use.
Cost[a]	2 mg (packaged in different amounts), boxes of 100–170 pieces = $48 (quantity used determines how long supply lasts) 4 mg (packaged in different amounts), boxes of 100–110 pieces = $63 (quantity used determines how long supply lasts)

[a] Cost data were established by averaging the retail price of the medication at national chain pharmacies in Atlanta, GA, Los Angeles, CA, Milwaukee, WI, Sunnyside, NY, and listed online during January 2008 and may not reflect discounts available to health plans and others.

Table 3.5. Clinical use of the nicotine inhaler (See FDA package insert for more complete information.)

	Clinical use of nicotine inhaler (FDA approved)
Patient selection	Appropriate as a first-line medication for treating tobacco use
Precautions, warnings, contraindications, and side effects (see FDA package insert for complete list)	*Pregnancy* – Pregnant smokers should be encouraged to quit without medication. The nicotine inhaler has not been shown to be effective for treating tobacco dependence in pregnant smokers. (The nicotine inhaler is an FDA pregnancy Class D agent.) The nicotine inhaler has not been evaluated in breastfeeding patients. *Cardiovascular diseases* – NRT is not an independent risk factor for acute myocardial events. NRT should be used with caution among particular cardiovascular patient groups: those in the immediate (within 2 weeks) postmyocardial infarction period, those with serious arrhythmias, and those with unstable angina pectoris. *Local irritation reactions* – Local irritation in the mouth and throat was observed in 40% of patients using the nicotine inhaler. Coughing (32%) and rhinitis (23%) also were common. Severity was generally rated as mild, and the frequency of such symptoms declined with continued use.
Dosage	A dose from the nicotine inhaler consists of a puff or inhalation. Each cartridge delivers a total of 4 mg of nicotine over 80 inhalations. Recommended dosage is 6–16 cartridges/day. Recommended duration of therapy is up to 6 months. Instruct patient to taper dosage during the final 3 months of treatment.
Availability	Prescription only
Prescribing instructions	*Ambient temperature* – Delivery of nicotine from the inhaler declines significantly at temperatures below 40°F. In cold weather, the inhaler and cartridges should be kept in an inside pocket or other warm area. *Absorption* – Acidic beverages (e.g., coffee, juices, soft drinks) interfere with the buccal absorption of nicotine, so eating and drinking anything except water should be avoided for 15 minutes before or during use of the inhaler. *Dosing information* – Patients often do not use enough *prn* NRT medicines to obtain optimal clinical effects. Use is recommended for up to 6 months, with gradual reduction in frequency of use over the last 6–12 weeks of treatment. Best effects are achieved by frequent puffing of the inhaler and using at least six cartridges/day.
Cost[a]	1 box of 168 10-mg cartridges = $196 (quantity used determines how long supply lasts)

[a] Cost data were established by averaging the retail price of the medication at national chain pharmacies in Atlanta, GA, Los Angeles, CA, Milwaukee, WI, Sunnyside, NY, and listed online during January 2008 and may not reflect discounts available to health plans and others.

Table 3.6. Clinical use of the nicotine lozenge (See FDA package insert for more complete information.)

	Clinical use of nicotine lozenge (FDA approved)
Patient selection	Appropriate as a first-line medication for treating tobacco use
Precautions, warnings, contraindications, and side effects (see FDA package insert for complete list)	*Pregnancy* – Pregnant smokers should be encouraged to quit without medication. The nicotine lozenge has not been shown to be effective for treating tobacco dependence for pregnant smokers. The nicotine lozenge has not been evaluated in breastfeeding patients. Because the lozenge was approved as an OTC agent, it was not evaluated by the FDA for teratogenicity. *Cardiovascular diseases* – NRT is not an independent risk factor for acute myocardial events. NRT should be used with caution among particular cardiovascular patient groups: those in the immediate (within 2 weeks) postmyocardial infarction period, those with serious arrhythmias, and those with unstable angina pectoris. *Side effects* – The most common side effects of the nicotine lozenge are nausea, hiccups, and heartburn. Individuals on the 4-mg lozenge also had increased rates of headache and coughing (less than 10% of participants).
Dosage	Nicotine lozenges are available in 2-mg and 4-mg (per piece) doses. The 2-mg lozenge is recommended for patients who smoke their first cigarette more than 30 minutes after waking, and the 4-mg lozenge is recommended for patients who smoke their first cigarette within 30 minutes of waking. Generally, smokers should use at least nine lozenges per day in the first 6 weeks; the lozenge should be used for up to 12 weeks, with no more than 20 lozenges to be used per day.
Availability	OTC only
Prescribing instructions	*Lozenge use* – The lozenge should be allowed to dissolve in the mouth rather than chewing or swallowing it. *Absorption* – Acidic beverages (e.g., coffee, juices, soft drinks) interfere with the buccal absorption of nicotine, so eating and drinking anything except water should be avoided for 15 minutes before or during use of the nicotine lozenge. *Dosing information* – Patients often do not use enough *prn* NRT medicines to obtain optimal clinical effects. Generally, patients should use 1 lozenge every 1–2 hours during the first 6 weeks of treatment, using a minimum of 9 lozenges/day, then decrease lozenge use to 1 lozenge every 2–4 hours during weeks 7–9, and then decrease to 1 lozenge every 4–8 hours during weeks 10–12.
Cost[a]	2 mg, 72 lozenges per box = $34 (quantity used determines how long supply lasts) 4 mg, 72 lozenges per box = $39 (quantity used determines how long supply lasts)

[a] Cost data were established by averaging the retail price of the medication at national chain pharmacies in Atlanta, GA, Los Angeles, CA, Milwaukee, WI, Sunnyside, NY, and listed online during January 2008 and may not reflect discounts available to health plans and others.

Table 3.7. Clinical use of the nicotine nasal spray (See FDA package insert for more complete information.)

	Clinical use of nicotine nasal spray (FDA approved)
Patient selection	Appropriate as a first-line medication for treating tobacco use
Precautions, warnings, contraindications, and side effects (see FDA package insert for complete list)	*Pregnancy* – Pregnant smokers should be encouraged to quit without medication. Nicotine nasal spray has not been shown to be effective for treating tobacco dependence in pregnant smokers. (Nicotine nasal spray is an FDA pregnancy Class D agent.) Nicotine nasal spray has not been evaluated in breastfeeding patients._ *Cardiovascular diseases* – NRT is not an independent risk factor for acute myocardial events. NRT should be used with caution among particular cardiovascular patient groups: those in the immediate (within 2 weeks) postmyocardial infarction period, those with serious arrhythmias, and those with unstable angina pectoris. *Nasal/airway reactions* – Some 94% of users report moderate to severe nasal irritation in the first 2 days of use; 81% still reported nasal irritation after 3 weeks, although rated severity typically was mild to moderate. Nasal congestion and transient changes in sense of smell and taste also were reported. Nicotine nasal spray should not be used in persons with severe reactive airway disease. *Dependency* – Nicotine nasal spray produces higher peak nicotine levels than other NRTs and has the highest dependence potential. Approximately 15–20% of patients report using the active spray for longer periods than recommended (6–12 months); 5% used the spray at a higher dose than recommended.
Dosage	A dose of nicotine nasal spray consists of one 0.5-mg dose delivered to each nostril (1 mg total). Initial dosing should be 1–2 doses per hour, increasing as needed for symptom relief. Minimum recommended treatment is 8 doses/day, with a maximum limit of 40 doses/day (5 doses/hour). Each bottle contains approximately 100 doses. Recommended duration of therapy is 3–6 months.
Availability	Prescription only
Prescribing instructions	*Dosing information* – Patients should not sniff, swallow, or inhale through the nose while administering doses, as this increases irritating effects. The spray is best delivered with the head tilted slightly back.
Cost[a]	$49 per bottle (quantity used determines how long supply lasts)

[a] Cost data were established by averaging the retail price of the medication at national chain pharmacies in Atlanta, GA, Los Angeles, CA, Milwaukee, WI, Sunnyside, NY, and listed online during January 2008 and may not reflect discounts available to health plans and others.

Table 3.8. Clinical use of the nicotine patch (See FDA package insert for more complete information.)

	Clinical use of the nicotine patch (FDA approved)
Patient selection	Appropriate as a first-line medication for treating tobacco use
Precautions, warnings, contraindications, and side effects (see FDA package insert for complete list)	*Pregnancy* – Pregnant smokers should be encouraged to quit without medication. The nicotine patch has not been shown to be effective for treating tobacco dependence treatment in pregnant smokers. (The nicotine patch is an FDA pregnancy Class D agent.) The nicotine patch has not been evaluated in breastfeeding patients. *Cardiovascular diseases* – NRT is not an independent risk factor for acute myocardial events. NRT should be used with caution among particular cardiovascular patient groups: those in the immediate (within 2 weeks) postmyocardial infarction period, those with serious arrhythmias, and those with unstable angina pectoris. *Skin reactions* – Up to 50% of patients using the nicotine patch will experience a local skin reaction. Skin reactions usually are mild and self-limiting, but occasionally worsen over the course of therapy. Local treatment with hydrocortisone cream (1%) or triamcinolone cream (0.5%) and rotating patch sites may ameliorate such local reactions. In fewer than 5% of patients, such reactions require the discontinuation of nicotine patch treatment. *Other side effects* – insomnia and/or vivid dreams
Dosage	Treatment of 8 weeks or less has been shown to be as efficacious as longer treatment periods. Patches of different doses sometimes are available as well as different recommended dosing regimens. The dose and duration recommendations in this table are examples. Clinicians should consider individualizing treatment based on specific patient characteristics, such as previous experience with the patch, amount smoked, degree of dependence, etc.
Availability	OTC or prescription

Type	Duration	Dosage
Step-Down Dosage	4 weeks then 2 weeks then 2 weeks	21 mg/24 hours 14 mg/24 hours 7 mg/24 hours
Single Dosage	Both a 22 mg/24 hours and an 11 mg/24 hours (for lighter smokers) dose are available in a one-step patch regimen.	

Table 3.8. Clinical use of the nicotine patch (See FDA package insert for more complete information.) (continued)

	Clinical use of the nicotine patch (FDA approved)
Prescribing instructions	*Location* – At the start of each day, the patient should place a new patch on a relatively hairless location, typically between the neck and waist, rotating the site to reduce local skin irritation. *Activities* – No restrictions while using the patch *Dosing information* – Patches should be applied as soon as the patient wakes on the quit day. With patients who experience sleep disruption, have the patient remove the 24-hour patch prior to bedtime, or use the 16-hour patch (designed for use while the patient is awake).
Cost[a]	7 mg, box = $37 (quantity used determines how long supply lasts) 14 mg, box – $47 (quantity used determines how long supply lasts) 21 mg, box = $48 (quantity used determines how long supply lasts)

[a] Cost data were established by averaging the retail price of the medication at national chain pharmacies in Atlanta, GA, Los Angeles, CA, Milwaukee, WI, Sunnyside, NY, and listed online during January 2008 and may not reflect discounts available to health plans and others.

Table 3.9. Clinical use of varenicline (See FDA package insert for more complete information.)

	Clinical use of varenicline (FDA approved)
Patient selection	Appropriate as a first-line medication for treating tobacco use
Precautions, warnings, contraindications, and side effects (see FDA package insert for complete list)	*Pregnancy* – Pregnant smokers should be encouraged to quit without medication. Varenicline has not been shown to be effective for treating tobacco dependence in pregnant smokers. (Varenicline is an FDA pregnancy Class C agent.) Varenicline has not been evaluated in breastfeeding patients. *Cardiovascular diseases* – Not contraindicated *Precautions* – Use with caution in patients with significant kidney disease (creatinine clearance < 30mL/min) or who are on dialysis. Dose should be reduced with these patients. Patients taking varenicline may experience impairment of the ability to drive or operate heavy machinery.

Table 3.9. Clinical use of varenicline (See FDA package insert for more complete information.) (continued)

	Clinical use of varenicline (FDA approved)
Precautions, warnings, contraindications, and side effects (see FDA package insert for complete list) (continued)	*Warning* – In February 2008, the FDA added a warning regarding the use of varenicline. Specifically, it noted that depressed mood, agitation, changes in behavior, suicidal ideation, and suicide have been reported in patients attempting to quit smoking while using varenicline. The FDA recommends that patients should tell their health care provider about any history of psychiatric illness prior to starting this medication, and clinicians should monitor patients for changes in mood and behavior when prescribing this medication. In light of these FDA recommendations, clinicians should consider eliciting information on their patients' psychiatric history. *Side effects* – Nausea, trouble sleeping, abnormal/vivid/strange dreams
Dosage	Start varenicline 1 week before the quit date at 0.5 mg once daily for 3 days, followed by 0.5 mg twice daily for 4 days, followed by 1 mg twice daily for 3 months. Varenicline is approved for a maintenance indication for up to 6 months. Note: Patient should be instructed to quit smoking on day 8, when dosage is increased to 1 mg twice daily.
Availability	Prescription only
Prescribing instructions	*Stopping smoking prior to quit date* – Recognize that some patients may lose their desire to smoke prior to their quit date or will spontaneously reduce the amount they smoke. *Dosing information* –To reduce nausea, take on a full stomach. To reduce insomnia, take second pill at supper rather than bedtime.
Cost[a]	1 mg, box of 56 = $131 (about 30-day supply)

[a] Cost data were established by averaging the retail price of the medication at national chain pharmacies in Atlanta, GA, Los Angeles, CA, Milwaukee, WI , Sunnyside, NY, and listed online during January 2008 and may not reflect discounts available to health plans and others.

Table 3.10. Clinical use of clonidine (See FDA package insert for more complete information.)

	Clinical use of clonidine (not FDA approved for smoking cessation)
Patient selection	Appropriate as a second-line medication for treating tobacco use
Precautions, warnings, contraindications, and side effects (see FDA package insert for complete list)	*Pregnancy* – Pregnant smokers should be encouraged to quit without medication. Clonidine has not been shown to be effective for tobacco cessation in pregnant smokers. (Clonidine is an FDA pregnancy Class C agent.) Clonidine has not been evaluated in breastfeeding patients. *Activities* – Patients who engage in potentially hazardous activities, such as operating machinery or driving, should be advised of a possible sedative effect of clonidine. *Side effects* – Most commonly reported side effects include dry mouth (40%), drowsiness (33%), dizziness (16%), sedation (10%), and constipation (10%). As an antihypertensive medication, clonidine can be expected to lower blood pressure in most patients. Therefore, clinicians should monitor blood pressure when using this medication. *Rebound hypertension* – When stopping clonidine therapy, failure to reduce the dose gradually over a period of 2–4 days may result in a rapid increase in blood pressure, agitation, confusion, and/or tremor.
Dosage	Doses used in various clinical trials have varied significantly, from 0.15–0.75 mg/day by mouth and from 0.10–0.20 mg/day transdermal (TTS), without a clear dose-response relation to treatment outcomes. Initial dosing is typically 0.10 mg b.i.d. PO or 0.10 mg/day TTS, increasing by 0.10 mg/day per week if needed. The dose duration also varied across the clinical trials, ranging from 3–10 weeks.
Availability	Oral – Prescription only Transdermal – Prescription only
Prescribing instructions	*Initiate* – Initiate clonidine shortly before (up to 3 days), or on the quit date. *Dosing information* – If the patient is using transdermal clonidine, at the start of each week, he or she should place a new patch on a relatively hairless location between the neck and waist. Users should not discontinue clonidine therapy abruptly.
Cost[a]	Oral – .1 mg, box of 60 = $13 (daily dosage determines how long supply lasts) Transdermal – 4-pack TTS = $106

[a] Cost data were established by averaging the retail price of the medication at national chain pharmacies in Atlanta, GA, Los Angeles, CA, Milwaukee, WI, Sunnyside, NY, and listed online during January 2008 and may not reflect discounts available to health plans and others.

Table 3.11. Clinical use of nortriptyline (See FDA package insert for more complete information.)

	Clinical use of nortriptyline (not FDA approved for smoking cessation)
Patient selection	Appropriate as a second-line medication for treating tobacco use
Precautions, warnings, contraindications, and side effects (see FDA package insert for complete list)	*Pregnancy* – Pregnant smokers should be encouraged to quit without medication. Nortriptyline has not been shown to be effective for tobacco cessation in pregnant smokers. (Nortriptyline is an FDA pregnancy Class D agent.) Nortriptyline has not been evaluated in breastfeeding patients. *Side effects* – Most commonly reported side effects include sedation, dry mouth (64–78%), blurred vision (16%), urinary retention, lightheadedness (49%), and shaky hands (23%). *Activities* – Nortriptyline may impair the mental and/or physical abilities required for the performance of hazardous tasks, such as operating machinery or driving a car; therefore, the patient should be warned accordingly. *Cardiovascular and other effects* – Because of the risk of arrhythmias and impairment of myocardial contractility, use with caution in patients with cardiovascular disease. Do not co-administer with MAO inhibitors.
Dosage	Doses used in smoking cessation trials have initiated treatment at a dose of 25 mg/day, increasing gradually to a target dose of 75–100 mg/day. Duration of treatment used in smoking cessation trials has been approximately 12 weeks, although clinicians may consider extending treatment for up to 6 months.
Availability	Nortriptyline HCl – prescription only
Prescribing instructions	*Initiate* – Therapy is initiated 10–28 days before the quit date to allow nortriptyline to reach steady state at the target dose. *Therapeutic monitoring* – Although therapeutic blood levels for smoking cessation have not been determined, therapeutic monitoring of plasma nortriptyline levels should be considered under American Psychiatric Association Guidelines for treating patients with depression. Clinicians may choose to assess plasma nortriptyline levels as needed.[163] *Dosing information* – Users should not discontinue nortriptyline abruptly because of withdrawal effects. Overdose may produce severe and life-threatening cardiovascular toxicity, as well as seizures and coma. Risk of overdose should be considered carefully before using nortriptyline.
Cost[a]	25 mg, box of 60 = $24 (daily dosage determines how long supply lasts)

[a] Cost data were established by averaging the retail price of the medication at national chain pharmacies in Atlanta, GA, Los Angeles, CA, Milwaukee, WI, Sunnyside, NY, and listed online during January 2008 and may not reflect discounts available to health plans and others.

B. For the Patient Unwilling To Quit

Promoting the Motivation To Quit

All patients entering a health care setting should have their tobacco use status assessed routinely. Clinicians should advise all tobacco users to quit and then assess a patient's willingness to make a quit attempt. For patients not ready to make a quit attempt at the time, clinicians should use a brief intervention designed to promote the motivation to quit.

Patients unwilling to make a quit attempt during a visit may lack information about the harmful effects of tobacco use and the benefits of quitting, may lack the required financial resources, may have fears or concerns about quitting, or may be demoralized because of previous relapse.[164-167] Such patients may respond to brief motivational interventions that are based on principles of Motivational Interviewing (MI),[168] a directive, patient-centered counseling intervention.[169] There is evidence that MI is effective in increasing future quit attempts;[170-174] however, it is unclear that MI is successful in boosting abstinence among individuals motivated to quit smoking.[173,175,176]

Clinicians employing MI techniques focus on exploring a tobacco user's feelings, beliefs, ideas, and values regarding tobacco use in an effort to uncover any ambivalence about using tobacco.[169,177,178] Once ambivalence is uncovered, the clinician selectively elicits, supports, and strengthens the patient's "change talk" (e.g., reasons, ideas, needs for eliminating tobacco use) and "commitment language" (e.g., intentions to take action to change smoking behavior, such as not smoking in the home). MI researchers have found that having patients use their own words to commit to change is more effective than clinician exhortations, lectures, or arguments for quitting, which tend to increase rather than lessen patient resistance to change.[177]

The four general principles that underlie MI are: *(1) express empathy, (2) develop discrepancy, (3) roll with resistance,* and *(4) support self-efficacy.*[168,179] Specific MI counseling strategies that are based on these principles are listed in Strategy B1. Because this is a specialized technique, it may be beneficial to have a member of the clinical staff receive training in motivational interviewing. The content areas that should be addressed in a motivational counseling intervention can be captured by the "5 R's": relevance, risks, rewards, roadblocks, and repetition (Strategy B2). Research suggests that the "5 R's" enhance future quit attempts.[169,180]

Strategy B1. Motivational interviewing strategies

Express empathy.	• Use open-ended questions to explore:
	   – The importance of addressing smoking or other tobacco use (e.g., "How important do you think it is for you to quit smoking?")
	   – Concerns and benefits of quitting (e.g., "What might happen if you quit?")
	• Use reflective listening to seek shared understanding:
	   – Reflect words or meaning (e.g., "So you think smoking helps you to maintain your weight.").
	   – Summarize (e.g., "What I have heard so far is that smoking is something you enjoy. On the other hand, your boyfriend hates your smoking, and you are worried you might develop a serious disease.").
	• Normalize feelings and concerns (e.g., "Many people worry about managing without cigarettes.").
	• Support the patient's autonomy and right to choose or reject change (e.g., "I hear you saying you are not ready to quit smoking right now. I'm here to help you when you are ready.").

Develop discrepancy.	• Highlight the discrepancy between the patient's present behavior and expressed priorities, values, and goals (e.g., "It sounds like you are very devoted to your family. How do you think your smoking is affecting your children?").
	• Reinforce and support "change talk" and "commitment" language:
	   – "So, you realize how smoking is affecting your breathing and making it hard to keep up with your kids."
	   – "It's great that you are going to quit when you get through this busy time at work."
	• Build and deepen commitment to change:
	   – "There are effective treatments that will ease the pain of quitting, including counseling and many medication options."
	   – "We would like to help you avoid a stroke like the one your father had."

Roll with resistance.	• Back off and use reflection when the patient expresses resistance:
	   – "Sounds like you are feeling pressured about your smoking."
	• Express empathy:
	   – "You are worried about how you would manage withdrawal symptoms."
	• Ask permission to provide information:
	   – "Would you like to hear about some strategies that can help you address that concern when you quit?"

Support self-efficacy.	• Help the patient to identify and build on past successes:
	   – "So you were fairly successful the last time you tried to quit."
	• Offer options for achievable small steps toward change:
	   – Call the quitline (1-800-QUIT-NOW) for advice and information.
	   – Read about quitting benefits and strategies.
	   – Change smoking patterns (e.g., no smoking in the home).
	   – Ask the patient to share his or her ideas about quitting strategies.

Strategy B2. Enhancing motivation to quit tobacco—the "5 R's"

Relevance	Encourage the patient to indicate why quitting is personally relevant, being as specific as possible. Motivational information has the greatest impact if it is relevant to a patient's disease status or risk, family or social situation (e.g., having children in the home), health concerns, age, gender, and other important patient characteristics (e.g., prior quitting experience, personal barriers to cessation).
Risks	The clinician should ask the patient to identify potential negative consequences of tobacco use. The clinician may suggest and highlight those that seem most relevant to the patient. The clinician should emphasize that smoking low-tar/low-nicotine cigarettes or use of other forms of tobacco (e.g., smokeless tobacco, cigars, and pipes) will not eliminate these risks. Examples of risks are: • *Acute risks:* Shortness of breath, exacerbation of asthma, increased risk of respiratory infections, harm to pregnancy, impotence, infertility. • *Long-term risks:* Heart attacks and strokes, lung and other cancers (e.g., larynx, oral cavity, pharynx, esophagus, pancreas, stomach, kidney, bladder, cervix, and acute myelocytic leukemia), chronic obstructive pulmonary diseases (chronic bronchitis and emphysema), osteoporosis, long-term disability, and need for extended care. • *Environmental risks:* Increased risk of lung cancer and heart disease in spouses; increased risk for low birth-weight, sudden infant death syndrome (SIDS), asthma, middle ear disease, and respiratory infections in children of smokers.
Rewards	The clinician should ask the patient to identify potential benefits of stopping tobacco use. The clinician may suggest and highlight those that seem most relevant to the patient. Examples of rewards follow: • Improved health • Food will taste better • Improved sense of smell • Saving money • Feeling better about oneself • Home, car, clothing, breath will smell better • Setting a good example for children and decreasing the likelihood that they will smoke • Having healthier babies and children • Feeling better physically • Performing better in physical activities • Improved appearance, including reduced wrinkling/aging of skin and whiter teeth

Strategy B2. Enhancing motivation to quit tobacco—the "5 R's" (continued)

Roadblocks	The clinician should ask the patient to identify barriers or impediments to quitting and provide treatment (problemsolving counseling, medication) that could address barriers. Typical barriers might include: • Withdrawal symptoms • Fear of failure • Weight gain • Lack of support • Depression • Enjoyment of tobacco • Being around other tobacco users • Limited knowledge of effective treatment options
Repetition	The motivational intervention should be repeated every time an unmotivated patient visits the clinic setting. Tobacco users who have failed in previous quit attempts should be told that most people make repeated quit attempts before they are successful.

C. For the Patient Who Has Recently Quit

Treatments for the Recent Quitter

Smokers who have recently quit face a high risk of relapse. Although most relapse occurs early in the quitting process,[96,101,181] some relapse occurs months or even years after the quit date.[181-184] Numerous studies have been conducted to identify treatments that can reduce the likelihood of future relapse. These studies attempt to reduce relapse either by including special counseling or therapy in the cessation treatment, or by providing additional treatment to smokers who have previously quit. In general, such studies have failed to identify either counseling or medication treatments that are effective in lessening the likelihood of relapse,[185] although there is some evidence that special mailings can reduce the likelihood of relapse.[186,187] Thus, at present, the best strategy for producing high long-term abstinence rates appears to be use of the most effective cessation treatments available; that is, the use of evidence-based cessation medication during the quit attempt and relatively intense cessation counseling (e.g., four or more sessions that are 10 minutes or more in length).

Ex-smokers often report problems that have been worsened by smoking withdrawal or that coexisted with their smoking. If a clinician encounters a tobacco user who recently quit, the clinician might reinforce the patient's success at quitting, review the benefits of quitting, and assist the patient in resolving any residual problems arising from quitting (Strategy C1). Such expressions of interest and involvement on the part of the clinician might encourage the patient to seek additional help with cessation should she or he ultimately relapse. When the clinician encounters a patient who is abstinent from tobacco and is no longer engaged in cessation treatment, the clinician may wish to acknowledge a patient's success in quitting. The abstinent former smoker also may experience problems related to cessation that deserve treatment in their own right (see Strategy C2).

Strategy C1. Intervening with the patient who has recently quit

The former tobacco user should receive congratulations on any success and strong encouragement to remain abstinent.

When encountering a recent quitter, use open-ended questions relevant to the topics below to discover if the patient wishes to discuss issues related to quitting:
- The benefits, including potential health benefits, the patient may derive from cessation
- Any success the patient has had in quitting (duration of abstinence, reduction in withdrawal, etc.)
- The problems encountered or anticipated threats to maintaining abstinence (e.g., depression, weight gain, alcohol, other tobacco users in the household, significant stressors)
- A medication check-in, including effectiveness and side effects if the patient is still taking medication

Strategy C2. Addressing problems encountered by former smokers

A patient who previously smoked might identify a problem that negatively affects health or quality of life. Specific problems likely to be reported by former smokers and potential responses follow:

Problems	Responses
Lack of support for cessation	• Schedule followup visits or telephone calls with the patient. • Urge the patient to call the national quitline network (1-800-QUIT-NOW) or other local quitline. • Help the patient identify sources of support within his or her environment. • Refer the patient to an appropriate organization that offers counseling or support.
Negative mood or depression	• If significant, provide counseling, prescribe appropriate medication, or refer the patient to a specialist.

Strategy C2. Addressing problems encountered by former smokers (continued)

Problems	Responses
Strong or prolonged withdrawal symptoms	• If the patient reports prolonged craving or other withdrawal symptoms, consider extending the use of an approved medication or adding/combining medications to reduce strong withdrawal symptoms.
Weight gain	• Recommend starting or increasing physical activity. • Reassure the patient that some weight gain after quitting is common and usually is self-limiting. • Emphasize the health benefits of quitting relative to the health risks of modest weight gain. • Emphasize the importance of a healthy diet and active lifestyle. • Suggest low-calorie substitutes such as sugarless chewing gum, vegetables, or mints. • Maintain the patient on medication known to delay weight gain (e.g., bupropion SR, NRTs—particularly 4-mg nicotine gum[147]—and lozenge. • Refer the patient to a nutritional counselor or program.
Smoking lapses	• Suggest continued use of medications, which can reduce the likelihood that a lapse will lead to a full relapse. • Encourage another quit attempt or a recommitment to total abstinence. • Reassure that quitting may take multiple attempts, and use the lapse as a learning experience. • Provide or refer for intensive counseling.

Chapter 4 Intensive Interventions for Tobacco Use and Dependence

Background

Intensive tobacco dependence treatment can be provided by any suitably trained clinician. The evidence in Chapter 6 shows that intensive tobacco dependence treatment is more effective than brief treatment. Intensive interventions (i.e., more comprehensive treatments that may occur over multiple visits for longer periods of time and that may be provided by more than one clinician) are appropriate for any tobacco user willing to participate in them; neither their effectiveness nor cost-effectiveness is limited to a subpopulation of tobacco users (e.g., heavily dependent smokers).[188-194] In addition, patients, even those not ready to quit, have reported increased satisfaction with their overall health care as tobacco counseling intensity increases.[50,88]

In many cases, intensive tobacco dependence interventions are provided by clinicians who specialize in the treatment of tobacco dependence. Such specialists are not defined by their certification, professional affiliation, or by the field in which they trained. Rather, specialists view tobacco dependence treatment as a primary professional role. Specialists possess the skills, knowledge, and training to provide effective interventions across a range of intensities. They often are affiliated with programs offering intensive treatment interventions or services (e.g., programs with staff dedicated to tobacco interventions in which treatment involves multiple counseling sessions, including quitlines). In addition to offering intensive treatments, specialists sometimes conduct research on tobacco dependence and its treatment.

As noted above, substantial evidence shows that intensive interventions produce higher success rates than do less intensive interventions. In addition, the tobacco dependence interventions offered by specialists represent an important treatment resource for patients even if they received tobacco dependence treatment from their own clinician.

The advent of state tobacco quitlines available through a national network at 1-800-QUIT-NOW (1-800-784-8669) means that intensive, specialist-delivered interventions are now available to smokers on an unprecedented basis. In addition to providing their own clinical tobacco dependence interventions, clinicians and health systems can take advantage of this availability by implementing systems that regularly refer patients to quitlines either directly or using fax referrals (e.g., via "fax-to-quit" referral procedures).[195-199]

Specialists also may contribute to tobacco control efforts through activities such as the following:

- Serving as a resource to nonspecialists who offer tobacco dependence services as part of general health care delivery. This might include training nonspecialists in counseling strategies, providing consultation on difficult cases or for inpatients, and providing specialized assessment services for high-risk populations.

- Developing, evaluating, and implementing changes in office/clinic procedures that increase the rates at which tobacco users are identified and treated.[200]

- Conducting evaluation research to determine the effectiveness of ongoing tobacco dependence treatment activities in relevant institutional settings.

- Developing and evaluating innovative treatment strategies that may increase the effectiveness and utilization of tobacco dependence treatments.

Strategies for Intensive Tobacco Dependence Intervention

Table 4.1 highlights Guideline findings based on meta-analyses and Panel opinion (see Chapters 6 and 7) that are particularly relevant to the implementation of intensive treatment programs. The findings in Table 4.1 support recommendations for components of an intensive intervention (Table 4.2). Of course, implementation of this strategy depends on factors such as resource availability and time constraints.

Table 4.1. Findings relevant to intensive interventions

Intensive counseling is especially effective. There is a strong dose-response relation between counseling intensity and quitting success. In general, the more intense the treatment intervention, the greater the rate of abstinence. Treatments may be made more intense by increasing (a) the length of individual treatment sessions and (b) the number of treatment sessions.
Many different types of providers (e.g., physicians, nurses, dentists, psychologists, social workers, cessation counselors, pharmacists) are effective at increasing quit rates; involving multiple types of providers can enhance abstinence rates.
Individual, group, and telephone counseling are effective tobacco use treatment formats.
Particular types of counseling strategies are especially effective. Practical counseling (problemsolving/skills-training approaches) and the provision of intratreatment social support are associated with significant increases in abstinence rates.
Medications such as bupropion SR, nicotine replacement therapies, and varenicline consistently increase abstinence rates. Therefore, their use should be encouraged for all smokers except in the presence of contraindications or for specific populations for which there is insufficient evidence of effectiveness (i.e., pregnant women, smokeless tobacco users, light smokers, and adolescents). In some instances, combinations of medications may be appropriate. In addition, combining counseling and medication increases abstinence rates.
Tobacco dependence treatments are effective across diverse populations (e.g., populations varying in gender, age, and race/ethnicity).

Table 4.2. Components of an intensive tobacco dependence intervention

Assessment	Assessments should determine whether tobacco users are willing to make a quit attempt using an intensive treatment program. Other assessments can provide information useful in counseling (e.g., stress level, dependence; see Chapter 6A, Specialized Assessment).
Program clinicians	Multiple types of clinicians are effective and should be used. One counseling strategy would be to have a medical/health care clinician deliver a strong message to quit and information about health risks and benefits, and recommend and prescribe medications recommended in this Guideline update. Nonmedical clinicians could then deliver additional counseling interventions.
Program intensity	There is evidence of a strong dose-response relation; therefore, when possible, the intensity of the program should be: *Session length* – longer than 10 minutes *Number of sessions* – 4 or more

Table 4.2. Components of an intensive tobacco dependence intervention (continued)

Program format	Either individual or group counseling may be used. Telephone counseling also is effective and can supplement treatments provided in the clinical setting. Use of self-help materials and cessation Web sites is optional. Followup interventions should be scheduled (see Chapter 6B).
Type of counseling and behavioral therapies	Counseling should include practical counseling (problemsolving/skills training) (see Table 6.19) and intratreatment social support (see Table 6.20).
Medication	Every smoker should be offered medications endorsed in this Guideline, except when contraindicated or for specific populations for which there is insufficient evidence of effectiveness (i.e., pregnant women, smokeless tobacco users, light smokers, and adolescents; see Table 3.2 for clinical guidelines and Tables 3.3–3.11 for specific instructions and precautions). The clinician should explain how medications increase smoking cessation success and reduce withdrawal symptoms. The first-line medications include: bupropion SR, nicotine gum, nicotine inhaler, nicotine lozenge, nicotine nasal spray, nicotine patch, and varenicline. Certain combinations of cessation medications also are effective. Combining counseling and medication increases abstinence rates.
Population	Intensive intervention programs may be used with all tobacco users willing to participate in such efforts.

Chapter 5 Systems Interventions— Importance to Health Care Administrators, Insurers, and Purchasers

Background

Efforts to integrate tobacco intervention into the delivery of health care require the active involvement of clinicians, health care systems, insurers, and purchasers of health insurance. Such integration represents an opportunity to increase rates of delivering tobacco dependence treatments, quit attempts, and successful smoking cessation.[201]

In contrast to strategies that target only the clinician or the tobacco user, systems strategies are intended to ensure that tobacco use is systematically assessed and treated at every clinical encounter. Importantly, these strategies are designed to work synergistically with clinician- and patient-focused interventions, ultimately resulting in informed clinicians and patients interacting in a seamless way that facilitates the treatment of tobacco dependence.[202-204]

Several considerations argue for the adoption of systems-level tobacco intervention efforts. First, such strategies have the potential to substantially improve population abstinence rates. Levy et al. estimated that, over time, widespread implementation of such strategies could produce a 2 percent to 3.5 percent reduction in smoking prevalence rates.[205] Second, despite recent progress in this area, many clinicians have yet to use evidence-based interventions consistently with their patients who use tobacco.[23,48,51] Some evidence indicates that institutional or systems support (e.g., adequate clinician training or automated smoker identification systems) improves the rates of clinical interventions.[206-208] Finally, agents such as administrators, insurers, employers, purchasers, and health care delivery organizations have the potential to craft and implement supportive systems, policies, and environmental prompts that can facilitate the delivery of tobacco dependence treatment for millions of Americans. For example, managed care organizations and other insurers influence medical care through formularies, performance feedback to clinicians, specific coverage criteria, and marketing approaches that prompt patient demand for particular services.[139,209] Purchasers also have begun to use tobacco measures in pay-for-performance initiatives in which managed care organizations, clinics, and individual physicians receive additional reimbursement by achieving specific tobacco treatment-related goals. Indeed, research clearly shows that systems-level changes can reduce smoking prevalence among enrollees of managed health care plans.[210-212]

Unfortunately, the potential benefits of a collaborative partnership among health care organizations, insurers, employers, and purchasers have not been fully realized. For example, treatments for tobacco use (both medication and counseling) are not provided consistently as paid services for subscribers of health insurance packages.[213-215] Although substantial progress has been made since the publication of the first Guideline in 1996,[1,216-218] neither private insurers nor state Medicaid programs consistently provide comprehensive coverage of evidence-based tobacco interventions.[206,214,219] Findings such as these resulted in the *Healthy People 2010* objective:

> *Increase insurance coverage of evidence-based treatment for nicotine dependency to 100 percent.*[220]

In sum, without supportive systems, policies, insurance coverage, and environmental prompts, the individual clinician likely will not assess and treat tobacco use consistently. Therefore, just as clinicians must assume responsibility to treat their patients for tobacco use, so must health care administrators, insurers, and purchasers assume responsibility to craft policies, provide resources, and display leadership that results in a health care system that delivers consistent and effective tobacco use treatment.

Cost-Effectiveness of Tobacco Use Treatments

Tobacco use treatments are not only clinically effective, but are cost-effective as well. Tobacco use treatments, ranging from clinician advice to medication to specialist-delivered intensive programs, are cost-effective in relation to other medical interventions such as treatment of hypertension and hyperlipidemia and to other preventive interventions such as periodic mammography.[194,221-224] In fact, tobacco use treatment has been referred to as the "gold standard" of health care cost-effectiveness.[225] Tobacco use treatment remains highly cost-effective, even though a single application of any effective treatment for tobacco dependence may produce sustained abstinence in only a minority of smokers. Finally, evidence-based tobacco dependence interventions produce a favorable return on investment from the perspective of both the employer and health plan due to reduced health care consumption and costs.[226-228] The cost-effectiveness of Guideline recommendations for tobacco use treatment is addressed in detail in Chapter 6.

Recommendations for Health Care Administrators, Insurers, and Purchasers

Health care delivery administrators, insurers, and purchasers can promote the treatment of tobacco dependence through a systems approach. Purchasers (often business entities or other employers, State or Federal units of government, or other consortia that purchase health care benefits for a group of individuals) should make tobacco assessment and coverage of treatment a contractual obligation of the health care insurers and/or clinicians who provide services to them. In addition to improving the health of their employees or subscribers, providing coverage for tobacco dependence treatment will result in lower rates of absenteeism[229,230] and lower utilization of health care resources.[229,231] Health care administrators and insurers should provide clinicians with assistance to ensure that institutional changes promoting tobacco dependence treatment are implemented universally and systematically. Various institutional policies would facilitate these interventions, including:

- Implementing a tobacco user identification system in every clinic (Systems Strategy 1).

- Providing adequate training, resources, and feedback to ensure that providers consistently deliver effective treatments (Systems Strategy 2).

- Dedicating staff to provide tobacco dependence treatment and assessing the delivery of this treatment in staff performance evaluations (Systems Strategy 3).

- Promoting hospital policies that support and provide tobacco dependence services (Systems Strategy 4).

- Including tobacco dependence treatments (both counseling and medication) identified as effective in this Guideline as paid or covered services for all subscribers or members of health insurance packages (Systems Strategy 5).

These strategies are based on the evidence described in Chapter 6, as well as on Panel opinion.

Strategies for Health Care Administrators, Insurers, and Purchasers

Systems Strategy 1. Implement a tobacco user identification system in every clinic

Action	Strategies for implementation
Implement an office-wide system that ensures that for *every* patient at every clinic visit, tobacco use status is queried and documented.	Office system change: Expand the vital signs to include tobacco use, or implement an alternative universal identification system. Responsible staff: Nurse, medical assistant, receptionist, or other individual already responsible for recording the vital signs. These staff must be instructed regarding the importance of this activity and serve as nonsmoking role models. Frequency of utilization: Every visit for every patient, regardless of the reason for the visit.[a] System implementation steps: Routine smoker identification can be achieved by modifying electronic medical record data collection fields or progress notes in paper charts to include tobacco use status as one of the vital signs. VITAL SIGNS Blood Pressure: _____ Pulse: _____ Weight: _____ Temperature: _____ Respiratory Rate: _____ Tobacco Use (circle one): Current Former Never

[a] Repeated assessment is not necessary in the case of the adult who has never used tobacco or who has not used tobacco for many years, and for whom this information is clearly documented in the medical record.

Systems Strategy 2. Provide education, resources, and feedback to promote provider intervention

Action	Strategies for implementation
Health care systems should ensure that clinicians have sufficient training to treat tobacco dependence, clinicians and patients have resources, and clinicians are given feedback about their tobacco dependence treatment practices.	*Educate* all staff. On a regular basis, offer training (e.g., lectures, workshops, inservices) on tobacco dependence treatments, and provide continuing education (CE) credits and/or other incentives for participation. *Provide resources* such as ensuring ready access to tobacco quitlines (e.g., 1-800-QUIT-NOW) and other community resources, self-help materials, and information about effective tobacco use medications (e.g., establish a clinic fax-to-quit service, place medication information sheets in examination rooms). *Report* the provision of tobacco dependence interventions on report cards or evaluative standards for health care organizations, insurers, accreditation organizations, and physician group practices (e.g., HEDIS, The Joint Commission, and Physician Consortium for Performance Improvement). *Provide feedback* to clinicians about their performance, drawing on data from chart audits, electronic medical records, and computerized patient databases. Evaluate the degree to which clinicians are identifying, documenting, and treating patients who use tobacco.

Systems Strategy 3. Dedicate staff to provide tobacco dependence treatment, and assess the delivery of this treatment in staff performance evaluations

Action	Strategies for implementation
Clinical sites should communicate to all staff the importance of intervening with tobacco users and should designate a staff person (e.g., nurse, medical assistant, or other clinician) to coordinate tobacco dependence treatments. Nonphysician personnel may serve as effective providers of tobacco dependence interventions.	*Designate* a tobacco dependence treatment coordinator for every clinical site. *Delineate* the responsibilities of the tobacco dependence treatment coordinator (e.g., ensuring the systematic identification of smokers, ready access to evidence-based cessation treatments [e.g., quitlines], and scheduling of followup visits). *Communicate* to each staff member (e.g., nurse, physician, medical assistant, pharmacist, or other clinician) his or her responsibilities in the delivery of tobacco dependence services. Incorporate a discussion of these staff responsibilities into training of new staff.

Systems Strategy 4. Promote hospital policies that support and provide inpatient tobacco dependence services

Action	Strategies for implementation
Provide tobacco dependence treatment to all tobacco users admitted to a hospital.	*Implement* a system to identify and document the tobacco use status of all hospitalized patients.
	Identify a clinician(s) to deliver tobacco dependence inpatient consultation services for every hospital and reimburse them for delivering these services.
	Offer tobacco dependence treatment to all hospitalized patients who use tobacco.
	Expand hospital formularies to include FDA-approved tobacco dependence medications.
	Ensure compliance with The Joint Commission regulations mandating that all sections of the hospital be entirely smoke-free and that patients receive cessation treatments.
	Educate hospital staff that first-line medications may be used to reduce nicotine withdrawal symptoms, even if the patient is not intending to quit at this time.

Systems Strategy 5. Include tobacco dependence treatments (both counseling and medication) identified as effective in this Guideline as paid or covered services for all subscribers or members of health insurance packages

Action	Strategies for implementation
Provide all insurance subscribers, including those covered by managed care organizations (MCOs), workplace health plans, Medicaid, Medicare, and other government insurance programs, with comprehensive coverage for effective tobacco dependence treatments, including medication and counseling.	*Cover* effective tobacco dependence treatments (counseling and medication) as part of the basic benefits package for all health insurance packages.
	Remove barriers to tobacco treatment benefits (e.g., copays, utilization restrictions).
	Educate all subscribers and clinicians about the availability of covered tobacco dependence treatments (both counseling and medication), and encourage patients to use these services.

Chapter 6 Evidence and Recommendations

Background

The recommendations summarized in Chapters 2, 3, 4, and 5 are the result of a review and analysis of the existing tobacco treatment literature. This chapter reports that review and analysis and describes the effectiveness of various treatments, assessments, and implementation strategies. This chapter also addresses which treatments or assessments are effective, how they should be used, and how they should be implemented within a health care system.

The Panel identified topics that warranted new analyses for the 2008 update based on several criteria: they were important, supported by substantial new literature, and/or addressed issues not considered in prior Guidelines. The number of topics selected for new analyses was limited by the Public Health Service Guideline Update contract parameters. The 2008 Guideline Update Panel selected 11 topics for new analysis (see Table 1.1), based in part on input from tobacco control researchers and practitioners. These 11 topics and related categories are represented in Table 6.1. Type of outcome analyses varied across the different topics. In most analyses, long-term abstinence (6 months or more) was the outcome measure of interest; in others, it was the rate of smoker identification or intervention delivery. In addition to these new topics, Table 6.2 lists the topics that previously were analyzed for the 1996 and 2000 Guidelines. Importantly, the Guideline Update Panel reviewed all recommendations from the 1996 and 2000 Guidelines that did not undergo updated meta-analyses. For these prior recommendations, the Panel reviewed relevant literature since 1999 to determine whether the prior recommendation merited retention, modification, or deletion. See Appendix D for comparison of 2000 and 2008 Guideline recommendations.

The analyses reported in this chapter almost exclusively addressed treatments for cigarette smoking, as opposed to the use of other forms of tobacco, as the small number of studies on the use of noncigarette tobacco products, other than smokeless tobacco, precluded their separate analysis.

Finally, the Panel attempted to analyze treatment and assessment strategies that constitute distinct approaches that exist in current clinical practice.

The Panel chose categories within each analyzed topic according to three major criteria. First, some categories reflected generally accepted dimensions or taxonomies. An example of this is the categorical nature of the clinician types (physician, psychologist, nurse, and so on). Second, information on the category had to be available in the published literature. Many questions of theoretical interest had to be abandoned simply because the requisite research literature was not available. Third, the category had to occur with sufficient frequency to permit meaningful statistical analysis. Therefore, the cutpoints of some continuous variables (e.g., total amount of contact time) were determined so there were a sufficient number of studies within each analytical category to permit meaningful analysis.

In ideal circumstances, the Panel could evaluate each characteristic by consulting randomized controlled trials relevant to the specific categories in question. Unfortunately, with the exception of medication interventions, very few or no randomized controlled trials are designed to address the effects of specific treatment or assessment characteristics of interest. Moreover, treatment characteristics frequently are confounded with one another. For example, comparisons among clinicians often are confounded with the type of counseling and the format and intensity of the interventions. Therefore, direct, unconfounded comparisons of categories within a particular analysis type often were impossible. These characteristics nevertheless were analyzed because of their clinical importance, and because it was possible to reduce confounding by careful selection of studies and by statistical control of some confounding factors.

Table 6.1. Topics meta-analyzed for the 2008 Guideline update

Characteristics analyzed	Categories of those characteristics
Quitline	• No quitline intervention • Use of a proactive quitline • Use of a proactive quitline in combination with medication • Number of quitline sessions
Combining counseling and medication	• Medication alone • Counseling alone • Medication and counseling combined

Table 6.1. Topics meta-analyzed for the 2008 Guideline update (continued)

Characteristics analyzed	Categories of those characteristics
Medications	• Placebo medication • Bupropion SR • Clonidine • Nicotine gum • Nicotine inhaler • Nicotine lozenge • Nicotine nasal spray • Nicotine patch • Nortriptyline • Varenicline • Long-term medication • Single medication • Combination of medications • High-dose nicotine patch
Providing tobacco treatment as a health care insurance benefit	• Not providing coverage for tobacco treatment • Providing services as a covered insurance benefit
Systems features	• No intervention • Clinician training • Clinician training and reminder systems
Specific populations	• Adolescent smokers, pregnant smokers, smokers with psychiatric disorders, including substance use disorders and smokers with low socioeconomic status/limited formal education (see Chapter 7 for description)

Table 6.2. Topics meta-analyzed for the 1996 and 2000 Guidelines and included in the 2008 Guideline update (but not re-analyzed)

Characteristics analyzed	Categories of those characteristics
Screen for tobacco use	• No screening system in place • Screening system in place
Advice to quit	• No advice to quit • Physician advice to quit
Intensity of person-to-person clinical contact	• No person-to-person intervention • Minimal counseling (longest session ≤ 3 minutes in duration) • Low intensity counseling (longest session > 3 minutes and ≤ 10 minutes in duration) • Higher intensity counseling (longest session > 10 minutes) • Total amount of contact time • Number of person-to-person treatment sessions

Table 6.2. Topics meta-analyzed for the 1996 and 2000 Guidelines and included in the 2008 Guideline update (but not re-analyzed) (continued)

Characteristics analyzed	Categories of those characteristics
Type of clinician	• No clinician • Self-help materials only • Nonphysician health care clinician (e.g., psychologist, counselor, social worker, nurse, dentist, graduate student, pharmacist, tobacco treatment specialist) • Physician • Number of types of clinicians
Formats of psychosocial intervention	• No contact • Self-help/self-administered (e.g., pamphlet, audiotape, videotape, mailed information, computer program) • Individual counseling/contact • Group counseling/contact • Proactive telephone counseling/contact • Number of types of formats
Self-help interventions	• No self-help intervention • Number of self-help interventions • Self-help interventions
Types of counseling and behavioral therapies	• No counseling • No person-to-person intervention or minimal counseling • General: problemsolving/coping skills/relapse-prevention/stress-management approach • Negative affect/depression intervention • Weight/diet/nutrition intervention • Extratreatment social support intervention • Intratreatment social support intervention • Contingency contracting/instrumental contingencies • Rapid smoking • Other aversive smoking techniques • Cigarette fading/smoking reduction prequit • Acupuncture
Over-the-counter (OTC) medication	• Placebo OTC nicotine patch therapy • OTC nicotine patch therapy

Additional topics that were important and clinically relevant—but did not lend themselves to analysis due to a lack of long-term abstinence data—nevertheless were considered by the Panel through a review of the existing literature. The strength of evidence associated with these recommended actions for clinical interventions was at the "B" or "C" level (see below), reflecting the fact that they are not based primarily on meta-analyses.

This chapter addresses the treatment and assessment characteristics outlined in Tables 6.1 and 6.2 and is divided into three sections: (1) evidence for counseling and psychosocial interventions; (2) evidence for medication interventions; and (3) evidence for systems changes. For each topic, background information, clinical recommendations, and the basis for those recommendations are provided. As described in Chapter 1, each recommendation was given a strength-of-evidence classification based on the criteria shown in Table 6.3. Finally, for many topics, recommendations for further research are provided.

Table 6.3. Summary of strength of evidence for recommendations

Strength-of-evidence classification	Criteria
Strength of Evidence = A	Multiple well-designed randomized clinical trials, directly relevant to the recommendation, yielded a consistent pattern of findings.
Strength of Evidence = B	Some evidence from randomized clinical trials supported the recommendation, but the scientific support was not optimal. For instance, few randomized trials existed, the trials that did exist were somewhat inconsistent, or the trials were not directly relevant to the recommendation.
Strength of Evidence = C	Reserved for important clinical situations in which the Panel achieved consensus on the recommendation in the absence of relevant randomized controlled trials.

A. Counseling and Psychosocial Evidence

1. Screening and Assessment

■ Screen for Tobacco Use

Recommendation: All patients should be asked if they use tobacco and should have their tobacco use status documented on a regular basis. Evidence has shown that clinic screening systems, such as expanding the vital signs to include tobacco use status or the use of other reminder systems such as chart stickers or computer prompts, significantly increase rates of clinician intervention. (Strength of Evidence = A)

The Panel relied on the meta-analyses from the original 1996 Guideline to determine the impact of tobacco screening systems. Tobacco screening systems were evaluated in terms of their impact on two outcomes: the rate of tobacco treatment by clinicians, and the rate of cessation by patients who smoke.

Identifying Tobacco Users: Impact on Clinical Intervention. Nine studies met the selection criteria and were meta-analyzed as part of the 1996 Guideline to assess the impact of screening systems on the rate of smoking cessation intervention by clinicians. The results of this meta-analysis are shown in Table 6.4. Implementing clinic systems designed to increase the assessment and documentation of tobacco use status markedly increases the rate at which clinicians intervene with their patients who smoke.

Table 6.4. Meta-analysis (1996): Impact of having a tobacco use status identification system in place on rates of clinician intervention with their patients who smoke (n = 9 studies)[a]

Screening system	Number of arms	Estimated odds ratio (95% C.I.)	Estimated rate of clinician intervention (95% C.I.)
No screening system in place to identify smoking status (reference group)	9	1.0	38.5
Screening system in place to identify smoking status	9	3.1 (2.2–4.2)	65.6 (58.3–72.6)

[a] Go to *www.surgeongeneral.gov/tobacco/gdlnrefs.htm* for the articles used in this meta-analysis.

Identifying Tobacco Users: Impact on Tobacco Cessation. Three studies met the selection criteria and were meta-analyzed as part of the 1996 Guideline to assess the impact of identifying smokers on actual rates of smoking cessation. The results of this meta-analysis are shown in Table 6.5. These results, combined with the results from Table 6.4, show that having a clinic system in place that identifies smokers increases rates of clinician intervention but does not, by itself, produce significantly higher rates of smoking cessation.

Strategy A1 (see Chapter 3A) and Systems Strategy 1 (see Chapter 5) detail an approach for including tobacco use status as a vital sign with systematic prompts and reminders. Although the data assessing this intervention were gathered exclusively from cigarette smokers, the Panel believed that these results are generalizable to all tobacco users. This approach is designed to produce consistent assessment and documentation of tobacco use. Evidence from controlled trials shows that this approach increases the probability that tobacco use is assessed and documented consistently.[54,232] However, documenting smoking status is not by itself sufficient to promote treatment by clinicians.[233] Systems changes beyond smoker identification strategies are likely to be needed to increase rates of cessation advice and intervention.[139,234-237]

Table 6.5. Meta-analysis (1996): Impact of having a tobacco use status identification system in place on abstinence rates among patients who smoke (n = 3 studies)[a]

Screening system	Number of arms	Estimated odds ratio (95% C.I.)	Estimated abstinence rate (95% C.I.)
No screening system in place to identify smoking status (reference group)	3	1.0	3.1
Screening system in place to identify smoking status	3	2.0 (0.8–4.8)	6.4 (1.3–11.6)

[a] Go to *www.surgeongeneral.gov/tobacco/gdlnrefs.htm* for the articles used in this meta-analysis.

■ Specialized Assessment

Recommendation: Once a tobacco user is identified and advised to quit, the clinician should assess the patient's willingness to quit at this time. (Strength of Evidence = C)

If the patient is willing to make a quit attempt at this time, interventions identified as effective in this Guideline should be provided. (See Chapters 3A and 4.)

If the patient is unwilling to quit at this time, an intervention designed to increase future quit attempts should be provided. (See Chapter 3B.)

Recommendation: Tobacco dependence treatment is effective and should be delivered even if specialized assessments are not used or available. (Strength of Evidence = A)

Every individual entering a health care setting should receive an assessment that determines his or her tobacco use status and interest in quitting. The patient should be asked, "Are you willing to make a quit attempt at this time?" Such an assessment (willing or unwilling) is a necessary first step in treatment. In addition, every patient should be assessed for physical or medical conditions that may affect the use of planned treatments (e.g., medication).

The clinician also may want to perform specialized assessments of individual and environmental attributes that provide information for tailoring treatment and that predict quitting success. Specialized assessments refer to the use of formal instruments (e.g., questionnaires, clinical interviews, or physiologic indices such as carbon monoxide, serum nicotine/cotinine levels, and/or pulmonary function) that may be associated with cessation outcome (in addition, the reader may find other assessments relevant to medication use and specific populations when selecting treatment). Some of the variables targeted by specialized assessments that predict quitting success are listed in Table 6.6.

Several considerations should be kept in mind regarding the use of specialized assessments. First, there is little consistent evidence that a smoker's status on a specialized assessment is useful for treatment matching. The one exception is that persons who are highly nicotine dependent may benefit more from higher nicotine gum or lozenge doses (see Medication Evidence; Section B of Chapter 6). More importantly, the Panel found that, regardless of their standing on specialized assessments, all smokers have the potential to benefit from tobacco dependence treatments. Therefore, delivery of tobacco dependence treatments should not depend on the use of specialized assessments. Finally, tailored interventions based on specialized assessments do not consistently produce higher long-term quit rates than do nontailored interventions of equal intensity. Some promising studies exist, however, that suggest that individualizing self-help materials may be beneficial (see Individually Tailored and Stepped-Care Interventions, page 92).[238-245] In addition, the Panel recognizes that some effective interventions, such as general problemsolving (see Types of Counseling and Behavioral Therapies, on page 96), entail treatment tailoring based on a systematic assessment that occurs as an integral part of treatment.

Table 6.6. Variables associated with higher or lower abstinence rates

Variables associated with higher abstinence rates	
Variable	Examples
High motivation	Tobacco user reports a strong motivation to quit.
Ready to change	Tobacco user is ready to quit within a 1-month period.
Moderate to high self-efficacy	Tobacco user is confident in his or her ability to quit.
Supportive social network	A smoke-free workplace and home; friends who do not smoke in the quitter's presence.
Variables associated with lower abstinence rates	
Variable	Examples
High nicotine dependence	Tobacco user smokes heavily (≥ 20 cigarettes/day), and/or has first cigarette of the day within 30 minutes after waking in the morning.
Psychiatric comorbidity and substance use	Tobacco user currently has elevated depressive symptoms, active alcohol abuse, or schizophrenia.
High stress level	Stressful life circumstances and/or recent or anticipated major life changes (e.g., divorce, job change).
Exposure to other smokers	Other smokers in the household.

The existing evidence suggests that treatment can be effective despite the presence of risk factors for relapse (e.g., high nicotine dependence, other smokers in the home), but abstinence rates in smokers with these characteristics tend to be lower than rates in those without these characteristics.[246-248]

■ Future Research

The following topics regarding specialized assessment require additional research:

- Whether treatment adjustment based on specialized assessments can improve long-term abstinence rates

- Whether working to change the social network can improve abstinence rates (e.g., intervening with other smokers in the household to change their smoking patterns, teaching quitting support, or encouraging a smokefree home)

- Disparities in screening and assessment in specific populations

2. Treatment Structure and Intensity

▪ Advice To Quit Smoking

Recommendation: All *physicians* should strongly advise every patient who smokes to quit because evidence shows that physician advice to quit smoking increases abstinence rates. (Strength of Evidence = A)

For these recommendations, the 2008 Guideline Panel relied on meta-analyses performed for the 1996 Guideline. Seven studies were included in the 1996 meta-analysis of the effectiveness of physician advice to quit smoking. In the studies used in this analysis, the modal length of clinician intervention was 3 minutes or less. Two studies in this analysis used interventions lasting about 5 minutes. Results of the meta-analysis on physician advice are shown in Table 6.7. This analysis shows that brief physician advice significantly increases long-term smoking abstinence rates. These results were also supported by a more recent, independent meta-analysis.[56]

Advice by physicians was examined in the Table 6.7 meta-analysis from the 1996 Guideline; there were too few studies to examine advice delivered by any other type of clinician, although one study found that advice to quit from health care providers in general did significantly increase quit rates.[249] The analysis for total amount of contact time (see Table 6.9) indicates that minimal counseling (advice) delivered by a variety of clinician types increases long-term abstinence rates. Also, studies have shown that dentists and dental hygienists can be effective in assessing and advising smokeless/spit tobacco users to quit[250] (see Chapter 7). Given the large number of smokers who visit a clinician each year, the potential public health impact of universal advice to quit is substantial.[56]

Table 6.7. Meta-analysis (1996): Effectiveness of and estimated abstinence rates for advice to quit by a physician (n = 7 studies)[a]

Advice	Number of arms	Estimated odds ratio (95% C.I.)	Estimated abstinence rate (95% C.I.)
No advice to quit (reference group)	9	1.0	7.9
Physician advice to quit	10	1.3 (1.1–1.6)	10.2 (8.5–12.0)

[a] Go to *www.surgeongeneral.gov/tobacco/gdlnrefs.htm* for the articles used in this meta-analysis.

Future Research

The following topics regarding advice to quit require additional research:

- Effectiveness of advice to quit smoking given by clinicians other than physicians (e.g., nurses, nurse practitioners, pharmacists, dentists, dental hygienists, tobacco treatment specialists, physician's assistants)

- Cumulative effectiveness of combined advice from physicians and other types of clinicians

Intensity of Clinical Interventions

Recommendation: Minimal interventions lasting less than 3 minutes increase overall tobacco abstinence rates. Every tobacco user should be offered at least a minimal intervention, whether or not he or she is referred to an intensive intervention. (Strength of Evidence = A)

Recommendation: There is a strong dose-response relation between the session length of person-to-person contact and successful treatment outcomes. Intensive interventions are more effective than less intensive interventions and should be used whenever possible. (Strength of Evidence = A)

Recommendation: Person-to-person treatment delivered for four or more sessions appears especially effective in increasing abstinence rates. Therefore, if feasible, clinicians should strive to meet four or more times with individuals quitting tobacco use. (Strength of Evidence = A)

These recommendations are supported by three separate meta-analyses conducted for the 2000 Guideline: one involving session length, one involving total amount of contact time, and one involving the number of sessions.

Table 6.8. Meta-analysis (2000): Effectiveness of and estimated abstinence rates for various intensity levels of session length (n = 43 studies)[a]

Level of contact	Number of arms	Estimated odds ratio (95% C.I.)	Estimated abstinence rate (95% C.I.)
No contact	30	1.0	10.9
Minimal counseling (< 3 minutes)	19	1.3 (1.01–1.6)	13.4 (10.9–16.1)
Low-intensity counseling (3-10 minutes)	16	1.6 (1.2–2.0)	16.0 (12.8–19.2)
Higher intensity counseling (> 10 minutes)	55	2.3 (2.0–2.7)	22.1 (19.4–24.7)

[a] Go to *www.surgeongeneral.gov/tobacco/gdlnrefs.htm* for the articles used in this meta-analysis.

Session Length. Forty-three studies met selection criteria for comparison across various session lengths. Whenever possible, session length was categorized based on the maximum amount of time the clinician spent with a smoker addressing tobacco dependence in a single contact. Minimal counseling interventions were defined as 3 minutes or less, low-intensity counseling was defined as greater than 3 minutes to 10 minutes, and higher intensity counseling interventions were defined as greater than 10 minutes. Interventions could involve multiple patient-clinician contacts, with the session length determined for coding purposes as the length of time of the longest session. These levels of person-to-person contact were compared with a no-contact reference group involving study conditions in which subjects received no person-to-person contact (e.g., self-help-only conditions). There is a dose-response relation between session length and abstinence rates. As Table 6.8 shows, all three session lengths (minimal counseling, low-intensity counseling, and higher intensity counseling) significantly increased abstinence rates over those produced by no-contact conditions. However, there was a clear trend for abstinence rates to increase across these session lengths, with higher intensity counseling producing the highest rates.

Total Amount of Contact Time. Thirty-five studies met the selection criteria for the analysis assessing the impact of total contact time. The amount of contact time was calculated from the text as the total time accumulated (the number of sessions multiplied by the session length). When the exact time was not known for minimal and low-intensity interventions, they were assigned median lengths of 2 and 6.5 minutes, respectively. The total amount of contact time was then categorized as no-contact, 1–3 minutes, 4–30 minutes, 31–90 minutes, 91–300 minutes, and greater than 300 minutes. As Table 6.9 shows, any contact time significantly increased abstinence rates over those produced by no contact. However, there was a clear trend for abstinence rates to increase across contact time, up to the 90-minute mark. There was no evidence that more than 90 minutes of total contact time substantially increases abstinence rates.

Table 6.9. Meta-analysis (2000): Effectiveness of and estimated abstinence rates for total amount of contact time (n = 35 studies)[a]

Total amount of contact time	Number of arms	Estimated odds ratio (95% C.I.)	Estimated abstinence rate (95% C.I.)
No minutes	16	1.0	11.0
1–3 minutes	12	1.4 (1.1–1.8)	14.4 (11.3–17.5)
4–30 minutes	20	1.9 (1.5–2.3)	18.8 (15.6–22.0)
31–90 minutes	16	3.0 (2.3–3.8)	26.5 (21.5–31.4)
91–300 minutes	16	3.2 (2.3–4.6)	28.4 (21.3–35.5)
> 300 minutes	15	2.8 (2.0–3.9)	25.5 (19.2–31.7)

[a] Go to *www.surgeongeneral.gov/tobacco/gdlnrefs.htm* for the articles used in this meta-analysis.

Number of Sessions. Forty-six studies involving at least some person-to-person contact met selection criteria for the analysis addressing the impact of number of treatment sessions. Zero or one session was used as the reference group. As shown in Table 6.10, multiple treatment sessions increase smoking abstinence rates over those produced by zero or one session. The evidence suggests a dose-response relation between number of sessions and treatment effectiveness.

It is important to note that although the use of more intensive interventions (i.e., longer sessions, more sessions) may produce enhanced abstinence rates, these interventions may have limited reach (affect fewer smokers) and may not be feasible in some primary care settings. For instance, not all smokers are interested in participating in an intensive intervention, and not all smokers may have access to or be able to afford services that can provide intensive interventions. Finally, the clinician can link the patient to additional treatment options, such as quitlines or other intensive cessation treatment programs, to provide additional person-to-person treatment.

■ Future Research

The following topics regarding intensity of person-to-person contact require additional research:

- Effects of treatment duration, timing, and spacing of sessions (i.e., the number of days or weeks over which treatment is spread). For instance, does front loading sessions (having the majority of the sessions during the first few weeks of a quit attempt) or spacing sessions throughout the quit attempt yield better long-term abstinence rates?

- Methods to increase the appeal and utilization of intensive treatments

- Effectiveness of intensive inpatient treatment programs

Table 6.10. Meta-analysis (2000): Effectiveness of and estimated abstinence rates for number of person-to-person treatment sessions (n = 46 studies)[a]

Number of sessions	Number of arms	Estimated odds ratio (95% C.I.)	Estimated abstinence rate (95% C.I.)
0–1 session	43	1.0	12.4
2–3 sessions	17	1.4 (1.1–1.7)	16.3 (13.7–19.0)
4–8 sessions	23	1.9 (1.6–2.2)	20.9 (18.1–23.6)
> 8 sessions	51	2.3 (2.1–3.0)	24.7 (21.0–28.4)

[a] Go to *www.surgeongeneral.gov/tobacco/gdlnrefs.htm* for the articles used in this meta-analysis.

■ Type of Clinician

Recommendation: Treatment delivered by a variety of clinician types increases abstinence rates. Therefore, all clinicians should provide smoking cessation interventions. (Strength of Evidence = A)

Recommendation: Treatments delivered by multiple types of clinicians are more effective than interventions delivered by a single type of clinician. Therefore, the delivery of interventions by more than one type of clinician is encouraged. (Strength of Evidence = C)

Clinician Types. Twenty-nine studies met selection criteria for the 2000 meta-analysis examining the effectiveness of various types of clinicians providing tobacco use treatment. These analyses compared the effectiveness of interventions delivered by different types of clinicians with interventions in which there were no clinicians (e.g., when there was no intervention or the intervention consisted of self-help materials only). Tobacco use treatments delivered by any single type of health care provider, such as a physician or other clinician (e.g., nurse, psychologist, dentist, or counselor), or by multiple clinicians, increase abstinence rates relative to interventions in which there is no clinician (e.g., self-help interventions). None of the studies in these analyses involved medication, but they did involve psychosocial intervention, principally counseling. Results are shown in Table 6.11. Results suggest that physicians and other clinicians are similarly effective in delivering tobacco cessation counseling. New research reviewed since the 2000 Guideline suggests that trained peer counselors also may be effective.[251-253]

Number of Clinician Types. Thirty-seven studies met selection criteria for the 2000 analysis examining the effectiveness of multiple clinicians used in smoking cessation interventions. "Multiple clinicians" refers to the number of different *types* of clinicians (if a nurse and a physician each delivered parts of an intervention, two types of clinicians would be involved). Tobacco use treatments delivered by two or more types of clinicians increase abstinence rates relative to those produced by interventions in which there is no clinician (Table 6.12). However, the number of clinician types is confounded with treatment intensity. For instance, if an individual meets with a physician for a medication consultation and then talks to a health educator about the quit plan, that is two clinicians and two sessions. The number of contacts may be more important than the number of clinicians providing treatment.

Table 6.11. Meta-analysis (2000): Effectiveness of and estimated abstinence rates for interventions delivered by different types of clinicians (n = 29 studies)[a]

Type of clinician	Number of arms	Estimated odds ratio (95% C.I.)	Estimated abstinence rate (95% C.I.)
No clinician	16	1.0	10.2
Self-help	47	1.1 (0.9–1.3)	10.9 (9.1–12.7)
Nonphysician clinician	39	1.7 (1.3–2.1)	15.8 (12.8–18.8)
Physician clinician	11	2.2 (1.5–3.2)	19.9 (13.7–26.2)

[a] Go to *www.surgeongeneral.gov/tobacco/gdlnrefs.htm* for the articles used in this meta-analysis.

Table 6.12. Meta-analysis (2000): Effectiveness of and estimated abstinence rates for interventions delivered by various numbers of clinician types (n = 37 studies)[a]

Number of clinician types	Number of arms	Estimated odds ratio (95% C.I.)	Estimated abstinence rate (95% C.I.)
No clinician	30	1.0	10.8
One clinician type	50	1.8 (1.5–2.2)	18.3 (15.4–21.1)
Two clinician types	16	2.5 (1.9–3.4)	23.6 (18.4–28.7)
Three or more clinician types	7	2.4 (2.1–2.9)	23.0 (20.0–25.9)

[a] Go to *www.surgeongeneral.gov/tobacco/gdlnrefs.htm* for the articles used in this meta-analysis.

Future Research

The following topics regarding type of clinician require additional research:

- Effectiveness of specific types of clinicians (e.g., quitline counselors, trained peer counselors, nurses, physician assistants, pharmacists, social workers)

- Relative effectiveness of various numbers and types of clinicians, with the intensity of the intervention held constant

Formats of Psychosocial Treatments

Recommendation: Proactive telephone counseling, group counseling, and individual counseling formats are effective and should be used in smoking cessation interventions. (Strength of Evidence = A)

Recommendation: Smoking cessation interventions that are delivered in multiple formats increase abstinence rates and should be encouraged. (Strength of Evidence = A)

Recommendation: Tailored materials, both print and Web-based, appear to be effective in helping people quit. Therefore, clinicians may choose to provide tailored self-help materials to their patients who want to quit. (Strength of Evidence = B)

Format Types. Overall format type (delivery mode) recommendations rest on the 2000 Guideline meta-analysis, although new focused analyses of proactive quitlines were conducted for the 2008 update. Fifty-eight studies met selection criteria and were included in the 2000 meta-analysis comparing different types of formats (see Table 6.13). Tobacco use treatment delivered by means of proactive telephone counseling/contact (quitlines, call-back counseling), individual counseling, and group counseling/contact all increase abstinence rates relative to no intervention.

Self-Help. The 2000 format meta-analysis also evaluated the effectiveness of self-help interventions (e.g., pamphlets/booklets/mailings/manuals, videotapes, audiotapes, referrals to 12-step programs, reactive telephone hotlines/helplines [see Glossary], computer programs/Internet, and lists of community programs). Interventions delivered by means of widely varied self-help materials (whether as stand-alone treatments or as adjuvants) appear to increase abstinence rates relative to no intervention in this particular analysis. However, the effect of self-help was weak and typically not significant across analyses conducted for the 2000 Guideline (see Tables 6.13 and 6.15).

Number of Formats. Fifty-four studies met selection criteria and were included in the 2000 meta-analysis comparing the number of format types used for tobacco use treatment. The self-help treatments included in this analysis occurred either by themselves or in addition to other treatments. Tobacco use treatment that used three or four format types was especially effective. Results of this analysis are shown in Table 6.14.

Self-Help: Focused Analyses. Because the format meta-analysis revealed self-help to be of marginal effectiveness, another analysis was undertaken in 2000 to provide additional, focused information on self-help. Studies were accepted for the 2000 analysis if the presence of self-help materials constituted the sole difference in treatment arms. In the main format analysis, some treatment arms differed on factors other than self-help *per se* (e.g., intensity of counseling). The treatments that accompanied self-help material in the focused analysis ranged from no advice or counseling to intensive counseling. The results of this analysis were comparable to those in the larger format analysis (i.e., self-help was of marginal effectiveness).

For the 2000 Guideline analysis, 21 studies met selection criteria to evaluate the effectiveness of providing multiple types of self-help interventions (e.g., pamphlets, videotapes, audiotapes, and reactive hotlines/helplines). The results provide little evidence that the provision of multiple types of self-help, when offered without any person-to-person intervention, significantly enhances treatment outcomes (see Table 6.15).

Two final 2000 meta-analyses addressed the impact of self-help brochures *per se*. In one analysis, brochures were used as the only intervention. In the other analysis, self-help brochures were used in addition to counseling. In neither analysis did self-help significantly boost abstinence rates.

Table 6.13. Meta-analysis (2000): Effectiveness of and estimated abstinence rates for various types of formats (n = 58 studies)[a]

Format Number	Number of arms	Estimated odds ratio (95% C.I.)	Estimated abstinence rate (95% C.I.)
No format	20	1.0	10.8
Self-help	93	1.2 (1.02–1.3)	12.3 (10.9–13.6)
Proactive telephone counseling	26	1.2 (1.1–1.4)	13.1 (11.4–14.8)
Group counseling	52	1.3 (1.1–1.6)	13.9 (11.6–16.1)
Individual counseling	67	1.7 (1.4–2.0)	16.8 (14.7–19.1)

[a] Go to *www.surgeongeneral.gov/tobacco/gdlnrefs.htm* for the articles used in this meta-analysis.

Table 6.14. Meta-analysis (2000): Effectiveness of and estimated abstinence rates for number of formats (n = 54 studies)[a]

Number of formats[b]	Number of arms	Estimated odds ratio (95% C.I.)	Estimated abstinence rate (95% C.I.)
No format	20	1.0	10.8
One format	51	1.5 (1.2–1.8)	15.1 (12.8–17.4)
Two formats	55	1.9 (1.6–2.2)	18.5 (15.8–21.1)
Three or four formats	19	2.5 (2.1–3.0)	23.2 (19.9–26.6)

[a] Go to *www.surgeongeneral.gov/tobacco/gdlnrefs.htm* for the articles used in this meta-analysis.
[b] Formats included self-help, proactive telephone counseling, group, or individual counseling.

Table 6.15. Meta-analysis (2000): Effectiveness of and estimated abstinence rates for number of types of self-help (n = 21 studies)[a]

Factor	Number of arms	Estimated odds ratio (95% C.I.)	Estimated abstinence rate (95% C.I.)
No self-help	17	1.0	14.3
One type of self-help	27	1.0 (0.9–1.1)	14.4 (12.9–15.9)
Two or more types	10	1.1 (0.9–1.5)	15.7 (12.3–19.2)

[a] Go to *www.surgeongeneral.gov/tobacco/gdlnrefs.htm* for the articles used in this meta-analysis.

Quitlines. Both the substantial growth in quitline research and the implementation of a national network of tobacco quitlines (available through 1-800-QUIT-NOW) led the 2008 Guideline Panel to identify quitline effectiveness as a topic deserving focused meta-analyses. Nine studies met selection criteria and were analyzed for the 2008 Guideline update comparing the effectiveness of a quitline intervention versus minimal or no contact or self-help materials. This differs from the 2000 meta-analysis (Table 6.13) in that the current analysis focused on study arms that used quitline intervention alone rather than telephone counseling that may have occurred with other types of interventions. For the purpose of this analysis, quitlines are defined as telephone counseling in which at least some of the contacts are initiated by the quitline counselor to deliver tobacco use interventions, including call-back counseling. Quitlines significantly increase abstinence rates compared to minimal or no counseling interventions (Table 6.16).[254] In a second 2008 meta-analysis of quitlines, six studies were analyzed comparing the effect of adding quitline counseling to medication versus medication alone. The addition of quitline counseling to medication significantly improves abstinence rates compared to medication alone (see Table 6.17). These analyses suggest a robust effect of quitline counseling and are consistent with a recent independent analysis[254] and with the recently released Centers for Disease Control and Prevention's *Guide to Community Preventive Services.*[92]

Table 6.16. Meta-analysis (2008): Effectiveness of and estimated abstinence rates for quitline counseling compared to minimal interventions, self-help, or no counseling (n = 9 studies)[a]

Intervention	Number of arms	Estimated odds ratio (95% C.I.)	Estimated abstinence rate (95% C.I.)
Minimal or no counseling or self-help	11	1.0	8.5
Quitline counseling	11	1.6 (1.4–1.8)	12.7 (11.3–14.2)

[a] Go to *www.surgeongeneral.gov/tobacco/gdlnrefs.htm* for the articles used in this meta-analysis.

Table 6.17. Meta-analysis (2008): Effectiveness of and estimated abstinence rates for quitline counseling and medication compared to medication alone (n = 6 studies)[a]

Intervention	Number of arms	Estimated odds ratio (95% C.I.)	Estimated abstinence rate (95% C.I.)
Medication alone	6	1.0	23.2
Medication and quitline counseling	6	1.3 (1.1–1.6)	28.1 (24.5–32.0)

[a] Go to *www.surgeongeneral.gov/tobacco/gdlnrefs.htm* for the articles used in this meta-analysis.

Individually Tailored and Stepped-Care Interventions. Recent research has focused on the use of individually tailored materials. Tailored materials are those that are designed to address smoker-specific variables, such as support sources, recency of quitting, and concerns about quitting. Tailored materials can either be print materials, such as letters mailed to patients, or Web-based materials such as interactive Web sites.[238,242] Some applications of tailoring have been shown to be effective and to have broad reach.[241,245,255,256] The Panel also considered the use of stepped-care interventions (see Glossary) and concluded that there is not enough evidence to recommend a stepped-care approach as a basis for tailoring.[257,258] However, these approaches warrant future research.

Computerized Interventions. E-health or Internet interventions have the potential to be accessed by a large percentage of the smoking population, permit extensive tailoring of content to the tobacco user's needs or characteristics, and, due to low personnel costs, are likely to be inexpensive to deliver. Such interventions may be used as stand-alone or adjuvant treatments. These programs typically collect information from the tobacco user and then use algorithms to tailor feedback or recommendations. They also typically permit the user to select from various features, including extensive information on quitting, tobacco dependence, and related topics. Current applications permit multiple iterations of feedback, development and monitoring of a quit plan, and proactive e-mail prompts to users.[259,260] Optimal features of Web site resources have not yet been identified; some sites may be confusing and may not exploit the tailoring potential of this medium.[261] Clearly, more research is needed to identify their optimal structures, features, and contents.[262-265]

E-health tobacco interventions generally have yielded positive results. In a recent review of the use of these interventions with adult tobacco users, Walters et al. found that 7 of 15 studies with adults reported significantly improved outcomes over control conditions.[259] Hall et al. combined computerized individualized feedback designed to motivate smokers using principles of the Stages of Change model with six 30-minute sessions of counseling and the nicotine patch. This was compared with untailored self-help material. Significant improvement due to the more intensive treatment was found at 18-month followup.[266] Strecher et al. compared a multifaceted Web-based intervention (tailored cessation guide based on cognitive-behavioral principles, a medication adherence intervention, tailored e-mails, and a behavioral support person) in concert with the nicotine patch. This was contrasted with the patch alone. Favorable outcomes were obtained at 3 months postquit.[241] Similar positive effects also have been reported for a population study using computer-generated reports based on the Stages of Change model[267] and a Web site study offered in a worksite program.[268] A study with adolescents[269] reported positive results due to access to a complex intervention that comprised an interactive computer intervention, clinician advice, brief motivational interviewing, and telephonic booster sessions. The control condition was information about eating more fruits and vegetables. Null results with computerized or computer-tailored interventions also have been obtained (see, e.g., Velicer et al.[270] and Aveyard et al.[271]). Moreover, in many of the studies yielding positive results, the Web-based intervention is just one element of a complex intervention, or is considerably more intense than the comparison intervention. Given the potential reach and low costs of such interventions, however, they remain a highly promising delivery system for tobacco dependence.

Future Research

The following topics regarding formats require additional research:

- Which combinations of formats are most effective

- Relative effectiveness of different types of self-help interventions, including computer-based interventions

- Effectiveness of tailoring

- Effectiveness of fax-to-quit programs and other programs designed to increase quitline use

- Effective features of Web-based interventions

- Effect of computer-delivered interventions as a format versus the effect of the content of the intervention

- Optimal methods to decrease barriers and increase the appeal and use of effective counseling treatments

Followup Assessment and Procedures

Recommendation: All patients who receive a tobacco dependence intervention should be assessed for abstinence at the completion of treatment and during subsequent contacts. (1) Abstinent patients should have their quitting success acknowledged, and the clinician should offer to assist the patient with problems associated with quitting (see Chapter 3C, For the Patient Who Has Recently Quit). (2) Patients who have relapsed should be assessed to determine whether they are willing to make another quit attempt. (Strength of Evidence = C)

If the patient is willing to make another quit attempt, provide or arrange additional treatment (see Chapter 3A, For the Patient Willing To Quit).

If the patient is not willing to try to quit, provide or arrange an intervention designed to increase future quit attempts (see Chapter 3B, For the Patient Unwilling To Quit).

All patients should be assessed with respect to their smoking status during followup clinical contacts. In particular, assessments within the first week after quitting should be encouraged.[272,273] Abstinent patients should receive reinforcement for their decision to quit, be congratulated on their success at quitting, and be encouraged to remain abstinent (see Chapter 3C, Strategy C1). The existing evidence does not show that these steps will prevent relapse, but continued involvement on the part of the clinician may increase the likelihood that the patient will consult the clinician in later quit attempts should they be needed. Clinicians also should inquire about and offer to help the patient with potential problems related to quitting (see Chapter 3C, Strategy C2), such as significant weight gain or residual withdrawal symptoms.

Patients who have relapsed should again be assessed for their willingness to quit. Patients who currently are motivated to make another quit attempt should be encouraged to use a tobacco dependence intervention (see Chapter 3A, For the Patient Willing To Quit). Clinicians may wish to increase the intensity of psychosocial treatment at this time or refer the patient to a tobacco dependence specialist/program for a more intensive treatment if the patient is willing. In addition, medication should be offered again to the patient, if appropriate. If the previous quit attempt included medication, the clinician should review whether the patient used the medication in an effective manner and determine whether the medication was helpful. Based on this assessment, the clinician should recommend retreatment with the same medication, another medication, or a combination of medications (see Tables 6.26–6.28). Patients who have relapsed and are unwilling to quit at the current time should receive a brief intervention designed to increase future quit attempts (see Chapter 3B).

■ Future Research

The following topics regarding followup assessment and treatments require additional research:

- Optimal timing and types of relapse prevention interventions

- Effectiveness of various formats for relapse prevention treatments (e.g., effectiveness of telephone contacts in reducing the likelihood of relapse after a minimal intervention)

3. Treatment Elements

■ Types of Counseling and Behavioral Therapies

Recommendation: Two types of counseling and behavioral therapies result in higher abstinence rates: (1) providing smokers with practical counseling (problemsolving skills/skills training), and (2) providing support and encouragement as part of treatment. These types of counseling elements should be included in smoking cessation interventions. (Strength of Evidence = B)

Sixty-four studies met selection criteria for meta-analyses in 2000 to examine the effectiveness of interventions using various types of counseling and behavioral therapies. The results, shown in Table 6.18, reveal that four specific types of counseling and behavioral therapy categories yield statistically significant increases in abstinence rates relative to no-contact (i.e., untreated control conditions). These categories are: (1) providing practical counseling such as problemsolving/skills training/stress management; (2) providing support during a smoker's direct contact with a clinician (intratreatment social support); (3) intervening to increase social support in the smoker's environment (extratreatment social support); and (4) using aversive smoking procedures (rapid smoking, rapid puffing, other smoking exposure). A separate analysis was conducted eliminating studies that included the use of U.S. Food and Drug Administration (FDA)-approved medications. The results of this analysis were substantially similar to the main analysis.

Table 6.18. Meta-analysis (2000): Effectiveness of and estimated abstinence rates for various types of counseling and behavioral therapies (n = 64 studies)[a]

Type of counseling and behavioral therapy	Number of arms	Estimated odds ratio (95% C.I.)	Estimated abstinence rate (95% C.I.)
No counseling/behavioral therapy	35	1.0	11.2
Relaxation/breathing	31	1.0 (0.7–1.3)	10.8 (7.9–13.8)
Contingency contracting	22	1.0 (0.7–1.4)	11.2 (7.8–14.6)
Weight/diet	19	1.0 (0.8–1.3)	11.2 (8.5–14.0)
Cigarette fading	25	1.1 (0.8–1.5)	11.8 (8.4–15.3)
Negative affect	8	1.2 (0.8–1.9)	13.6 (8.7–18.5)
Intratreatment social support	50	1.3 (1.1–1.6)	14.4 (12.3–16.5)
Extratreatment social support	19	1.5 (1.1–2.1)	16.2 (11.8–20.6)
Practical counseling (general problemsolving/skills training)	104	1.5 (1.3–1.8)	16.2 (14.0–18.5)
Other aversive smoking	19	1.7 (1.04–2.8)	17.7 (11.2–24.9)
Rapid smoking	19	2.0 (1.1–3.5)	19.9 (11.2–29.0)

[a] Go to *www.surgeongeneral.gov/tobacco/gdlnrefs.htm* for the articles used in this meta-analysis.

The 2008 Guideline Panel decided not to recommend extratreatment social support in the current Guideline update. This change was based on recent literature on extratreatment social support that does not show a strong effect for helping smokers identify and utilize support outside of the treatment relationship.[274-276] Aversive smoking was recommended in the 2000 Guideline. However, new studies that have been conducted since the 2000 Guideline, including a Cochrane Review, cast doubt on the effectiveness of aversive smoking.[277] Because of this and the side effects of this treatment, the Guideline Panel decided not to recommend the use of aversive smoking therapy in the 2008 update.

The strength of evidence for the 2008 Guideline update recommendations regarding practical counseling and intratreatment social support did not warrant an "A" rating for several reasons. First, the evidence reviewed indicated that tobacco use treatments rarely used a particular type of counseling or behavioral therapy in isolation. Second, various types of counseling and behavioral therapies tended to be correlated with other treatment characteristics. For instance, some types of counseling and behavioral therapies were more likely to be delivered using a greater number of sessions across longer time periods. Third, all of these types of counseling and behavioral therapies were compared with no-contact/control conditions. Therefore, the control conditions in this meta-analysis did not control for nonspecific or placebo effects of treatment. This further restricted the ability to attribute effectiveness to particular types of counseling and behavioral therapies *per se*. Fourth, the studies used in this analysis often tailored the types of counseling and behavioral therapies to the needs of specific populations being studied, thereby affecting the generalizability of the study results. Fifth, there was considerable heterogeneity within each type of counseling and behavioral therapy.

Tables 6.19 and 6.20 outline elements of practical counseling (problemsolving/skills training) and intratreatment social support, respectively. These tables are designed to help clinicians using these counseling and behavioral therapies. It must be noted, however, that these treatment labels are nonspecific and include heterogeneous treatment elements. The effectiveness of encouragement and support as part of treatment is consistent with the literature regarding the importance of providing a caring, empathic, and understanding context in making other health behavior changes.[278-280]

Table 6.19. Common elements of practical counseling (problemsolving/skills training)

Practical counseling (problemsolving/ skills training) treatment component	Examples
Recognize danger situations – Identify events, internal states, or activities that increase the risk of smoking or relapse.	• Negative affect and stress • Being around other tobacco users • Drinking alcohol • Experiencing urges • Smoking cues and availability of cigarettes
Develop coping skills – Identify and practice coping or problemsolving skills. Typically, these skills are intended to cope with danger situations.	• Learning to anticipate and avoid temptation and trigger situations • Learning cognitive strategies that will reduce negative moods • Accomplishing lifestyle changes that reduce stress, improve quality of life, and reduce exposure to smoking cues • Learning cognitive and behavioral activities to cope with smoking urges (e.g., distracting attention; changing routines)

Table 6.19. Common elements of practical counseling (problemsolving/skills training) (continued)

Practical counseling (problemsolving/ skills training) treatment component	Examples
Provide basic information – Provide basic information about smoking and successful quitting.	• The fact that any smoking (even a single puff) increases the likelihood of a full relapse • Withdrawal symptoms typically peak within 1–2 weeks after quitting but may persist for months. These symptoms include negative mood, urges to smoke, and difficulty concentrating. • The addictive nature of smoking

Table 6.20. Common elements of intratreatment supportive interventions

Supportive treatment component	Examples
Encourage the patient in the quit attempt.	• Note that effective tobacco dependence treatments are now available. • Note that one-half of all people who have ever smoked have now quit. • Communicate belief in patient's ability to quit.
Communicate caring and concern.	• Ask how patient feels about quitting. • Directly express concern and willingness to help as often as needed. • Ask about the patient's fears and ambivalence regarding quitting.
Encourage the patient to talk about the quitting process.	Ask about: • Reasons the patient wants to quit. • Concerns or worries about quitting. • Success the patient has achieved. • Difficulties encountered while quitting.

Acupuncture. A separate meta-analysis was conducted in 2000 to evaluate the effectiveness of acupuncture. Evidence, as shown in Table 6.21, did not support the effectiveness of acupuncture as a tobacco use treatment. The acupuncture meta-analysis comparing "active" acupuncture with "control" acupuncture (see Glossary) revealed no difference in effectiveness between the two types of procedures. These results suggest that any effect of acupuncture might be produced by other factors such as positive expectations about the procedure. These results are consistent with the more recent Cochrane analysis.[281] Moreover, the Guideline Panel did not identify scientific literature to support the effectiveness of the more recent electrostimulation or laser acupuncture treatments for tobacco use.

Hypnosis. The 1996 Guideline did not conduct a separate meta-analysis on hypnosis because few studies met inclusion criteria, and those that did used very heterogeneous hypnotic procedures. There was no common or standard intervention technique to analyze. Literature screening for the 2000 Guideline revealed no new published studies on the treatment of tobacco dependence by hypnosis that met the inclusion criteria; therefore, this topic was not reexamined. Moreover, an independent review of nine hypnotherapy trials by the Cochrane Group found insufficient evidence to support hypnosis as a treatment for smoking cessation.[282] In contrast to the Cochrane Review and other reviews, a small recent study reported preliminary positive results with hypnotherapy.[283]

Other Interventions. The number of studies was insufficient to accurately appraise the effectiveness of other types of counseling and behavioral therapies, such as physiological feedback, restricted environmental stimulation therapy,[284] and the use of incentives.[285]

Table 6.21. Meta-analysis (2000): Effectiveness of and estimated abstinence rates for acupuncture (n = 5 studies)[a]

Treatment	Number of arms	Estimated odds ratio (95% C.I.)	Estimated abstinence rate (95% C.I.)
Placebo	7	1.0	8.3
Acupuncture	8	1.1 (0.7–1.6)	8.9 (5.5–12.3)

[a] Go to *www.surgeongeneral.gov/tobacco/gdlnrefs.htm* for the articles used in this meta-analysis.

■ Future Research

The following topics regarding types of counseling and behavioral therapies require additional research:

- Effectiveness of motivational interventions, cigarette fading, and physiological feedback of smoking effects

- Mechanisms through which counseling interventions exert their effects

- Effectiveness of specific counseling interventions among various patient populations (e.g., those with cancers; chronic obstructive pulmonary disease [COPD]; psychiatric disorders, including substance use disorders; and atherosclerosis)

- Effectiveness of smokefree policies, particularly smokefree homes and worksites, on increasing interest in, and the effectiveness of, tobacco dependence treatment[286]

- Effectiveness of family systems interventions as a means to increase support

■ Combining Counseling and Medication

Recommendation: The combination of counseling and medication is more effective for smoking cessation than either medication or counseling alone. Therefore, whenever feasible and appropriate, both counseling and medication should be provided to patients trying to quit smoking. (Strength of Evidence = A)

Recommendation: There is a strong relation between the number of sessions of counseling, when it is combined with medication, and the likelihood of successful smoking cessation. Therefore, to the extent possible, clinicians should provide multiple counseling sessions, in addition to medication, to their patients who are trying to quit smoking. (Strength of Evidence = A)

Evidence in this Guideline update supports the independent effectiveness of both counseling interventions and medication interventions. In the 2008 Guideline update, the Panel evaluated whether combining counseling and medication improved cessation rates relative to using either of these treatments alone.

Providing Counseling in Addition to Medication. Eighteen studies met selection criteria to evaluate the effectiveness of providing counseling in addition to medication versus medication alone. The results of this 2008 meta-analysis indicate that providing counseling in addition to medication significantly enhances treatment outcomes (see Table 6.22). These same 18 studies also were analyzed to examine the relation of counseling intensity when it was used in combination with a medication. Results revealed that two or more sessions significantly enhance treatment outcomes, and more than eight sessions produced the highest abstinence rates (see Table 6.23). The counseling provided in these studies was delivered either in person or via telephone.

Table 6.22. Meta-analysis (2008): Effectiveness of and estimated abstinence rates for the combination of counseling and medication vs. medication alone (n = 18 studies)[a]

Treatment	Number of arms	Estimated odds ratio (95% C.I.)	Estimated abstinence rate (95% C.I.)
Medication alone	8	1.0	21.7
Medication and counseling	39	1.4 (1.2–1.6)	27.6 (25.0–30.3)

[a] Go to *www.surgeongeneral.gov/tobacco/gdlnrefs.htm* for the articles used in this meta-analysis.

Table 6.23. Meta-analysis (2008): Effectiveness of and estimated abstinence rates for the number of sessions of counseling in combination with medication vs. medication alone (n = 18 studies)[a]

Treatment	Number of arms	Estimated odds ratio (95% C.I.)	Estimated abstinence rate (95% C.I.)
0–1 session plus medication	13	1.0	21.8
2–3 sessions plus medication	6	1.4 (1.1–1.8)	28.0 (23.0–33.6)
4–8 sessions plus medication	19	1.3 (1.1–1.5)	26.9 (24.3–29.7)
More than 8 sessions plus medication	9	1.7 (1.3–2.2)	32.5 (27.3–38.3)

[a] Go to *www.surgeongeneral.gov/tobacco/gdlnrefs.htm* for the articles used in this meta-analysis.

Providing Medication in Addition to Counseling. The effect of adding medication to counseling also was examined. Nine studies met inclusion criteria and provided 24 arms to compare medication and counseling with counseling alone. The results of this 2008 meta-analysis indicate that providing medication in addition to counseling significantly enhances treatment outcomes (see Table 6.24).

Table 6.24. Meta-analysis (2008): Effectiveness of and estimated abstinence rates for the combination of counseling and medication vs. counseling alone (n = 9 studies)[a]

Treatment	Number of arms	Estimated odds ratio (95% C.I.)	Estimated abstinence rate (95% C.I.)
Counseling alone	11	1.0	14.6
Medication and counseling	13	1.7 (1.3–2.1)	22.1 (18.1–26.8)

[a] Go to *www.surgeongeneral.gov/tobacco/gdlnrefs.htm* for the articles used in this meta-analysis.

Medication and/or counseling are effective and should be provided as stand-alone interventions when it is not feasible to do both or the patient is not interested in both. By combining medication and counseling, however, the clinician can significantly improve abstinence rates. The clinician providing the medication does not need to be the clinician providing the counseling. It may be that a physician, dentist, physician assistant, or nurse practitioner could prescribe medicine, and counseling could be provided by a health educator, dental hygienist, tobacco treatment specialist, pharmacist, or quitline. Adherence to treatment, both medication and counseling, is important for optimal outcomes. Even though there is compelling evidence that both counseling and medications increase smoking cessation success, the clinician should encourage the patient to make a quit attempt even if she or he declines such treatment.

Future Research

The following topics regarding the combination of counseling and medication require additional research:

- Optimal timing and length of counseling and medication interventions (e.g., timing and spacing of postquit counseling sessions)

- Effectiveness and acceptability/appeal of different counseling formats and techniques (e.g., computer-based counseling, quitline counseling, motivational interviewing)

- Strategies to address misconceptions about effective counseling and medication treatments

- Relative cost-effectiveness of various treatment combinations

■ For Smokers Not Willing To Make a Quit Attempt At This Time

Recommendation: Motivational intervention techniques appear to be effective in increasing a patient's likelihood of making a future quit attempt. Therefore, clinicians should use motivational techniques to encourage smokers who are not currently willing to quit to consider making a quit attempt in the future. (Strength of Evidence = B)

Evidence suggests that a variety of motivational interventions can increase the motivation for behavior change. These interventions have varied contents and labels (e.g., individualized motivational intervention, motivational consulting, and motivational interviewing; see e.g., Chan et al.,[170] Butler et al.,[171] and Brown et al.[173]). The motivational intervention that has perhaps the greatest level of support and content specificity is motivational interviewing.

Motivational interviewing (MI) is a specific counseling strategy that is intended to increase a person's motivation for behavior change.[168] MI comprises a variety of strategies that are designed to help individuals resolve ambivalence about such change.[175] The technique has been used successfully to help individuals attempt and achieve many types of behavior change, including reduced drinking and illicit drug use, and reduction of HIV risk behaviors.[175,287,288]

Several studies have shown that MI techniques appear to be effective in motivating smokers to make quit attempts. A randomized controlled trial of an MI-based intervention among 137 smokers with cancer found that MI significantly increased quit attempts compared to an advice condition.[289] Another study found that a single session of MI, versus either brief psychoeducational counseling or advice, significantly increased the proportion of patients with schizophrenia who contacted a tobacco dependence treatment provider and attended an initial treatment session.[174] A third study showed that two 45-minute individual counseling sessions based on MI principles yielded higher levels of intention to quit smoking among adolescents than did a brief advice condition.[173] No differences in quitting attempts or quitting success were seen in that study, however. Studies that used motivational approaches that shared features of MI (but that were not

MI) yielded a mixed pattern of results, with some studies showing significant increases in quit attempts (see, e.g., Butler et al.[171]); others showed only trends in that direction.[170] Finally, one study that targeted unmotivated smokers showed that counseling based on the "5 R's" (see Chapter 3, Strategy B2) significantly increased the odds of making a quit attempt that lasted at least 24 hours.[169]

The available evidence shows that the reviewed motivational interventions such as MI increase quit attempts when used with individuals not already interested in quitting. The evidence does not show that such interventions are reliably effective as cessation treatments,[173,175,290] nor is there consistent evidence that MI-induced quit attempts translate into higher long-term abstinence rates. Evidence also shows that such interventions are more effective in smokers with little pre-existing motivation to quit.[171,173] Finally, some evidence suggests that extensive training is needed before competence is achieved in the MI technique.[175,291]

Physiological Monitoring/Biological Marker Feedback To Motivate Smokers To Quit

Investigators have sought to determine whether feedback regarding either smoking effects or disease risk motivates quit attempts. Modest evidence indicates that such feedback motivates quit attempts.[292] One small study found that multifaceted feedback involving CO level, vital capacity measurement, and discussion of pulmonary symptoms led to more quit attempts among smokers identified during routine medical screening.[293] In a second study, feedback regarding CO level and genetic susceptibility to cancer was associated with a greater likelihood of quit attempts 1 year later.[294] Although these results are encouraging, there is too little information to evaluate definitively the effects of physiological feedback.[284] In addition, there is insufficient information as to how this feedback affects those at different levels of readiness to quit. It also is unclear whether feedback that a person is *not* at high risk would encourage continued smoking. Finally, data are mixed regarding the effectiveness of feedback as a cessation versus motivational intervention. That is, data are mixed as to whether or not feedback increases abstinence rates.[284,295,296]

Future Research

The following topics require additional research:

- Effectiveness of motivational interviewing and related techniques, including the impact of brief motivational interviewing strategies delivered in primary care settings

- Effectiveness of physiological monitoring and biological marker feedback to motivate smokers to quit and increase abstinence rates

B. Medication Evidence

Recommendation: Clinicians should encourage all patients attempting to quit to use effective medications for tobacco dependence treatment, except where contraindicated or for specific populations for which there is insufficient evidence of effectiveness (i.e., pregnant women, smokeless tobacco users, light smokers, and adolescents). (Strength of Evidence = A)

As with other chronic diseases, the most effective treatment of tobacco dependence requires the use of multiple clinical modalities. Medications are a vital element of a multicomponent approach. The clinician should encourage all patients initiating a quit attempt to use one or a combination of effective medications, although medication use may not be appropriate with some patient groups (e.g., those with medical contraindications, those smoking fewer than 10 cigarettes a day, pregnant/breastfeeding women, smokeless tobacco users, and adolescent smokers). The Guideline Panel identified seven first-line (FDA-approved) medications (bupropion SR, nicotine gum, nicotine inhaler, nicotine lozenge, nicotine nasal spray, nicotine patch, and varenicline) and two second-line (non-FDA-approved for tobacco use treatment) medications (clonidine and nortriptyline) as being effective for treating smokers. Each has been documented to increase significantly rates of long-term smoking abstinence. These results are consistent with other independent reviews.[158,297-300] No other medication treatments were consistently supported by the available scientific evidence.

In this update, the Panel conducted an inclusive meta-analysis of medications that complements the inclusive meta-analysis of psychosocial interventions that was conducted for the 2000 Guideline. For this meta-analysis, all medication trials with at least two studies of a particular medication, at an appropriate dose and duration, were entered into one analysis. This inclusive medication meta-analysis allows for the comparison of particular medications to both placebo controls and other active medications (Table 6.26), and makes greater use of all information in the available studies. Note also that, although all of these studies were published in peer-reviewed journals, a number of the studies were supported by the pharmaceutical industry.

The medication meta-analysis included predominantly studies with "self-selected" populations (see Chapter 1, Overview and Methods). In addition, in medication studies both experimental and control subjects in the studies typically received substantial counseling. Both of these factors tend to produce higher abstinence rates than typically are observed among self-quitters.

The studies submitted to the inclusive medications meta-analysis were screened and categorized prior to analysis. Screening removed medications for which there were too few acceptable studies to submit to meta-analysis (e.g., the nicotine lozenge, selegeline), and removed study arms that were confounded (e.g., two different medication conditions had counseling adjuvants of different intensities). Decisions about cutscores for treatment duration and dose categories were designed to be consistent with package insert information and data on effectiveness (i.e., prior data indicated rough clinical equivalence of certain dosages). Therefore, although there was an attempt to achieve some uniformity across the medications, decisions about dose and duration categories necessarily were made on a medication-by-medication basis. It is important to note that some medication categories, and some medication recommendations, do not conform with manufacturers' recommendations (e.g., the use of a nicotine patch dose > 25 mg per day). Table 6.25 shows the dosage and duration inclusion criteria for normal course, long-term, and high-dose medication classifications. In the case of medication combinations, the combinations typically comprised two standard-length medication regimens. In one combination, however, *ad libitum* NRT (gum or spray) was paired with long-term nicotine patch use ("patch [long-term] + *Ad Lib* NRT"). Different medications were grouped together into a single use category (e.g., grouping nicotine gum and spray together into the "Long-term *Ad Lib* NRT" condition) when the grouping was clinically and conceptually meaningful and when it permitted greater use of the available research evidence. Analyses were conducted for both 6- and 12-month outcomes, and the results of the

12-month analyses were very similar to the 6-month results shown in Table 6.26.

Table 6.25. Coding rules for medication duration and dose

Medication	Coding	Meaning
Nicotine Patch	Usual duration	6–14 weeks
	Long duration	> 14 weeks
	Usual dose/day	15 mg/16 hours/day 21 mg/24 hours/day
	High dose	> 25 mg/day
Nicotine Gum	Usual duration	6–14 weeks
	Long duration	> 14 weeks
Nicotine Inhaler and Nasal Spray	Usual duration	Up to 6 months
	Long duration	> 6 months
Bupropion SR	Usual duration	Up to 14 weeks
	Usual dose/day	150 mg once daily or twice daily
Varenicline	Usual duration	Up to 14 weeks
	Usual dose/day	1 mg daily or 1 mg twice daily (analyzed separately)

Recommendations Regarding Individual Medications: First-Line Medications

First-line medications are those that have been found to be safe and effective for tobacco dependence treatment and that have been approved by the FDA for this use, except in the presence of contraindications or with specific populations for which there is insufficient evidence of effectiveness (i.e., pregnant women, smokeless tobacco users, light smokers, and adolescents). These first-line medications have an established empirical record of effectiveness, and clinicians should consider these agents first in choosing a medication. For the 2008 update, the first-line medications are listed in Table 6.26 by size of the odds ratio and in the text alphabetically by generic name.

Table 6.26. Meta-analysis (2008): Effectiveness and abstinence rates for various medications and medication combinations compared to placebo at 6-months postquit (n = 83 studies)[a]

Medication	Number of arms	Estimated odds ratio (95% C.I.)	Estimated abstinence rate (95% C.I.)
Placebo	80	1.0	13.8
Monotherapies			
Varenicline (2 mg/day)	5	3.1 (2.5–3.8)	33.2 (28.9–37.8)
Nicotine Nasal Spray	4	2.3 (1.7–3.0)	26.7 (21.5–32.7)
High-Dose Nicotine Patch (> 25 mg) (These included both standard or long-term duration)	4	2.3 (1.7–3.0)	26.5 (21.3–32.5)
Long-Term Nicotine Gum (> 14 weeks)	6	2.2 (1.5–3.2)	26.1 (19.7–33.6)
Varenicline (1 mg/day)	3	2.1 (1.5–3.0)	25.4 (19.6–32.2)
Nicotine Inhaler	6	2.1 (1.5–2.9)	24.8 (19.1–31.6)
Clonidine	3	2.1 (1.2–3.7)	25.0 (15.7–37.3)
Bupropion SR	26	2.0 (1.8–2.2)	24.2 (22.2–26.4)
Nicotine Patch (6–14 weeks)	32	1.9 (1.7–2.2)	23.4 (21.3–25.8)
Long-Term Nicotine Patch (> 14 weeks)	10	1.9 (1.7–2.3)	23.7 (21.0–26.6)
Nortriptyline	5	1.8 (1.3–2.6)	22.5 (16.8–29.4)
Nicotine Gum (6–14 weeks)	15	1.5 (1.2–1.7)	19.0 (16.5–21.9)
Combination therapies			
Patch (long-term; > 14 weeks) + *ad lib* NRT (gum or spray)	3	3.6 (2.5–5.2)	36.5 (28.6–45.3)
Patch + Bupropion SR	3	2.5 (1.9–3.4)	28.9 (23.5–35.1)
Patch + Nortriptyline	2	2.3 (1.3–4.2)	27.3 (17.2–40.4)
Patch + Inhaler	2	2.2 (1.3–3.6)	25.8 (17.4–36.5)
Patch + Second generation antidepressants (paroxetine, venlafaxine)	3	2.0 (1.2–3.4)	24.3 (16.1–35.0)
Medications not shown to be effective			
Selective Serotonin Re-uptake Inhibitors (SSRIs)	3	1.0 (0.7–1.4)	13.7 (10.2–18.0)
Naltrexone	2	0.5 (0.2–1.2)	7.3 (3.1–16.2)

[a] Go to *www.surgeongeneral.gov/tobacco/gdlnrefs.htm* for the articles used in this meta-analysis.

■ Bupropion SR (Sustained Release)

Recommendation: Bupropion SR is an effective smoking cessation treatment that patients should be encouraged to use. (Strength of Evidence = A)

Bupropion SR was the first non-nicotine medication shown to be effective for smoking cessation and was approved by the FDA for that use in 1997. Its possible mechanisms of action include blockade of neuronal re-uptake of dopamine and norepinephrine and blockade of nicotinic acetylcholinergic receptors. It is contraindicated in patients with a seizure disorder, a current or prior diagnosis of bulimia or anorexia nervosa, use of a monoamine oxidase (MAO) inhibitor within the previous 14 days, or in patients taking another medication that contains bupropion. Bupropion SR is available exclusively as a prescription medication and can be used in combination with nicotine replacement therapies. Suggestions regarding the clinical use of bupropion SR are provided in Table 3.3.

Twenty-four studies generated the 26 arms that served as the basis for estimating the bupropion SR effect. The bupropion SR dose was 150 mg for 3 of these study arms, and 300 mg for the other 22 of these arms (one study did not report dose). As Table 6.26 reveals, bupropion SR approximately doubles the likelihood of long-term (> 5 month) abstinence from tobacco use as compared to placebo treatment. These results are consistent with other independent reviews.[299]

■ Nicotine Replacement Therapies (NRTs)

Nicotine replacement therapy (NRT) medications deliver nicotine with the intent to replace, at least partially, the nicotine obtained from cigarettes and to reduce the severity of nicotine withdrawal symptoms.

Nicotine Gum

Recommendation: Nicotine gum is an effective smoking cessation treatment that patients should be encouraged to use. (Strength of Evidence = A)

Recommendation: Clinicians should offer 4 mg rather than 2 mg nicotine gum to highly dependent smokers. (Strength of Evidence = B)

Nicotine gum currently is available exclusively as an OTC medication and is packaged with important instructions on correct usage, including chewing (see Table 3.4 for information on the clinical use of nicotine gum). Nine studies generated the 15 study arms that served as the basis for estimating the effect of nicotine gum. In addition, another four studies generated the six arms that served as the basis for the estimation of effects of long-term gum use (directed use beyond 14 weeks). Two arms used gum for 52 weeks, and the other four arms used gum for 24–26 weeks. Table 6.26 reveals that regular course and long-term nicotine gum use increased the likelihood of long-term abstinence by about 50 percent compared to placebo treatment. These results are consistent with other independent reviews.[300]

Nicotine Inhaler

Recommendation: The nicotine inhaler is an effective smoking cessation treatment that patients should be encouraged to use. (Strength of Evidence = A)

The nicotine inhaler currently is available exclusively as a prescription medication. The nicotine inhaler is not a true pulmonary inhaler, but rather deposits nicotine in the oropharynx, from which it is absorbed across the mucosa. See Table 3.5 for suggestions regarding the clinical use of the nicotine inhaler. Six studies generated the six arms that served as the basis for estimating the nicotine inhaler effect. As Table 6.26 shows, the inhaler approximately doubled smokers' likelihood of long-term abstinence from tobacco as compared to placebo treatment. These results are consistent with other independent reviews.[300]

Nicotine Lozenge

Recommendation: The nicotine lozenge is an effective smoking cessation treatment that patients should be encouraged to use. (Strength of Evidence = B)

Nicotine lozenge is available exclusively as an OTC medication and is packaged with important instructions for correct usage (see Table 3.6). Only one randomized controlled trial of the nicotine lozenge was available for review.[301] Therefore, the nicotine lozenge was not included in the inclusive meta-analysis (Table 6.26). The data from this study of more than 1,800 smokers found that the 2-mg lozenge for low-dependent smokers (smoke a first cigarette 30 minutes or more after waking) approximately doubled and the 4-mg lozenge for highly dependent smokers (smoke a first cigarette within 30 minutes of waking) approximately tripled the odds of abstinence at 6 months postquit as compared to placebo treatment. See Table 6.27 for the study results. These results are consistent with other independent reviews.[300]

Table 6.27. Effectiveness of the nicotine lozenge: Results from the single randomized controlled trial

Lozenge dose	N for active/N for placebo	Odds Ratio (95% C.I.)	Continuous abstinence rates at 6 months (Active/Placebo)
2 mg	459/458	2.0 (1.4–2.8)	24.2/14.4
4 mg	450/451	2.8 (1.9–4.0)	23.6/10.2

Nicotine Nasal Spray

Recommendation: Nicotine nasal spray is an effective smoking cessation treatment that patients should be encouraged to use. (Strength of Evidence = A)

The nicotine nasal spray currently is available exclusively as a prescription medication. See Table 3.7 for suggestions regarding the clinical use of the nicotine nasal spray. Four studies generated the four study arms that served as the basis for estimating the nasal spray effect. As Table 6.26 reveals, the nasal spray more than doubles the likelihood of long-term abstinence from tobacco as compared to placebo treatment.

Nicotine Patch

Recommendation: The nicotine patch is an effective smoking cessation treatment that patients should be encouraged to use. (Strength of Evidence = A)

Nicotine patches currently are available both as an OTC medication and as a prescription medication. Awareness of this prescription option is important for insurance plans that include coverage only for prescription medications. Suggestions for the clinical use of the nicotine patch are provided in Table 3.8.

Twenty-five studies generated the 32 study arms that served as the basis for estimating the nicotine patch effect. Of these 32 arms, the peak dose used was 14 or 15 mg in 6 study arms and 21–25 mg in 25 arms (one study did not report dose). As Table 6.26 shows, the nicotine patch almost doubled the likelihood of long-term abstinence compared to placebo treatment. These results are consistent with other independent reviews.[300]

The meta-analysis also addressed the effectiveness of long-term and high-dose nicotine patch therapy. As noted in Table 6.25, high-dose therapy was coded when the highest dose used exceeded 25 mg. This often was achieved by using two patches per day as a dosing regimen. Four studies generated four analyzable study arms with peak patch dosages of 30 mg (2 arms), 35 mg (1 arm), and 42 mg (1 arm). In some of these high-dose arms, patch use was of regular duration (14 weeks or less), although in other arms the duration of directed patch use exceeded 14 weeks.

Table 6.25 shows that long-term patch therapy was coded when the duration of directed patch use exceeded 14 weeks. All of the long-term patch studies used regular-dose patch regimens (15–25 mg). Eight studies generated 10 study arms that served as the basis for estimating the effect of long-term patch therapy. Table 6.26 shows that both long-term therapy and high-dose patch therapy approximately doubled the likelihood that a smoker would achieve long-term abstinence relative to placebo treatment. Thus, neither high-dose nor long-term patch therapy appeared to produce benefit above and beyond that of nicotine patch therapy at the regular duration (6–14 weeks) and dose (14–25 mg).

A time trend analysis of the nicotine patch studies based on data from the current meta-analysis revealed no significant change in the effectiveness of the nicotine patch during the approximately 15 years it has been available.

■ Varenicline

Recommendation: Varenicline is an effective smoking cessation treatment that patients should be encouraged to use. (Strength of Evidence = A)

Varenicline is a non-nicotine medication that was approved by the FDA for the treatment of tobacco dependence in 2006. Its mechanism of action is presumed to be due to its partial nicotine receptor agonist and antagonist effects. It is well tolerated in most patients. However, a recent publication reported two case reports of exacerbations of existing psychiatric illness, schizophrenia and bipolar illness, in patients who took varenicline.[302,303] In contrast, one recent smoking cessation study using varenicline included smokers with mental illness (depression, bipolar disorder, and/or psychosis) and reported no evidence that varenicline worsened the patients' mental illness.[304] Importantly, the FDA noted that patients with psychiatric illness were not included in the studies conducted for the approval of this medication.

In February 2008, the FDA added a warning regarding the use of varenicline. Specifically, it noted that depressed mood, agitation, changes in behavior, suicidal ideation, and suicide have been reported in patients attempting to quit smoking while using varenicline. The FDA recommends (1) that patients tell their health care provider about any history of psychiatric illness prior to starting this medication; and (2) that clinicians monitor patients for changes in mood and behavior when prescribing this medication. In light of these FDA recommendations, clinicians should consider eliciting information on their patients' psychiatric history.

Because varenicline is eliminated almost entirely unchanged in the urine, it should be used with caution in patients with severe renal dysfunction (creatinine clearance < 30 ml per min). Varenicline is available exclusively as a prescription medication and is not recommended for use in combination with NRT because of its nicotine antagonist properties. One recent review[297] found that varenicline increased odds of quitting over that of bupropion SR with a minimal to moderate side effect profile. Suggestions regarding the clinical use of varenicline are presented in Table 3.9.

The FDA dosing recommendation for varenicline is a total of 2 mg per day (1 mg twice daily). However, there is evidence that a dose of 1 mg per day also is effective.[305] Therefore, the effectiveness of both doses was addressed in the inclusive meta-analysis. Four studies generated five study arms that served as the basis for estimating the effect of 2 mg varenicline. Two studies generated the three study arms that served as the basis for estimating the effect of 1 mg varenicline. As Table 6.26 shows, the 1 mg total daily dose of varenicline approximately doubles, and the 2 mg total daily dose of varenicline approximately triples, a smoker's likelihood of long-term abstinence from tobacco as compared to placebo treatment. This suggests that the 1 mg per day dose is a viable alternative to the 2 mg per day dose, should the patient experience dose-related side effects.

Evidence indicates that varenicline is well-tolerated for periods up to 1 year[306] and that extended treatment may prove useful in reducing the likelihood of relapse.[307] More research is needed, however, to evaluate varenicline as a relapse prevention medication, to assess its long-term effects, and to evaluate its effectiveness in specific populations.

■ Interactions of First-Line Tobacco Use Medications With Other Drugs

The goal of treating tobacco use and dependence is abstinence from tobacco products. In achieving this goal, the metabolic effects of tobacco abstinence must be understood with respect to potential changes in homeostasis that occur in response to quitting and, eventually, the elimination of nicotine from the body. This is particularly important for smokers who are on other medications for chronic disease state management because they essentially are in a homeostatic metabolic condition and the titration of their chronic disease medications may have been influenced by their smoking status.

The polycyclic aromatic hydrocarbons in tobacco smoke are metabolic inducers of some isoforms of the hepatic cytochrome P450.[308] Thus, when smokers quit and the P450 system returns to its basal level of functioning, the concentration of drugs metabolized by these particular CYP isoforms may increase. As a result, smokers who quit can experience side effects from supratherapeutic drug levels of caffeine, theophylline, fluvoxamine, olanzapine, and clozapine. This can have serious consequences for selective drugs such as clozapine, with its associated agranulocytosis.[309]

Although nicotine is metabolized by CYP2A6, it does not appear to induce, in a clinically significant way, CYP enzymes. Thus, when a smoker is switched from cigarettes to a nicotine replacement product, changes in drug metabolism are similar to those seen when quitting without NRT.

Nicotine produces sympathetic activation that may reduce the sedative effects of benzodiazepines, and the vasoconstrictive effects of nicotine may decrease subcutaneous absorption of insulin. Nicotine also may attenuate the ability of beta-blockers to lower blood pressure and heart rate and may lessen opioid analgesia. When nicotine replacement products are withdrawn, adjustments in these types of medications may be necessary.

The metabolism of bupropion is mediated primarily by CYP2B6. Three categories of drugs could have clinically significant interactions with bupropion: drugs affecting CYP2B6, drugs metabolized by CYP2D6, and general enzyme inducers/inhibitors.[310] Drugs that affect CYP2B6 metabolism, such as cyclophosphamide and orphenadrine, potentially could alter bupropion metabolism. Bupropion and its metabolites inhibit CYP2D6[311,312] and could affect the impact of agents metabolized by this enzyme (e.g., tricyclic antidepressants, antipsychotics, type 1C anitarrhythmics, or certain beta-blockers). Due to the extensive metabolism of bupropion, enzyme inducers (e.g., carbamazepine, phenobarbital, phenytoin) and inhibitors (e.g., valproate, cimetidine) may alter its plasma concentration. Bupropion can lower seizure threshold. It should be used with caution with medications that can also lower seizure threshold.[310,313] Specifically, use of bupropion within 14 days of discontinuation of therapy with any MAO inhibitor is contraindicated.

Varenicline is eliminated unchanged by kidney excretion and thus is believed to pose no metabolic effects. Cimetidine inhibits the renal secretion of varenicline, although the magnitude of the interaction is small. No significant drug-drug interactions are known.[314]

Recommendations Regarding Second-Line Medications

Second-line medications are medications for which there is evidence of effectiveness for treating tobacco dependence, but they have a more limited role than first-line medications because: (1) the FDA has not approved them for a tobacco dependence treatment indication; and (2) there are more concerns about potential side effects than exist with first-line medications. Second-line medications should be considered for use on a case-by-case basis after first-line medications (either alone or in combination) have been used without success or are contraindicated. The listing of the second-line medications is alphabetical by generic name.

Clonidine

Recommendation: Clonidine is an effective smoking cessation treatment. It may be used under a physician's supervision as a second-line agent to treat tobacco dependence. (Strength of Evidence = A)

Three studies generated three analyzable study arms that served as the basis for estimating clonidine's effects on long-term abstinence. These studies all were conducted prior to 1997. Table 6.26 reveals that the use of clonidine approximately doubles abstinence rates when compared to a placebo. These studies varied the clonidine dose from 0.1 to 0.75 mg per day. The drug was delivered either transdermally or orally. It should be noted that abrupt discontinuation of clonidine can result in symptoms such as nervousness, agitation, headache, and tremor, accompanied or followed by a rapid rise in blood pressure and elevated catecholamine levels.

Clonidine is used primarily as an antihypertensive medication and has not been approved by the FDA as a medication for treating tobacco use and dependence. Therefore, clinicians need to be aware of the specific warnings regarding this medication as well as its side-effect profile. Additionally, a specific dosing regimen for the use of clonidine in smoking cessation has not been established. The Guideline Panel chose to recommend clonidine as a second-line as opposed to first-line agent because of the warnings associated with clonidine discontinuation, variability in dosages used to test this medication, and lack of FDA approval. As such, clonidine should be considered for treating tobacco use under a physician's monitoring with patients unable to use first-line medications because of contraindications or with patients who were unable to quit when using first-line medications. An independent review[298] indicated that clonidine is effective in promoting smoking abstinence, but prominent side effects limit its usefulness. Suggestions regarding clinical use of clonidine are provided in Table 3.10.

■ Nortriptyline

Recommendation: Nortriptyline is an effective smoking cessation treatment. It may be used under a physician's supervision as a second-line agent to treat tobacco dependence. (Strength of Evidence = A)

Four studies generated the five analyzable study arms that served as the basis for estimating the effect of nortriptyline on long-term abstinence. Nortriptyline dosages were 75 mg per day (3 arms) and 100 mg per day (2 arms), with treatment lasting from 6 to 13 weeks across the five arms. As Table 6.26 shows, nortriptyline almost doubles a smoker's likelihood of achieving long-term abstinence from tobacco as compared to placebo treatment. A recent independent review[158] also indicated that nortriptyline is effective in treating tobacco dependence. Suggestions regarding the clinical use of nortriptyline are provided in Table 3.11. Nortriptyline is used primarily as an antidepressant and has not been evaluated or approved by the FDA as a medication for treating tobacco use and dependence. Clinicians need to be aware of the specific warnings regarding this medication as well as its side-effect profile. Because of the side-effect profile and the lack of FDA approval for tobacco dependence treatment, nortriptyline is recommended as a second-line rather than a first-line agent. As such, nortriptyline should be considered for treating tobacco use under a physician's direction with patients unable to use first-line medications because of contraindications or with patients who were unable to quit using first-line medications.

Combination Medications

Recommendation: Certain combinations of first-line medications have been shown to be effective smoking cessation treatments. Therefore, clinicians should consider using these combinations of medications with their patients who are willing to quit. Effective combination medications are:

- **Long-term (> 14 weeks) nicotine patch + other NRT (gum and spray)**

- **The nicotine patch + the nicotine inhaler**

- **The nicotine patch + bupropion SR (Strength of Evidence = A)**

The number and variety of analyzable articles was sufficient to assess the effectiveness of five combinations of medications relative to placebo. Only the patch + bupropion combination has been approved by the FDA for smoking cessation.

▪ Nicotine Patch + Bupropion SR

Three studies yielded three analyzable study arms that served as the basis for estimating the effect of the nicotine patch + bupropion SR on long-term abstinence. Both the patch and bupropion SR were used at standard durations and doses (see Table 6.25).

■ Nicotine Patch + Nicotine Inhaler

Two studies generated two arms that served as the basis for estimating the effect of the nicotine patch + the nicotine inhaler. The 15-mg patch was used in both studies at a regular treatment duration. The directed duration of use of the inhaler was 12 weeks in one arm and 26 weeks in the other arm.

■ Long-Term Nicotine Patch Use + *Ad Libitum* NRT

Three studies yielded three analyzable study arms that served as the basis for estimating the effect of long-term nicotine patch use + *ad libitum* NRT use. All arms involved nicotine patch therapy that exceeded 14 weeks, with durations that ranged from 18 to 24 weeks. The *ad libitum* NRT condition involved nicotine gum in two arms and the nicotine nasal spray in one arm. The two gum arms both used 2-mg gum, with directed use lasting 26 weeks in one arm and 52 weeks in another arm. The third arm involved nicotine nasal spray, with directed use lasting 52 weeks.

■ Nicotine Patch + Nortriptyline

Two studies generated three analyzable arms that served as the basis for estimating the effects of the nicotine patch + nortriptyline. The 21-mg nicotine patch served as the highest patch dose in all study arms, and the nortriptyline dose was 75 mg per day in one arm and 100 mg per day in the other arm. Both medications were used for standard durations (8–14 weeks).

■ Nicotine Patch + Second Generation Antidepressants

Three studies yielded three analyzable arms that served as the basis for estimating the effects of second generation antidepressants + the nicotine patch. The antidepressants used included the specific serotonin re-uptake inhibitor paroxetine (20 mg per day for 9 weeks for 2 arms), and the atypical antidepressant venlafaxine (22 mg per day for 21 weeks). The 21- or 22-mg patch served as the highest patch dose, with the duration of patch therapy being 6 or 8 weeks.

■ Effectiveness of Medication Combinations

Table 6.26 displays the 2008 meta-analytic results describing the effectiveness data for the five medication combinations. The data reveal that the nicotine patch + bupropion SR, the nicotine patch + inhaler, the long-term nicotine patch + *ad libitum* NRT, the nicotine patch + nortriptyline, and the nicotine patch + second generation antidepressants all significantly increased a smoker's likelihood of abstinence relative to placebo treatment. A meta-analysis using 12-month abstinence rates had similar results. The first three medication combinations involve only first-line medications and therefore are recommended for use as first-line treatments.

Decisions about use of a medication combination may be based on considerations other than abstinence. Evidence indicates, for instance, that a combination of medication may result in greater suppression of tobacco withdrawal symptoms than does the use of a single medication.[148,315,316] Patient preferences also may play a role, because some combinations of medications may produce more side effects and cost more than individual medications.[315,317,318]

Relative Effectiveness of Medications

Information on the relative effectiveness of medications may help the clinician and patient select an appropriate medication intervention. To this end, all medication conditions in Table 6.26 were compared with the nicotine patch. The nicotine patch was selected as a comparison condition because more study arms were available for this condition than for any other, and because this condition was of moderate effectiveness relative to other conditions (see Table 6.26; OR = 1.9). Contrasts between all treatments were not conducted because of concerns about Type I error due to multiple testing. Also, a conservative Hochberg[319] adjustment to the alpha level was used so that only treatments that were substantially different in effectiveness would be found to be significantly different. These comparisons of the different medications should be viewed as suggestive rather than definitive. For instance, the studies of one type of medication may differ from studies evaluating a different medication on numerous bases such as year of publication, type of population, and newness of the medication. It is possible that such differences could have affected the relative size of the odds ratios obtained for the different medications. Existing studies that provide head-to-head comparisons of medications (which were included in this meta-analysis) provide an additional source of information on this topic.

The *a posteriori* tests resulted in three treatment conditions being statistically different from the effectiveness of the nicotine patch when it is used at regular doses and durations. The 2 mg per day varenicline and the combination of long-term patch use + *ad libitum* NRT (gum or spray) were both found to produce significantly greater likelihood of long-term abstinence than the patch by itself (see Table 6.28). Two treatments produced a lower likelihood of long-term abstinence: selective serotonin re-uptake inhibitors (SSRIs) and naltrexone. The analyses presented in Table 6.28 represent 6-month abstinence rates. Similar conclusions were reached in a meta-analysis of 12-month abstinence rates.

Table 6.28. Meta-analysis (2008): Effectiveness of and abstinence rates of medications relative to the nicotine patch (n = 83 studies)[a]

Medication	Number of arms	Estimated odds ratio (95% C. I.)
Nicotine Patch (reference group)	32	1.0
Monotherapies		
Varenicline (2 mg/day)	5	1.6 (1.3–2.0)
Nicotine Nasal Spray	4	1.2 (0.9–1.6)
High-Dose Nicotine Patch (> 25 mg; standard or long-term)	4	1.2 (0.9–1.6)
Long-Term Nicotine Gum (> 14 weeks)	6	1.2 (0.8–1.7)
Varenicline (1 mg/day)	3	1.1 (0.8–1.6)
Nicotine Inhaler	6	1.1 (0.8–1.5)
Clonidine	3	1.1 (0.6–2.0)
Bupropion SR	26	1.0 (0.9–1.2)
Long-Term Nicotine Patch (> 14 weeks)	10	1.0 (0.9–1.2)
Nortriptyline	5	0.9 (0.6–1.4)
Nicotine Gum	15	0.8 (0.6–1.0)
Combination therapies		
Patch (long-term; > 14 weeks) + NRT (gum or spray)	3	1.9 (1.3–2.7)
Patch + Bupropion SR	3	1.3 (1.0–1.8)

Table 6.28. Meta-analysis (2008): Effectiveness of and abstinence rates of medications relative to the nicotine patch (n = 83 studies)[a] (continued)

Medication	Number of arms	Estimated odds ratio (95% C. I.)
Combination therapies		
Patch + Nortriptyline	2	0.9 (0.6–1.4)
Patch + Inhaler	2	1.1 (0.7–1.9)
Second-generation antidepressants & Patch	3	1.0 (0.6–1.7)
Medications not shown to be effective		
Selective Serotonin Re-uptake Inhibitors (SSRIs)	3	0.5 (0.4–0.7)
Naltrexone	2	0.3 (0.1-0.6)

[a] Go to *www.surgeongeneral.gov/tobacco/gdlnrefs.htm* for the articles used in this meta-analysis.

■ Precessation NRT Use

Recent studies have investigated the use of NRT prior to a quit attempt. Some of these studies involved smokers who are planning to quit, and others involved smokers who were not willing to quit but who were willing to reduce their smoking. The use of NRT while smoking contradicts NRT package inserts. The existence of multiple studies on this prequit medication strategy led the Panel to review this topic as part of this Guideline update. The results of this review (see below) suggest that NRT prior to quitting may be effective in increasing abstinence rates, but the Panel chose not to recommend this intervention (see below). If this strategy is used clinically, patients should be advised to cease NRT use if they develop symptoms of nicotine toxicity (e.g., nausea, vomiting, dizziness).

Precessation Use of NRT Among Patients Making a Quit Attempt. Two randomized controlled studies examined the effect of initiating the use of NRT prior to a quit attempt among patients making a quit attempt. One study examined the use of nicotine patches, either active or placebo, 2 weeks prior to quitting, after which all participants received active patches for 12 weeks following the quit day.[320] Results revealed no differences in adverse events, and smokers who had received the active patches during the prequit period were more likely to be abstinent at 6 months postquit. In a second study, Rose and colleagues[321] found that precessation patch use significantly increased abstinence rates at 4 weeks postquit but not at 6 months.

Finally, a small pilot study found that prequit patch use was well tolerated by smokers wanting to quit.[322] Given the limited data on this strategy, the Panel declined to recommend precessation use of NRT among patients making a quit attempt. However, this topic warrants further research.

Use of NRT Among Patients Unwilling to Make a Quit Attempt at This Time. Research has examined the use of NRT in patients who are not currently willing to make a quit attempt but who state that they are willing to reduce their smoking. In general, these studies found that NRT used in this way increased the likelihood that smokers will make a quit attempt and succeed in quitting. Sufficient studies were available to meta-analyze this topic for the Guideline update. Five studies generated five arms that met criteria for the analysis of the effect of NRT compared to placebo with smokers not willing to quit (but who were willing to reduce the number of cigarettes smoked and use a nicotine replacement medication). As Table 6.29 shows, the use of NRT more than doubled the likelihood that a smoker would be abstinent at 12 months, despite the smoker's unwillingness to make a quit attempt at the time of initial assessment. The nicotine replacement products in these studies included nicotine gum (2 or 4 mg for 6–12 months), the nicotine inhaler (10 mg for 6–24 months), the nicotine patch (16-hour 15-mg patch for up to 6 months), or the choice of a combination of these medications.

Because of the selective participant inclusion criteria and other aspects of this research, it is unclear that the results described above would be relevant to the broader population of smokers unwilling to quit. For instance, most patients in the studies included in the analysis in Table 6.29 were not offered a cessation intervention prior to study induction. It is possible that some of the participants would have opted for a free cessation treatment had it been offered. Also, in some instances, the recruitment material may have made it clear that treatment was available only for those uninterested in quitting. It is unclear how this perceived contingency affected the sample. Further, it is not clear if the results would be true for only those interested in reducing their smoking and not for uninterested patients, in general. Additionally, there was concern that if clinicians routinely asked about interest in cutting down, this might suggest to tobacco users that reduction confers health benefits, is a recommended strategy for persons trying to quit, or is a recommended goal of treatment (rather than quitting smoking)—and that these perceptions might decrease the proportion of smokers willing to make a quit attempt. Because of such concerns, the Panel decided not to recommend medication use as a standard intervention for smokers unwilling to quit. A recent Cochrane analysis[323] found that NRT significantly increased quit rates among smokers not initially motivated to quit. The authors concluded, however, that there was insufficient evidence to recommend this as a standard treatment approach with this population. The Panel believes that this topic warrants further research.

Table 6.29. Meta-analysis (2008): Effectiveness of and abstinence rates for smokers not willing to quit (but willing to change their smoking patterns or reduce their smoking) after receiving NRT compared to placebo (n = 5 studies)[a]

Intervention	Number of arms	Estimated odds ratio (95% C.I.)	Estimated abstinence rate (95% C.I.)
Placebo	5	1.0	3.6
Nicotine replacement (gum, inhaler, or patch)	5	2.5 (1.7–3.7)	8.4 (5.9–12.0)

[a] Go to *www.surgeongeneral.gov/tobacco/gdlnrefs.htm* for the articles used in this meta-analysis.

Medications Not Recommended by the Guideline Panel

▮ Antidepressants Other Than Bupropion SR and Nortriptyline

Smoking is significantly more prevalent among individuals with a past history of depression, and these individuals have more difficulty quitting smoking than do smokers without a past history of depression.[324-328] One antidepressant, bupropion SR, has been documented as effective for treating tobacco use and approved by the FDA for this use (see Bupropion SR [sustained release], page 110). Nortriptyline also has been documented to be effective (see Nortriptyline, page 117), although the FDA has not evaluated this medication for treatment of tobacco dependence. The Panel's review of the extant literature revealed a sufficient body of research to evaluate one class of antidepressants that is dissimilar from both bupropion SR and nortriptyline: selective serotonin re-uptake inhibitors (SSRIs).

▪ Selective Serotonin Re-Uptake Inhibitors (SSRIs)

Two studies yielded three analyzable arms that served as the basis for estimating the effects of SSRIs. Sertraline (200 mg per day) served as the medication in one arm, and fluoxetine (30 to 60 mg per day) served as the medication in the other two arms. The treatment duration was 10 weeks in all arms. Results showed that treatment with SSRIs did not significantly increase the likelihood of abstinence relative to placebo treatment. These results are consistent with other independent reviews[299] (see Table 6.26).

▪ Anxiolytics/Benzodiazepines/Beta-Blockers

A few trials have evaluated anxiolytics and other agents that reduce the somatic signs or the symptoms of anxiety. Early individual trials of pro-pranolol, a beta-blocker,[329] and diazepam, an anxiolytic,[330] did not reveal a beneficial effect for these drugs compared with control interventions. Likewise, of the early studies assessing the anxiolytic buspirone that met inclusion criteria, only one revealed evidence of effectiveness relative to placebo.[331] Further studies of buspirone have failed to replicate this effect.[332-334] These results are consistent with other independent reviews.[333] Because of a lack of data, no meta-analyses were conducted, and no conclusions were drawn regarding the effectiveness of anxiolytics in smoking cessation.

▪ Opioid Antagonists/Naltrexone

Two studies yielded the analyzable study arms that served as the basis for estimating the effects of the opiate antagonist naltrexone. Table 6.26 reveals that naltrexone treatment did not increase the likelihood of abstinence relative to placebo treatment. These results are consistent with other independent reviews.[335] Two studies[336,337] also examined whether naltrexone added to the effectiveness of the nicotine patch. The studies used different naltrexone and patch dosing regimens. The patch use regimen in one study did not meet meta-analysis inclusion criteria. Therefore, these patch + naltrexone studies could not be submitted to meta-analysis. Neither study reported significant benefit from adding naltrexone to the nicotine patch.

Silver Acetate

Due to limitations of the literature available regarding silver acetate, this agent was not included in the inclusive meta-analysis. Several randomized clinical trials[338-340] of silver acetate, however, revealed no beneficial effects for smoking cessation; a Cochrane review concurs with this finding.[341]

Mecamylamine

In the single study that compared mecamylamine alone to placebo, no effectiveness was noted.[342] Another early study compared a combination of mecamylamine plus the nicotine patch to placebo and found a significant effect for this combination.[343] A more recent study comparing nicotine patch alone to nicotine patch plus mecamylamine found no significant differences.[344] These findings are consistent with other independent reviews.[345] Because of these findings, the Panel drew no conclusions regarding mecamylamine as a monotherapy.

Extended Use of Medications

For some patients, it may be appropriate to continue medication treatment for periods longer than is usually recommended. Results of the inclusive meta-analysis indicated that long-term patch and gum use are effective. Evidence indicates that the long-term use of gum may be more effective than a shorter course of gum therapy (Table 6.26). The Lung Health Study, of almost 4,000 smokers with evidence of early COPD, reported that approximately one-third of long-term quitters still were using nicotine gum at 12 months,[346] and some for as long as 5 years, with no serious side effects.[347] Other studies also have found that, among patients given free access to nicotine gum, 15 to 20 percent of successful abstainers continue to use the gum for a year or longer.[348] Thus, it may be that certain groups of smokers may benefit from long-term medication use. Although weaning should be encouraged for all patients using medications, continued use of such medication clearly is preferable to a return to smoking with respect to health consequences. This is because, unlike smoking, these medications do not (a) contain non-nicotine toxic substances (e.g., "tar," carbon monoxide, formaldehyde, benzene); (b) produce sharp surges in blood nicotine levels; and/or (c) produce strong dependence.[349,350] Finally, it should be noted that the medication treatment that produced the largest effects on abstinence rates, of those analyzed, involved long-term nicotine patch therapy + *ad libitum* NRT (Table 6.26).

▐ Use of NRT in Cardiovascular Patients

Soon after the nicotine patch was released, the media reported a possible link between the use of this medication and cardiovascular risk. This question has been studied systematically since that time. Separate analyses now have documented the lack of an association between the nicotine patch and acute cardiovascular events,[351-356] even in patients who continued to smoke while on the nicotine patch,[357] although a recent study raised questions regarding NRT use in intensive care units.[358] Because of inaccurate media coverage in the past, it may be important to inform patients who are reluctant to use NRTs that there is no evidence of increased cardiovascular risk with these medications. Note that package inserts recommend caution in patients with acute cardiovascular diseases (see Tables 3.3 3.11).

▐ Future Research

The following pharmacotherapeutic topics require additional research:

- Relative effectiveness and safety of the seven FDA-approved medications, in general and for specific subpopulations (e.g., women; adolescents; older smokers; smokeless tobacco users; individuals with psychiatric disorders, including substance use disorders; postmyocardial infarction patients) and for long-term treatment

- Use of combined tobacco dependence medications in general and for specific subpopulations (e.g., highly dependent smokers)

- Effectiveness of long-term medications

- Effectiveness of prequit NRT use in increasing abstinence rates

- Strategies to address widespread misconceptions about effective smoking cessation medications and common barriers to their appropriate use

- Effectiveness of MAO inhibitors, especially for those with depression

Use of Over-the-Counter Medications

Recommendation: Over-the-counter nicotine patch therapy is more effective than placebo, and its use should be encouraged. (Strength of evidence = B)

No new studies were identified for the 2008 update that examined the effectiveness of nicotine patch versus placebo patch in an OTC setting. Based on the 2000 Guideline, there were three placebo-controlled studies with six arms that met selection criteria for the meta-analysis of medication interventions in OTC settings. These three studies specifically examined the effect of patch versus placebo. The only additional treatments in these studies were a self-help manual, instructions contained in the package, or written directions for using the patch. As shown in Table 6.30, the use of the nicotine patch in OTC settings nearly doubles abstinence rates when compared to a placebo. These results are consistent with a more recent (2003) meta-analysis of active versus placebo patch in an OTC setting that found an odds ratio of 2.5 (95% C.I. = 1.8–3.6) for active nicotine patch.[359] A study that did not meet inclusion criteria for meta-analysis reported low abstinence rates when the nicotine patch was used in the OTC setting.[360] Too few studies were done in the OTC setting to permit meta-analysis of the OTC effect of any other medication. The "B" strength of evidence rating reflects the Panel's concern about the external validity of the studies designed to reflect the OTC context.

The FDA has approved nicotine gum, the nicotine lozenge, and the nicotine patch for OTC use. The patches and gum are identical to those previously available only via prescription. Although the OTC status of these medications has increased their availability and use,[361] this does not reduce the clinician's responsibility to intervene with smokers or insurers/managed care organizations/payers to cover the costs of such treatment. Moreover, OTC availability may enhance the capacity of a broad array of clinicians to intervene comprehensively when treating tobacco dependence.

All clinicians have specific responsibilities regarding these products, such as encouraging their use when appropriate, identifying patients with specific contraindications, providing counseling and followup, encouraging total abstinence during a quit attempt, offering instruction on appropriate use, addressing common patient misconceptions, and providing prescriptions when needed for select populations to ensure reimbursement (e.g., Medicaid patients). Additionally, patients should be urged to read the package insert and consult with their pharmacist. Finally, the clinician should advise patients regarding the selection and use of medications, whether purchased OTC or by prescription. Debate has arisen in the field regarding the effectiveness of OTC NRT use. For instance, a population-based study found no long-term effects of OTC nicotine patch use.[34] However, cross-sectional surveys have methodolgical constraints (e.g., patients may self-select certain treatments based on dependence or perceived difficulty of quitting).[362]

Table 6.30. Meta-analysis (2000): Effectiveness of and estimated abstinence rates for OTC nicotine patch therapy (n = 3 studies)[a]

OTC therapy	Number of arms	Odds Ratio (95% C.I.)	Estimated abstinence rate (95% C.I.)
Placebo	3	1.0	6.7
OTC nicotine patch therapy	3	1.8 (1.2–2.8)	11.8 (7.5–16.0)

[a] Go to *www.surgeongeneral.gov/tobacco/gdlnrefs.htm* for the articles used in this meta-analysis.

Future Research

Important topics for future research are:

- Effectiveness of nicotine patch, gum, and lozenge when access is OTC

- Extent to which individuals use medications appropriately when access is OTC

- Extent to which the effectiveness of OTC medication is enhanced by other treatments (e.g., pharmacist counseling, telephone counseling, computer self-help resources, clinician interventions)

- Extent to which OTC status increases or reduces the use of medications by poor or minority populations

- Strategies for improving the accessibility and appropriate use of OTC medications

C. Systems Evidence

Clinician Training and Reminder Systems

Recommendation: All clinicians and clinicians-in-training should be trained in effective strategies to assist tobacco users willing to make a quit attempt and to motivate those unwilling to quit. Training appears to be more effective when coupled with systems changes. (Strength of Evidence = B)

Meta-analyses were conducted to analyze the effects of clinician training and other systems changes. It was necessary to include studies in these analyses in which higher level units (clinicians or clinical sites) served as units of randomization. This strategy was adopted because relatively few studies in this area of research randomized individual patients to treatment or intervention conditions. Studies randomized at higher level units were considered for the analyses only if the study's analytic plan accounted for the dependency of data nested under such units or if the outcome, such as providing advice to quit, was analyzed at the same level as the randomization (e.g., clinician or clinic level). In fact, however, the few studies that analyzed data at the level of the clinician or clinic shared no common outcomes and could not be used in the meta-analysis.

Table 6.31 depicts meta-analytic results for studies that examined the effects of training on abstinence outcomes. Only two studies, somewhat heterogenous, were available for this analysis. Thus, although the meta-analysis showed a significant effect of training, the Panel elected to assign this recommendation a "B" strength of evidence.

Table 6.31. Meta-analysis (2008): Effectiveness of and estimated abstinence rates for clinician training (n = 2 studies)[a]

Intervention	Number of arms	Odds Ratio (95% C.I.)	Estimated abstinence rate (95% C.I.)
No intervention	2	1.0	6.4
Clinician training	2	2.0 (1.2–3.4)	12.0 (7.6–18.6)

[a] Go to *www.surgeongeneral.gov/tobacco/gdlnrefs.htm* for the articles used in this meta-analysis.

Clinician training and other systems changes are intended to increase rates of tobacco use assessment and intervention. Therefore, additional meta-analyses were conducted to ascertain the effects of systems changes on outcomes such as clinician assessment of smoking status ("Ask"), provision of treatment ("Assist"), and arranging for treatment followup ("Arrange"). Thus, these meta-analyses focused on systems change impact on specific clinician behaviors. In the analyzed studies, clinician behavior was assessed via patient report or chart review (not via clinician report). Analyses of such clinician behaviors are of public health significance because of evidence that the provision of treatment has been shown to lead to higher tobacco cessation rates.

As noted in Table 6.32, training clinicians increases the percentage of smokers who receive treatment, such as a discussion of benefits/obstacles to quitting or strategies to prevent relapse, medication, and provision of support. Further, combining clinician training with a charting system, such as chart reminder stickers or treatment algorithms attached to the chart, increases rates of tobacco use assessment (Table 6.33), setting a quit date (Table 6.34), providing materials (Table 6.35), and arranging for followup (Table 6.36). Thus, clinician training, especially when coupled with other systems changes such as reminder systems, increases the rates at which clinicians engage in tobacco interventions that reliably boost tobacco cessation. The *Guide to Community Preventive Services*[92] found insufficient evidence to recommend provider education systems as stand-alone interventions, separate from other system changes, but does recommend provider education when part of other system changes such as reminder systems.

Table 6.32. Meta-analysis (2008): Effectiveness of clinician training on rates of providing treatment ("Assist") (n = 2 studies)[a]

Intervention	Number of arms	Odds Ratio (95% C.I.)	Estimated rate (95% C.I.)
No intervention	2	1.0	36.2
Clinician training	2	3.2 (2.0–5.2)	64.7 (53.1–74.8)

[a] Go to *www.surgeongeneral.gov/tobacco/gdlnrefs.htm* for the articles used in this meta-analysis.

Table 6.33. Meta-analysis (2008): Effectiveness of clinician training combined with charting on asking about smoking status ("Ask") (n = 3 studies)[a]

Intervention	Number of arms	Odds Ratio (95% C.I.)	Estimated rate (95% C.I.)
No intervention	3	1.0	58.8
Training and charting	3	2.1 (1.9–2.4)	75.2 (72.7–77.6)

[a] Go to *www.surgeongeneral.gov/tobacco/gdlnrefs.htm* for the articles used in this meta-analysis.

Table 6.34. Meta-analysis (2008): Effectiveness of training combined with charting on setting a quit date ("Assist") (n = 2 studies)[a]

Intervention	Number of arms	Odds Ratio (95% C.I.)	Estimated rate (95% C.I.)
No intervention	2	1.0	11.4
Training and charting	2	5.5 (4.1–7.4)	41.4 (34.4–48.8)

[a] Go to *www.surgeongeneral.gov/tobacco/gdlnrefs.htm* for the articles used in this meta-analysis.

Table 6.35. Meta-analysis (2008): Effectiveness of training combined with charting on providing materials ("Assist") (n = 2 studies)[a]

Intervention	Number of arms	Odds Ratio (95% C.I.)	Estimated rate (95% C.I.)
No intervention	2	1.0	8.7
Training and charting	2	4.2 (3.4–5.3)	28.6 (24.3–33.4)

[a] Go to *www.surgeongeneral.gov/tobacco/gdlnrefs.htm* for the articles used in this meta-analysis.

Table 6.36. Meta-analysis (2008): Effectiveness of training combined with charting on arranging for followup ("Arrange") (n = 2 studies)[a]

Intervention	Number of arms	Odds Ratio (95% C.I.)	Estimated rate (95% C.I.)
No intervention	2	1.0	6.7
Training and charting	2	2.7 (1.9–3.9)	16.3 (11.8– 22.1)

[a] Go to *www.surgeongeneral.gov/tobacco/gdlnrefs.htm* for the articles used in this meta-analysis.

These meta-analyses support the finding that clinician training increases the delivery of effective tobacco use treatments. Training elements provided in these interventions included didactic presentation of material, group discussions, and role playing. These studies also examined a range of clinician training, from formal training during residency to onsite clinician training within the community.

Training should be directed at both clinicians-in-training as well as practicing clinicians. Training should be reinforced throughout the clinicians' education and practice.[363-368] Such training has been shown to be cost-effective.[369] For clinicians-in-training, most clinical disciplines currently neither provide training nor require competency in tobacco use interventions,[370] although this is improving slowly.[371,372] One survey of U.S. medical schools found that most medical schools (69%) did not require clinical training in tobacco dependence treatment.[373] The National Cancer Institute's Prevention and Cessation Education in Medical Schools (PACE) reported that, in 2004, about 36 percent of medical school courses offered about 10 hours of tobacco-related teaching over 4 years,[374] and PACE has developed competencies for graduating medical students.[375]

Similarly, the American Dental Education Association has guidelines recommending tobacco use cessation clinical activities (TUCCA) education for dental and dental hygiene students and, in 1998, 51 percent of dental schools reported clinical training in this area.[376] Tobacco-related curricula may be taught as part of a preventive medicine or substance abuse course or as a class by itself. Similar recommendations would be relevant to virtually all other clinical disciplines. Training in tobacco use interventions should not only transmit essential treatment skills (see Chapter 3), but also should inculcate the belief that tobacco dependence treatment is a standard of good clinical practice.[130,208,250]

Several factors would promote the training of clinicians in tobacco intervention activities:[370]

- Inclusion of education and training in tobacco dependence treatments in the required curricula of all clinical disciplines

- Evaluation of effective tobacco dependence treatment knowledge and skills in licensing and certification exams for all clinical disciplines

- Adoption by medical specialty societies of a uniform standard of competence in tobacco dependence treatment for all members

Finally, clinicians who currently use any tobacco product should participate in treatment programs to stop their own tobacco use permanently. Clinicians are important role models for their patients, and those who use tobacco probably are less likely to counsel their patients to quit.[377] Therefore, it is heartening that many types of clinicians have dramatically decreased their own tobacco use during the past 40 years,[378] although this has not been universal.

▣ Future Research

The following topics regarding clinician training require additional research:

- Effectiveness of training programs for other health disciplines, such as nursing, psychology, dentistry (including hygienists), social work, and pharmacy

- Effective elements in successful training programs (e.g., continuing medical education, interactive components)

- Combined effect of multiple systems changes, such as clinician training, reminder systems, clinician feedback, incentive payments, and recruitment of opinion leaders

Cost-Effectiveness of Tobacco Dependence Interventions

Recommendation: The tobacco dependence treatments shown to be effective in this Guideline (both counseling and medication) are highly cost-effective relative to other reimbursed treatments and should be provided to all smokers. (Strength of Evidence = A)

Recommendation: Sufficient resources should be allocated for systems support to ensure the delivery of efficacious tobacco use treatments. (Strength of Evidence = C)

Smoking exacts a substantial financial burden on the United States. A recent report of the Centers for Disease Control and Prevention estimated that tobacco dependence costs the Nation more than $96 billion per year in direct medical expenses and $97 billion in lost productivity.[28] Given these substantial costs, research has focused on the economic impact and cost-effectiveness of tobacco cessation interventions.

Tobacco use treatments, ranging from brief clinician advice to specialist-delivered intensive programs, including medication, have been shown not only to be clinically effective, but also to be extremely cost-effective relative to other commonly used disease prevention interventions and medical treatments. Cost-effectiveness analyses have shown that tobacco dependence treatment compares favorably with routinely reimbursed medical interventions such as the treatment of hypertension and hypercholesterolemia, as well as preventive screening interventions such as periodic mammography or Papanicolaou smears.[222,224,379-382] For example, the cost per life-year saved of tobacco dependence treatment has been estimated at $3,539,[194] which compares favorably to hypertension screening for men ages 45 to 54 ($5,200) and annual cervical screening for women ages 34 to 39 ($4,100).[383] Treating tobacco dependence also is important economically in that it can prevent the development of a variety of costly chronic diseases, including heart disease, cancer, and pulmonary disease. In fact, tobacco dependence treatment has been referred to as the "gold standard" of health care cost-effectiveness.[225]

Cost-effectiveness can be measured in a variety of ways, including cost per quality-adjusted-life-year saved (QALY), cost per quit, health care costs and utilization pre- and postquit, and return on investment (ROI) for coverage of tobacco dependence treatment.

Cost per Quality-Adjusted-Life-Year Saved and Cost per Quit

Numerous analyses have estimated the cost per QALY saved resulting from use of effective tobacco dependence interventions.[187,222,380,384-389] In general, evidence-based tobacco use interventions compare favorably with other prevention and chronic disease interventions such as treatment of hypertension and mammography screening when using this criterion. Specific analyses have estimated the costs of tobacco use treatment to range from a few hundred to a few thousand dollars per QALY saved.[228,385] Separate analyses have computed the estimated costs of treatment in terms of the cost per quit. Compared to other interventions, the cost of tobacco use treatments has been modest, ranging from a few hundred to a few thousand dollars per quit.[194,212,384,390-393]

Managed Care Organizations (MCOs) often assess the per member per month (PMPM) cost of a benefit, and the PMPM cost for tobacco use treatment has been assessed in a variety of settings. In general, the PMPM cost for tobacco use treatments has been low relative to other covered benefits, ranging from about $0.20 to about $0.80 PMPM.[210,228,391,394]

Health Care Costs and Utilization Pre- and Postquit

A substantial body of research has investigated the effect of tobacco use treatment on health care costs.[395-399] A synthesis of these findings suggests that: (1) among individuals who quit tobacco use, health care costs typically increase during the year in which smokers quit then decline progressively, falling below those of continuing smokers for 1 to 10 years after quitting; (2) in general, smokers' health care costs begin to rise in the time period immediately prior to quit attempts; and (3) higher health care utilization predicts smoking cessation among smokers with and without chronic diseases. These findings suggest that quitting smoking often occurs in response to serious and expensive health problems. Such research also suggests that increases in health care costs, including hospitalizations, during the year of quitting may be a cause rather than a consequence of successful smoking cessation.

Return on Investment for Coverage of Tobacco Dependence Treatment

The ROI tool is used frequently to estimate the amount of time it takes for an expenditure to earn back some or all of its initial investment. The economic arguments supporting the decision to provide insurance coverage for tobacco use treatments would be enhanced if the costs of such coverage are modest compared to economic benefits resulting from successful cessation (reductions in health care expenditures, increased productivity, and/or other costs).

Studies have documented that tobacco dependence treatments provide a timely return on investment when considered by the employer. Such analyses have concluded that providing coverage for tobacco use treatment for employees often produces substantial net financial savings through increased health care savings, increased productivity, reduced absenteeism, and reduced life insurance payouts.[229,400-402]

Financial savings are more difficult to attain for a health plan given factors such as member turnover, the difficulty of attributing reduced health care expenditures to tobacco dependence, and the absence of economic benefits resulting from productivity gains. Although most analyses have not demonstrated cost savings, insurance coverage of evidence-based tobacco dependence treatments are highly cost-effective relative to other frequently paid-for health care services. One recent effort to simulate the financial implications of covering tobacco use treatments by MCOs found that at 5 years, coverage of tobacco use treatment cost an MCO a modest $0.61 PMPM, with quitters gaining an average of 7.1 years of life and a direct coverage cost of about $3,500 for each life-year saved.[228] The authors concluded that coverage of such cost-effective tobacco use treatment programs by MCOs should be strongly encouraged. Another study examined the trend in health care costs for former smokers over 7 years postquitting compared to continuing smokers.[395] The authors found that, by the seventh year, former smokers' cumulative costs (including increased cost in the year they quit) were lower than those of continuing smokers. A more recent analysis concluded that at 10 years, the ROI of providing a comprehensive tobacco use treatment benefit, considering only health care costs, ranged from 75 percent to 92 percent, indicating that health care savings alone have repaid more than three-fourths of the investment.[229] Other analyses have shown that multiple tobacco use treatment components, including telephone counseling and various medications,[227,403,404] yield a favorable ROI. The American Health Insurance Plans (AHIP) has provided a Web link for health plans to compute their ROI for the provision of tobacco use treatment: *www.businesscaseroi.org/roi/default.aspx*.

Tobacco cessation treatment is particularly cost-effective in certain populations, such as hospitalized patients and pregnant women. For hospitalized patients, successful tobacco abstinence not only reduces general medical costs in the short term, but also reduces the number of future hospitalizations.[9,355,405] Tobacco dependence interventions for pregnant women are especially cost-effective because they result in fewer low birth-weight babies and perinatal deaths; fewer physical, cognitive, and behavioral problems during infancy and childhood; and yield important health benefits for the mother.[406,407] One study found that interventions with U.S. pregnant smokers could net savings up to $8 million in direct neonatal inpatient costs given the cost of an intervention ($24–$34) versus the costs saved ($881) for each woman who quits smoking during pregnancy.[408] Another study showed that, for each low-income pregnant smoker who quit, Medicaid saved $1,274.[409] A simulation study found that a 1 percent decrease in smoking prevalence among U.S. pregnant women would save $21 million (1995 dollars) in direct medical costs in the first year.[406,410,411]

Tobacco Dependence Treatment as a Part of Assessing Health Care Quality

Recommendation: Provision of Guideline-based interventions to treat tobacco use and dependence should remain in standard ratings and measures of overall health care quality (e.g., NCQA HEDIS). These standard measures should also include measures of outcomes (e.g., use of cessation treatment, short- and long-term abstinence rates) that result from providing tobacco dependence interventions. (Strength of Evidence = C)

The provision of tobacco dependence treatment should be increased by: (1) attention to health organization "report cards" (e.g., HEDIS, The Joint Commission, Physician Consortium for Performance Improvement, National Quality Forum, Ambulatory Quality Alliance),[89,412-414] which support smoker identification and treatment; (2) accreditation criteria used by The Joint Commission and other accrediting bodies that include the presence of effective tobacco assessment and intervention policies; and (3) increasing the use of tobacco-related measures in pay-for-performance initiatives.

Future Research

The following topics regarding cost-effectiveness and health systems require additional research:

- Cost-effectiveness of the various tobacco dependence treatments, both short- and long-term

- Optimal ways to remove systemic barriers that prevent clinicians from effectively delivering tobacco dependence treatments

- Systemic interventions to encourage provider and patient utilization of effective tobacco dependence treatments

- Relative costs and economic impacts of different formats of effective treatments (e.g., proactive telephone counseling, face-to-face contact, medication)

- Impact of using tobacco intervention performance measures on clinician intervention and patient outcomes, including the use of such measures in "pay for performance" programs

Providing Treatment for Tobacco Use and Dependence as a Covered Benefit

Recommendation: Providing tobacco dependence treatments (both medication and counseling) as a paid or covered benefit by health insurance plans has been shown to increase the proportion of smokers who use cessation treatment, attempt to quit, and successfully quit. Therefore, treatments shown to be effective in the Guideline should be included as covered services in public and private health benefit plans. (Strength of Evidence = A)

Multiple studies have assessed the impact of including tobacco dependence treatment as a covered health insurance benefit for smokers. Most studies have documented that such health insurance coverage increases both treatment utilization rates and the rates of cessation,[210,212,391,415] although some research is not consistent with these findings.[416] A recent Cochrane analysis (2005) concluded that health care financing systems that offered full payment for tobacco use treatment increased self-reported prolonged abstinence rates at relatively low costs when compared with a partial benefit or no benefit. Moreover, the presence of prepaid or discounted prescription drug benefits increases patients' receipt of medication and smoking abstinence rates.[231,348,417] These studies emphasize that removing all cost barriers yields the highest rates of treatment utilization.

Three studies met criteria to be included in a 2008 Guideline update meta-analysis of the effects of providing tobacco use treatments as a covered health insurance benefit. Three different outcomes were examined: rates of treatment provision, quit attempts, and quit rates. As can be seen in Tables 6.37 through 6.39, compared to not having tobacco use treatment as a covered benefit, individuals with the benefit were more likely to receive treatment, make a quit attempt, and abstain from smoking.

Table 6.37. Meta-analysis (2008): Estimated rates of intervention for individuals who received tobacco use interventions as a covered health insurance benefit (n = 3 studies)[a]

Treatment	Number of arms	Estimated odds ratio (95% C.I.)	Estimated intervention rate (95% C.I.)
Individuals with no covered health insurance benefit	3	1.0	8.9
Individuals with the benefit	3	2.3 (1.8–2.9)	18.2 (14.8–22.3)

[a] Go to *www.surgeongeneral.gov/tobacco/gdlnrefs.htm* for the articles used in this meta-analysis.

Table 6.38. Meta-analysis (2008): Estimated rates of quit attempts for individuals who received tobacco use interventions as a covered health insurance benefit (n = 3 studies)[a]

Treatment	Number of arms	Estimated odds ratio (95% C.I.)	Estimated quit attempt rate (95% C.I.)
Individuals with no covered benefit	3	1.0	30.5
Individuals with the benefit	3	1.3 (1.01–1.5)	36.2 (32.3–40.2)

[a] Go to *www.surgeongeneral.gov/tobacco/gdlnrefs.htm* for the articles used in this meta-analysis.

Table 6.39. Meta-analysis (2008): Estimated abstinence rates for individuals who received tobacco use interventions as a covered benefit (n = 3 studies)[a]

Treatment	Number of arms	Estimated odds ratio (95% C.I.)	Estimated abstinence rate (95% C.I.)
Individuals with no covered benefit	3	1.0	6.7
Individuals with the benefit	3	1.6 (1.2–2.2)	10.5 (8.1–13.5)

[a] Go to *www.surgeongeneral.gov/tobacco/gdlnrefs.htm* for the articles used in this meta-analysis.

It may be in the best interests of insurance companies, MCOs, purchasers, and governmental bodies within a specific geographic area to work collaboratively to ensure that tobacco dependence interventions are a covered benefit and that enrollees are aware of these benefits. This would allow the financial benefits of the successful use of these services to be realized by all of the health plans within a community.

Future Research

- Impact of promotion or communication of tobacco dependence treatment benefits on utilization and resulting population health and economic effects

- Cost-effectiveness of specific elements of tobacco dependence treatment

- Appropriate level of payment needed to optimize clinician delivery of tobacco dependence treatment

Chapter 7 | Specific Populations and Other Topics

Background

Many factors could affect the acceptability, use, and effectiveness of tobacco dependence treatments. This raises the question of whether interventions should be tailored or modified on the basis of personal characteristics or contextual factors such as gender, race/ethnicity, age, comorbidity, or hospitalization status. Should pregnant smokers receive tobacco dependence medication? Do tobacco dependence interventions interfere with nontobacco chemical dependency treatments? These and other specific populations and issues are considered in this chapter. The answers to these questions are relevant to a range of clinicians who routinely deal with specific populations of smokers (e.g., obstetricians, gynecologists, pediatricians, psychiatrists, internists, cardiologists, nurses, pharmacists, dentists, and dental hygienists).

Recommendation: The interventions found to be effective in this Guideline have been shown to be effective in a variety of populations. In addition, many of the studies supporting these interventions comprised diverse samples of tobacco users. Therefore, interventions identified as effective in this Guideline are recommended for all individuals who use tobacco, except when medication use is contraindicated or with specific populations in which medication has not been shown to be effective (pregnant women, smokeless tobacco users, light smokers, and adolescents). (Strength of Evidence = B)

Effective Treatments for Specific Populations

The above recommendation applies to the broad population of smokers, including HIV-positive smokers; hospitalized smokers; lesbian/gay/bisexual/transgender smokers; those with low socioeconomic status (SES)/limited formal education; smokers with medical comorbidities; older smokers; smokers with psychiatric disorders, including substance use disorders; racial and ethnic minorities; and women smokers. It does not apply to adolescents, pregnant smokers, light smokers, and smokeless tobacco users (see below).

The recommendation that tobacco dependence treatments be used with broad populations of tobacco users arises from several considerations. One is that many of the randomized trials that generated the treatment recommendations comprised diverse samples. A second consideration is that the studies that tested interventions in homogeneous, specific populations show that interventions that are effective in one population tend to be effective in other populations. Finally, the relative safety of the tobacco dependence treatments versus the hazards of continued tobacco use supports some extrapolation from extant data. Table 7.1 reviews the randomized clinical trial (RCT) evidence of effectiveness of various treatments in different populations. Unless specifically stated, this table presents evidence from individual, screened RCTs rather than from meta-analyses. It is not intended to provide a comprehensive review of the relevant literature, but rather to provide some key findings from that review. Importantly, adolescents, pregnant smokers, light smokers, and smokeless tobacco users each have their own sections of this Guideline update, given that they usually are excluded from the RCTs used to evaluate the effectiveness of interventions presented in this Guideline and may have other special issues (e.g., safety).

Table 7.1. Evidence of effectiveness of tobacco dependence interventions in specific populations

Population of Smokers	Review of Evidence
HIV-positive	No long-term RCTs have examined the effectiveness of interventions in this population. More research is needed. • One study with 3-month followup indicated that telephone counseling is promising.[418] • Pilot data indicate that effective treatments work with this population.[419]
Hospitalized patients	2007 Cochrane analyses[420] revealed that intensive intervention (inpatient contact plus followup for at least 1 month) was associated with a significantly higher quit rate compared to control conditions (OR = 1.65; 95% CI = 1.44–1.90, 17 trials). Specific additional Cochrane findings: • Posthospitalization followup appears to be a key component of effective interventions. • No significant effect of medication was seen in this population. However, the effect sizes were comparable to those obtained in other clinical trials, suggesting that nicotine replacement therapy (NRT) and bupropion SR may be effective in this population.

Table 7.1. Evidence of effectiveness of tobacco dependence interventions in specific populations (continued)

Population of Smokers	Review of Evidence
Hospitalized patients (continued)	• Intervention is effective regardless of the patient's reason for admission. There was no strong evidence that clinical diagnosis of the medically comorbid condition affected the likelihood of quitting. Interventions that have been shown to be effective in individual studies are: counseling and medication[57,355,421-423] and other psychosocial interventions, including self-help via brochure or audio/videotape; chart prompt reminding physician to advise smoking cessation; hospital counseling; and postdischarge counseling telephone calls.[424,425] Some data suggest NRT might not be appropriate in intensive care patients.[358]
Lesbian, gay, bisexual, transgender	No long-term RCTs have examined the effectiveness of interventions specifically in this population.
Low SES/limited formal education[a]	• Meta-analysis (2008): 5 studies met selection criteria and contributed to a 2008 Guideline meta-analysis comparing counseling vs. usual care or no counseling among individuals with low SES/limited formal education. Meta-analytic results showed that counseling is effective in treating smokers with low SES/limited formal education (OR = 1.42; 95% C.I. = 1.04–1.92) (Abstinence rate without counseling = 13.2%; with counseling, abstinence rate = 17.7% [95% C.I. = 13.7%–22.6%]) • Interventions included in the meta-analysis were motivational messages with and without telephone counseling for low-income mothers and low-income African Americans,[172,426] proactive telephone counseling in addition to nicotine patches,[427,428] tailored bedside counseling and followup for hospitalized African-American patients.[429]
Medical co-morbidities	Tobacco use treatments have been shown to be effective among smokers with a variety of comorbid medical conditions. The comorbid conditions and effective interventions include: • Cardiovascular disease: psychosocial interventions;[430-439] exercise;[440,441] bupropion SR,[439,442] but one study did not find significant long-term effects;[443] nicotine patch, gum, or inhaler.[439] • Lung/COPD patients: intensive cessation counseling,[444] intensive behavioral (relapse prevention) program combined with nicotine replacement therapy,[445] bupropion SR,[446,447] nortriptyline,[447] nicotine patch or inhaler.[448] • Cancer: counseling and medication,[251,449,450] motivational counseling.[451]

Table 7.1. Evidence of effectiveness of tobacco dependence interventions in specific populations (continued)

Population of Smokers	Review of Evidence
Older smokers	• Research has demonstrated the effectiveness of the "4 A's" (ask, advise, assist, and arrange followup) in patients ages 50 and older.[452-454] Counseling interventions,[455-457] physician advice,[118,456] buddy support programs,[458] age-tailored self-help materials,[456,459-461] telephone counseling,[460,461] and the nicotine patch[454,462,463] all have been shown to be effective in treating tobacco use in adults 50 and older.
Psychiatric disorders, including substance use disorders[a]	• Meta-analysis (2008): Four studies met selection criteria and were relevant to a 2008 Guideline meta-analysis comparing antidepressants (bupropion SR and nortriptyline) vs. placebo for individuals with a past history of depression. Meta-analytic results showed that antidepressants, specifically bupropion SR and nortriptyline, are effective in increasing long-term cessation rates in smokers with a past history of depression (OR = 3.42; 95% C.I. = 1.70–6.84; abstinence rates = 29.9%, 95% C.I. = 17.5%–46.1%). Note that these studies typically included intensive psychosocial interventions for all participants.
	• Although psychiatric disorders may place smokers at increased risk for relapse, such smokers can be helped by tobacco dependence treatments.[464-468]
	• Some data suggest that bupropion SR and NRT may be effective for treating smoking in individuals with schizophrenia and may improve negative symptoms of schizophrenia and depressive symptoms.[467,469-472] Data suggest that individuals on atypical antipsychotics may be more responsive to bupropion SR for treatment of tobacco dependence than those taking standard antipsychotics.[472]
	• Current evidence is insufficient to determine whether smokers with psychiatric disorders benefit more from tobacco use treatments tailored to psychiatric disorder/symptoms than from standard treatments.[266,473]
	• Evidence indicates that tobacco use interventions, both counseling and medication, are effective in treating smokers who are receiving treatment for chemical dependency.[464,474-476]
	• There is little evidence that tobacco dependence interventions interfere with recovery from nontobacco chemical dependencies among patients who are in treatment for such dependencies.[475,477-482] One study suggests that delivery of smoking cessation interventions concurrent with alcohol dependence interventions may compromise alcohol abstinence outcomes, although there was no difference in smoking abstinence rates.[483]

Table 7.1. Evidence of effectiveness of tobacco dependence interventions in specific populations (continued)

Population of Smokers	Review of Evidence
Psychiatric disorders, including substance use disorders[a] (continued)	• The use of varenicline has been associated with depressed mood, agitation, suicidal ideation, and suicide. The FDA recommends that patients tell their health care provider about any history of psychiatric illness prior to starting varenicline and that clinicians monitor for changes in mood and behavior when prescribing this medication. In light of these FDA recommendations, clinicians should consider eliciting information on their patients' psychiatric history. For more information, see the FDA package insert.
Racial/ethnic minorities	RCTs have examined the effectiveness of interventions in specific racial/ethnic minority populations: African Americans • Bupropion SR,[484] in-person motivational counseling,[176] nicotine patch,[485] clinician advice,[486,487] counseling,[488] biomedical feedback,[489] tailored self-help manuals and materials, and telephone counseling[486,490] have been shown to be effective with African-American smokers. Asian and Pacific Islanders • No long-term RCTs have examined the effectiveness of interventions specifically in this population. Hispanics • Nicotine patch;[491] telephone counseling;[492] self-help materials, including a mood management component;[493] and tailoring[494] have been shown to be effective with Hispanic smokers. American Indians and Alaska Natives • Screening for tobacco use, clinician advice, clinic staff reinforcement, and followup materials have been shown to be effective for American Indian and Alaska Native populations.[495]
Women	• Evidence shows that both men and women benefit from bupropion SR, NRT, and varenicline;[496] evidence is mixed as to whether women show as great a benefit from NRT as do men.[150,155-157,496-498] • Psychosocial interventions, including proactive phone counseling[462] individually tailored followup,[499] and advice to quit geared toward children's health[500] are effective with women. There is some evidence that exercise is effective for women;[501] however, these findings are not consistent.[502]

[a] Go to *www.surgeongeneral.gov/tobacco/gdlnrefs.htm* for the articles used in this meta-analysis.

Clinical Issues for Specific Populations

There are population-specific concerns and clinical issues regarding prevalence and treatment of tobacco dependence (see Table 7.2).

Table 7.2. Clinical issues for treating specific populations

Issue	Approach
Language	• Ensure that interventions are provided in a language the patient understands. Most quitlines provide counseling in Spanish, and some provide counseling in other languages.[503] • All textual materials used (e.g., self-help brochures) should be written at an appropriate reading level. This is particularly important given epidemiological data showing that tobacco use rates are markedly higher among individuals of lower educational attainment.[504,505]
Culture	• Interventions should be culturally appropriate to be relevant and acceptable to the patient.[506] The extent to which cultural tailoring enhances intervention effectiveness requires further research.[490] • Clinicians should remain sensitive to individual differences and spiritual and health beliefs that may affect treatment acceptance, use, and success in all populations (see Chapter 6A, Specialized Assessment).
Medical comorbidity	• Examine the possibility of medication interactions (See Chapter 6B, Interactions of First-Line Tobacco Use Medications With Other Drugs).[308] • Address how exposure to tobacco can alter the liver's ability to metabolize different medications (HIV-positive patients).

HIV-Positive Smokers

HIV-positive individuals are more likely to smoke than the general population.[507-510] Currently, HIV-positive individuals are living longer, due to treatment advances, making the issue of cigarette smoking in this population a significant clinical concern.[511,512] HIV-positive smokers have higher mortality rates and report lower quality of life than HIV-positive nonsmokers.[513,516] In addition, HIV-positive smokers appear to be at greater risk for developing invasive pneumococcal diseases and CNS infections compared with non-HIV infected individuals.[514,517] Also, compared to nonsmoking HIV-positive individuals, smoking among HIV-positive persons is associated with increased risk of several opportunistic infections[518-520] and spontaneous pneumothorax.[521] Data suggest that HIV-positive smokers underestimate the effects of smoking on their health, and some state that they will not live long enough for the health effects of smoking to matter.[507,522] In addition, some HIV-positive smokers report that smoking is an effective way to cope with the stress of their illness.[522]

■ Future Research

The following topics regarding HIV-positive smokers require additional research:

- Effectiveness of medications and counseling/behavioral interventions, including tailored interventions

- Effectiveness of motivational interviewing and educational approaches in increasing motivation to quit

- Effectiveness of community and social support networks in bolstering quitting motivation and improving treatment outcomes

Hospitalized Smokers

It is vital that hospitalized patients attempt to quit using tobacco because tobacco use may interfere with their recovery and overall health. Among cardiac patients, second heart attacks are more common in those who continue to smoke.[9,523] Lung, head, and neck cancer patients who are successfully treated for their cancer but who continue to smoke are at elevated risk for a second cancer.[524-531] Additionally, smoking negatively affects COPD as well as bone and wound healing.[531-538]

Hospitalized patients may be particularly motivated to make a quit attempt for two reasons. First, the illness resulting in hospitalization may have been caused or exacerbated by tobacco use, highlighting the patient's perceived vulnerability to the health risks of smoking[539] and making the hospitalization a "teachable moment." Second, every hospital in the United States must now be smoke-free if it is to be accredited by The Joint Commission. As a result, every hospitalized smoker is temporarily housed in a smoke-free environment. In addition, more hospitals are adopting policies establishing tobacco-free campuses, thus extending smoke-free space from indoor facilities to surrounding outdoor environments.[540-542] For these reasons, clinicians should use hospitalization as an opportunity to promote smoking cessation.[11,543,544] This also is an opportunity for clinicians to prescribe medications to alleviate withdrawal symptoms. If patients have positive experiences with the alleviation of their withdrawal symptoms, they may be more likely to use intensive treatments in a future quit attempt or maintain their hospital-enforced abstinence. Patients in long-term care facilities also should receive tobacco dependence interventions identified as effective in this Guideline. Suggested interventions for hospitalized patients can be found in Table 7.3.

Table 7.3. Suggested interventions for hospitalized patients

For every hospitalized patient, the following steps should be taken:
• Ask each patient on admission if he or she uses tobacco and document tobacco use status.
• For current tobacco users, list tobacco use status on the admission problem list and as a discharge diagnosis.
• Use counseling and medications to help all tobacco users maintain abstinence and to treat withdrawal symptoms.
• Provide advice and assistance on how to quit during hospitalization and remain abstinent after discharge.
• Arrange for followup regarding smoking status. Supportive contact should be provided for at least a month after discharge.

The importance of posthospitalization followup has been demonstrated by research.[355,545-546] However, there are systems-level issues that may complicate the ability of hospital-based clinicians to follow up with smoking patients. The development of fax-to-quit links with quitline services may be an effective and efficient way for hospitals to refer patients for smoking cessation followup.[195,199,547]

■ Future Research

The following topics regarding hospitalized patients require additional research:

- Effectiveness of interventions provided by different hospital personnel, including nurses and respiratory therapists

- Effectiveness of counseling and medications with hospitalized patients

- Relapse prevention once the patient leaves the hospital, including use of fax-to-quit programs

Lesbian/Gay/Bisexual/Transgender (LGBT) Smokers

LGBT individuals, both adolescents and adults, are more likely to smoke than the general population,[548-550] and tobacco marketing is targeted at these communities.[551-554] LGBT individuals are more likely to have other risk factors for smoking, including daily stress related to prejudice and stigma.[555-558]

■ Future Research

The following topics regarding LGBT smokers require additional research:

- Accessibility and acceptability of tobacco dependence interventions

- Rates of intervention use and effectiveness of both medications and counseling treatments, including quitlines

- Effectiveness of tailored interventions

Low SES/Limited Formal Education

Individuals with low SES and/or limited formal education, including the homeless, bear a disproportionate burden from tobacco.[559] Addressing this particular disparity is an important part of improving the overall health of the American public.[560] These patients are more likely to: smoke,[561,562] have limited access to effective treatment,[563,564] be misinformed about smoking cessation medications,[565] be exposed to more permissive environmental and workplace smoking policies,[562] and be targeted by tobacco companies.[566] They are less likely to receive cessation assistance.[564] Moreover, smokers with low SES/limited formal education are more likely to be uninsured or on Medicaid than are other smokers.[567] Only 25 percent of smokers on Medicaid reported receiving any practical assistance with quitting. However, low SES smokers or those with limited formal education express significant interest in quitting[404,507,508,568] and appear to benefit from treatment.[569,570] Due to the prevalence of smoking in this population, it is vital that clinicians intervene with such individuals. It is important that interventions, particularly written materials, be delivered in a manner that is understandable to the patient.

■ Future Research

The following topics regarding low SES/limited formal education smokers require additional research:

- Effectiveness of and compliance with medications shown to be effective with general populations of smokers

- Effectiveness and utilization of novel treatment delivery settings (e.g., pharmacy-based, community-based, worksite)

- Effectiveness of quitlines, including ability of this population to access services using this modality

- Strategies for addressing misconceptions about effective cessation treatment that may be more common in these populations

- Cost-effectiveness of cessation interventions delivered as part of chronic disease management programs

Medical Comorbid Conditions, Including Cancer, Cardiac Disease, COPD, Diabetes, and Asthma

Smokers with comorbid medical conditions such as cancer, cardiac disease, COPD, diabetes, and asthma are important to target for tobacco use treatments, given the role that smoking plays in exacerbating these conditions.[447,538,571-581] Clinicians treating smokers with these conditions have an ideal "teachable moment" in that they are treating a disease that may have been caused or exacerbated by smoking and that can be ameliorated by quitting[198,582-588] but not by cutting down. Using chronic disease management programs to integrate tobacco dependence interventions into treatment may be an effective and efficient way to deliver tobacco use interventions to these populations.

■ Future Research

The following topics regarding smokers with comorbid medical conditions require additional research:

- Effectiveness of counseling and cessation medications among individuals with diabetes and asthma

- Impact and effectiveness of specialized assessment and tailored interventions in these populations

Older Smokers

It is estimated that more than 18 million Americans age 45 and older smoke cigarettes, accounting for 41 percent of all adult smokers in the United States;[589] 4.5 million adults over age 65 smoke cigarettes.[590] Even smokers over the age of 65 can benefit greatly from abstinence.[9,405,523,591] Older smokers who quit can reduce their risk of death from coronary heart disease, COPD, and lung cancer and decrease their risk of osteoporosis.[544,592,593] Moreover, abstinence can promote more rapid recovery from illnesses that are exacerbated by smoking and can improve cerebral circulation.[453,594,595] In fact, age does not appear to diminish the desire to quit[596] or the benefits of quitting smoking,[166,597] and treatments shown to be effective in this Guideline have been shown to be effective in older smokers (see Table 7.1). However, smokers over the age of 65 may be less likely to receive smoking cessation medications identified as effective in this Guideline.[598] Issues particular to this population (e.g., mobility, medications) make the use of proactive telephone counseling appear particularly promising. Importantly, Medicare has expanded benefits for tobacco cessation counseling and prescription medications (through Medicare Part D) for tobacco dependence treatment.[219]

■ Future Research

The following topics regarding older smokers require additional research:

- Effectiveness of tailored as well as general counseling interventions for older smokers in promoting tobacco abstinence

- Effectiveness and side effects of medications

- Effective methods to motivate older smokers to make a quit attempt

Psychiatric Disorders, Including Substance Use Disorders

Psychiatric disorders are more common among smokers than in the general population. For instance, as many as 30 to 60 percent of patients seeking tobacco dependence treatment may have a past history of depression,[599,600] and 20 percent or more may have a past history of alcohol abuse or dependence.[601-603] Smoking occurs at rates well above the population average among abusers of alcohol and drugs (i.e., greater than 70 percent),[604-607] and one study found that these individuals have increased mortality from tobacco-related diseases.[608] These individuals may present themselves less frequently for tobacco dependence treatment. However, such treatments could be conveniently delivered within the context of chemical dependence or mental health clinics.[609]

As noted in the Specialized Assessment section in Chapter 6A, smokers currently experiencing a psychiatric disorder are at heightened risk for relapse to smoking after a cessation attempt.[246,466,610-613]

All smokers with psychiatric disorders, including substance use disorders, should be offered tobacco dependence treatment, and clinicians must overcome their reluctance to treat this population.[614] However, the clinician may wish to offer the tobacco dependence treatment when psychiatric symptoms are not severe. Although patients in inpatient psychiatric units are able to stop smoking with few adverse effects (e.g., little increase in aggression),[615-617] stopping smoking or nicotine withdrawal may exacerbate a patient's comorbid condition. For instance, stopping smoking may elicit or exacerbate depression among patients with a prior history of affective disorder.[325,618,619] One study suggests that alcohol treatment should precede tobacco dependence treatment to maximize the effect of the alcohol treatment.[483] Considerable research, however, also indicates that tobacco dependence treatment does not interfere with patients' recovery from the abuse of other substances.[474,475,477,480-482,620] Treating tobacco dependence in individuals with psychiatric disorders is made more complex by the potential for multiple psychiatric diagnoses and multiple psychiatric medications. Stopping tobacco use may affect the pharmacokinetics of certain psychiatric medications.[308,621] Therefore, clinicians should closely monitor the level or effects of psychiatric medications in smokers making a quit attempt.[75]

■ Future Research

The following topics regarding psychiatric disorders, including substance use disorders, require additional research:

- Relative effectiveness and reach of different tobacco dependence medications and counseling strategies in patients with psychiatric comorbidity, including depression

- Effectiveness and impact of tobacco dependence treatments within the context of nontobacco chemical dependency treatments

- Importance and effectiveness of specialized assessment and tailored interventions in these populations

- Impact of stopping tobacco use on psychiatric disorders and their management

Racial and Ethnic Minority Populations

Some racial and ethnic minority populations in the United States—African Americans, American Indians and Alaska Natives, Asians and Pacific Islanders, Hispanics—experience higher mortality in a number of disease categories compared with others. For example, African Americans experience substantial excess mortality from cancer, cardiovascular disease, and infant death, all of which are directly affected by tobacco use.[622-626] Moreover, they experience greater exposure to tobacco advertising.[627-629] American Indian and Alaska Natives have some of the highest documented rates of infant mortality caused by SIDS,[630,631] which also is affected by tobacco use and exposure to secondhand smoke. Therefore, the need to deliver effective tobacco dependence interventions to ethnic and racial minority smokers is critical. Unfortunately, evidence indicates that large proportions of some racial/ethnic groups lack adequate access to primary care providers and are more likely to have low SES.[632,633] These populations may be less aware of Medicaid or other available benefits[564,633-635] and more likely to harbor misconceptions about tobacco dependence treatments.[636-639] Finally, these populations may be less likely to receive advice to stop smoking[640,641] or use tobacco dependence treatment[635,637,642] than are other individuals. This suggests that special efforts and resources should be provided to meet the treatment needs of these underserved populations.[4,643]

The differences between racial and ethnic minorities and whites in smoking prevalence, smoking patterns, pharmacokinetics of nicotine, and quitting behavior in the United States are well documented.[587,642,644-656] In addition, smoking prevalence and patterns vary substantially across and within minority subgroups (e.g., gender, level of acculturation, tribal communities).[636,657-663] Racial and ethnic minority groups also differ from whites in awareness of the health effects of smoking[636,664-667] and awareness of the benefits of proven treatments, and some racial and ethnic minority populations report a greater sense of fatalism that may affect disease prevention efforts.[637,660] On the other hand, both tobacco dependence and desire to quit appear to be prevalent across varied racial and ethnic groups.[642,667-671] In fact, smokers in several racial and ethnic groups attempt to quit as often as or more often than nonminority smokers, but use effective treatments less often and have lower success rates.[642,672]

▌Future Research

The following topics regarding racial and ethnic minorities require additional research:

- Effectiveness of specific tobacco dependence interventions, including medications and quitlines, in these populations (e.g., American Indian and Alaska Native smokers)

- Effectiveness of culturally adapted versus generic interventions for different racial and ethnic minority populations

- Identification and development of interventions to address the specific barriers or impediments to treatment delivery, use, or success (e.g., SES, inadequate access to medical care, treatment misconceptions, not viewing tobacco use as problematic)

- Identification of motivators of cessation that are especially effective with members of racial and ethnic minority populations (e.g., fear of illness requiring long-term care and disability)

Women

Data suggest that women are more likely to seek assistance in their quit attempts than are men.[673] Research suggests that women benefit from the same interventions as do men, although the data are mixed on whether they benefit as much as men.[156,157] Women may face different stressors and barriers to quitting that may be addressed in treatment. These include greater likelihood of depression, greater weight control concerns, hormonal cycles, greater nonpharmacologic motives for smoking (e.g., for social-ization), educational differences, and others.[248] This suggests that women may benefit from tobacco dependence treatments that address these issues, although few studies have examined programs targeted at one gender.

■ Future Research

The following topics regarding gender differences require additional re-search:

- Gender differences in the effectiveness of tobacco dependence treat-ments found to be effective in this Guideline, including counseling and the effectiveness of varenicline and combination medications

- Impact of gender-specific motives that may increase quit attempts and success (e.g., quitting to improve fertility and reproductive health, pregnancy outcomes, physical appearance, and osteoporosis)

Other Specific Populations and Topics

Children and Adolescents

Recommendation: Clinicians should ask pediatric and adolescent patients about tobacco use and provide a strong message regarding the importance of totally abstaining from tobacco use. (Strength of Evidence = C)

Recommendation: Counseling has been shown to be effective in treat-ment of adolescent smokers. Therefore, adolescent smokers should be provided with counseling interventions to aid them in quitting smok-ing. (Strength of Evidence = B)

Recommendation: Secondhand smoke is harmful to children. Cessation counseling delivered in pediatric settings has been shown to be effec-tive in increasing abstinence among parents who smoke. Therefore, to protect children from secondhand smoke, clinicians should ask par-ents about tobacco use and offer them cessation advice and assistance. (Strength of Evidence = B)

■ Background

Tobacco use is a pediatric concern. In the United States, about 4,000 children and adolescents under age 18 smoke their first cigarette each day, and an estimated 1,200 children and adolescents become daily cigarette smokers each day.[44,674] Among adults who ever smoked daily, 90 percent tried their first cigarette before age 21.[675] It is estimated that in 2006, 3.3 million U.S. adolescents aged 12 to 17 were current (past month) users of tobacco products and 2.6 million were current cigarette smokers.[43] Although use of cigarettes and cigars declined slightly from 2005 among this age group, the use of smokeless tobacco increased.[43] If current patterns persist, an estimated 6.4 million youth will die prematurely from a smoking-related disease.[675] Young people experiment with or begin regular use of tobacco for a variety of reasons, including social and parental norms, advertising, movies and popular media, peer influence, parental smoking, weight control, and curiosity.[676-685] Nicotine dependence, however, is established rapidly even among adolescents.[686-689] Because of the importance of primary prevention, clinicians should ensure that they deliver tobacco prevention and cessation messages to pediatric patients and their parents. Because tobacco use often begins during preadolescence,[690] clinicians should routinely assess and intervene with this population. Intervention research remains a priority for this population. Current reviews of smoking prevention and cessation interventions for adolescents have, so far, demonstrated limited evidence of effectiveness.[691,692] A 2007 national survey of youth tobacco cessation programs showed a lack of such programs in communities most in need—those in which youth smoking prevalence is increasing.[693] Prevention strategies useful in more general settings can be found in the Institute of Medicine report *Growing Up Tobacco Free*[694] and in the 2000 Surgeon General's Report *Reducing Tobacco Use*[6] and recently have been addressed by several authors.[695,696]

Young people vastly underestimate the addictive potential of nicotine. Adolescent smokers, both occasional and daily smokers, are more likely than nonsmokers to think they can quit at any time.[697] However, only about 4 percent of smokers aged 12 to 19 successfully quit smoking each year,[698,699] and the rate of failed adolescent quit attempts exceeds that of adult smokers.[32] Adolescents are very interested in quitting; 82 percent of 11- to 19-year-olds who smoke are thinking about quitting,[700] and 77 percent have made a serious quit attempt in the past year.[701,702] Adolescent quit attempts are rarely planned, and adolescents tend to choose unassisted rather than assisted quit methods,[32] even though young people who enroll in a tobacco cessation program are twice as likely to succeed in their quit attempt.[703,704]

Tobacco Use Treatments in Children and Adolescents

Counseling. Seven studies met selection criteria and were included in a new 2008 analysis comparing counseling to usual care among adolescent smokers. Results of this analysis are shown in Table 7.4. As can be seen from this analysis, the use of counseling approximately doubles long-term abstinence rates when compared to usual care or no treatment. In these studies usual care may have included brief advice, self-help pamphlets, reading materials, or a referral. Note that although counseling does significantly boost abstinence rates, absolute abstinence rates were quite low, attesting to the need for improved counseling interventions for adolescents. An inspection of the included studies revealed significant heterogeneity among analyzed articles. Thus, the Panel decided to make a "B" level recommendation rather than "A" level recommendation. A recent Cochrane meta-analysis produced mixed findings for counseling as a tobacco use treatment for youth.[705]

Table 7.4. Meta-analysis (2008): Effectiveness of and estimated abstinence rates for counseling interventions with adolescent smokers (n = 7 studies)[a]

Adolescent smokers	Number of arms	Estimated odds ratio (95% C.I.)	Estimated abstinence rate (95% C.I.)
Usual care	7	1.0	6.7
Counseling	7	1.8 (1.1–3.0)	11.6 (7.5–17.5)

[a] Go to *www.surgeongeneral.gov/tobacco/gdlnrefs.htm* for the articles used in this meta-analysis.

There were too few studies to perform meta-analyses on specific counseling techniques (e.g., motivational interviewing). The adolescent intervention studies that yielded significant effects used interventions that varied in intensity, format, and content. One study used an intervention that had one in-person counseling session and one telephone call; the other two interventions comprised six and eight sessions of counseling delivered in a group format. The counseling content of these interventions involved efforts to enhance motivation, establish rapport, set goals, promote problemsolving and skill training, and prevent relapse.[482,706,707] One recent meta-analysis found significant effects for studies that employed cognitive-behavioral strategies (self-monitoring and coping skills), social influence strategies (addressing social influences that serve to promote or maintain smoking), and motivational strategies (techniques to clarify desire for change and reduce ambivalence toward change).[704]

A series of studies comparing intensive group sessions based on social/ cognitive therapy to a 10- to 20-minute brief intervention produced promising results, at least when measured at the end of treatment, across diverse adolescent populations.[708-716] Interventions should be developmentally appropriate across the adolescent age span (e.g., appropriate for a 12-year-old vs. an 18-year-old). Additionally, counseling and other interventions have been recommended for young adults ages 18 to 24 years old.[717]

Recent studies indicate that adolescent smokers are identified and counseled to quit in about 33 to 55 percent of physician visits[120,718,719] and about 20 percent of dental visits.[120] Receipt of assistance in quitting was reported by 42 percent of adolescents and followup by only 16 percent of adolescents.[719] Yet, in a survey of 5,000 adolescents (all of the 11th graders in the Memphis City Schools), more than 79 percent reported they would acknowledge their smoking if asked.[718] Therefore, clinicians need to assess adolescent tobacco use, offer counseling, and follow up with these patients. Asking about tobacco use and advising adolescents to quit are the entry points for providing effective interventions. Clinicians may use motivational interventions such as those listed in Chapter 3B, which can be adapted for use with adolescents.[173,706,720,721] It is important for clinicians to intervene with adolescents in a manner that respects confidentiality and privacy (e.g., interviewing adolescents without parents present).

Counseling Provided to Parents During the Pediatric Visit. Recent research suggests that tobacco use interventions provided to parents in pediatric clinics or during child hospitalizations increase parents' interest in stopping smoking,[198,722] parents' quit attempts[198,199] and parents' quit rates,[172,723,724] although one study failed to find such an effect.[428]

Children and adolescents also benefit if parents are given information on secondhand smoke exposure. A review of the studies conducted by the expert Panel showed that giving parents information on the harms of secondhand smoke reduces childhood exposure to such smoke and may reduce parental smoking rates.[198,725]

Questions have been raised about whether and how clinicians caring for children and adolescents might offer treatment for tobacco dependence to their parents who smoke. Would such treatment interfere with the doctor-patient relationship that parents might have with their physicians? In response to this concern, the American Medical Association adopted a policy statement in 2005 supporting the practice of pediatricians addressing parental smoking.[726]

Tobacco Use Medications. Although nicotine replacement has been shown to be safe in adolescents, there is little evidence that these medications and bupropion SR are effective in promoting long-term smoking abstinence among adolescent smokers.[727-731] As a result, they are not recommended as a component of pediatric tobacco use interventions. One small pilot study (N = 22) found some positive initial effects for bupropion SR.[730] However, other studies have found no difference between placebo and patch at 10 or 12 weeks postquit[727] or between placebo versus gum or patch at 6 months postquit.[729,732] The majority of these studies also included an intensive counseling component (6 or more sessions).

Future Research

The following topics regarding adolescents and children require additional research:

- Effectiveness of using the 5 A's in pediatric clinics to treat both adolescents and parents

- Safety and effectiveness of medications in adolescents, including bupropion SR, NRT, varenicline, and a nicotine vaccine

- Effectiveness of counseling interventions designed specifically to motivate youth to stop using tobacco

- Effectiveness of child-focused versus family-focused or peer-focused interventions as well as interventions accessed via the Internet, quitlines, and school-based programs

- Strategies for increasing the efficacy, appeal, and reach of counseling treatments for adolescent smokers

Light Smokers

Recommendation: Light smokers should be identified, strongly urged to quit, and provided counseling cessation interventions. (Strength of Evidence = B)

The field of tobacco dependence research has not achieved consensus regarding the definition of a light smoker. For the purposes of this Guideline, the Panel considered a light smoker to be anyone who smokes fewer than 10 cigarettes per day, given that these individuals frequently are excluded from the RCTs that are the basis of some of the treatment recommendations. This definition includes individuals who may not smoke daily. Light smoking does not refer to smoking low-tar/low-nicotine cigarettes. Despite lower consumption levels, light smokers are at risk for developing smoking-related diseases.[733,734] A large, longitudinal study in Norway (N = 42,722) found an increase in risk of death from ischemic heart disease and other tobacco-related causes for both men and women who smoked one to four cigarettes per day.[735] Similar results were found in a Finnish cohort, in which men who reported being "occasional smokers" demonstrated increased cardiovascular morbidity and mortality.[736]

Light smoking is becoming more common, perhaps due to smoking restrictions and increases in the price of cigarettes.[734,737] A recent National Health Interview Survey (NHIS) survey found that among adult smokers in the United States, approximately 25.4 percent report smoking 10 or fewer cigarettes per day, and 11.6 percent smoke 5 or fewer cigarettes per day.[738] Many light smokers want to quit but have difficulty doing so.[734] This is consistent with evidence that many light smokers are dependent, even though they smoke relatively few cigarettes.[739] Light smokers also are less likely to receive treatment than are heavier smokers.[734,740]

Light smokers should be provided counseling treatments identified as effective in this Guideline. One study found that health education was more effective than motivational interviewing for African-American light smokers (≤ 10 cigarettes per day).[176]

Tobacco Use Medications. Two studies examined the effectiveness of medications with light smokers. One study found that use of the nicotine lozenge significantly increased 12-month abstinence rates among light smokers ($\leq$ 15 cigarettes per day) compared to placebo.[741] Another study found no difference in effectiveness of 2-mg gum versus placebo.[176]

Future Research

The following topic regarding light smokers requires additional research:

- Effectiveness of specific counseling and medication interventions with lighter smokers

Noncigarette Tobacco Users

Recommendation: Smokeless tobacco users should be identified, strongly urged to quit, and provided counseling cessation interventions. (Strength of Evidence = A)

Recommendation: Clinicians delivering dental health services should provide brief counseling interventions to all smokeless tobacco users. (Strength of Evidence = A)

Recommendation: Users of cigars, pipes, and other noncigarette forms of smoking tobacco should be identified, strongly urged to quit, and offered the same counseling interventions recommended for cigarette smokers. (Strength of Evidence = C)

Like cigarette smoking, the use of smokeless tobacco, such as chewing tobacco, snuff, or moist snuff, produces addiction to nicotine and has serious health consequences.[742-744] Smokeless tobacco use was reported among 4 percent of adult men, but less than 1 percent of women in 2005.[591,745] Health risks from these products include abrasion of teeth, gingival recession, periodontal bone loss, leukoplakia, and oral and pancreatic cancer.[745,746] Thus, the use of smokeless tobacco is not a safe alternative to smoking,[747] nor is there evidence to suggest that it is effective in helping smokers quit.

Evidence shows that counseling treatments are effective in treating smokeless tobacco users.[748-750] Therefore, clinicians should offer quitting advice and assistance to their patients who use tobacco, regardless of the formulation of the tobacco product. Some information may be particularly relevant in the treatment of smokeless tobacco use. For instance, a large majority of moist snuff users have identifiable oral lesions, and emphasizing this information during an oral exam may be useful in motivating a quit attempt. A close review of the literature showed that dental health clinicians (e.g., dental hygienists) delivering brief advice to quit using smokeless tobacco, in the context of oral hygiene feedback, can increase abstinence rates.[250,751]

Cigar smokers are at increased risk for coronary heart disease; COPD; periodontitis; and oral, esophageal, laryngeal, lung, and other cancers; with evidence of dose-response effects.[752-756] The prevalence of cigar smoking was 5 percent for men and less than 1 percent for women.[590] Although cigarette sales have declined over the last decade, cigar sales have increased in the United States, increasing 15.3 percent in 2005,[757] and sales of "little cigars" were at an all-time high in 2006.[758] Cigar smokers are known to discount the health effects of cigar smoking, believing it to be less detrimental than cigarettes.[752,759]

Clinicians should be aware of and address the use of other noncigarette tobacco products, including pipes, water pipes (also known as hookahs and narghile), cigarillos, loose tobacco, bidis, and betel quid. The use of cigars, pipes, and bidis is associated with cancers of the lung, stomach, oral cavity, larynx, and esophagus.[760] Further, the evidence is mixed as to whether or not individuals who use noncigarette tobacco products, either alone or in addition to cigarettes, find it more or less difficult, in comparison to cigarette smokers, to become abstinent from tobacco.[761,762]

Tobacco Use Medications. Current evidence is insufficient to suggest that the use of tobacco cessation medications increases long-term abstinence among users of smokeless tobacco. Studies conducted to date with various medications have not shown that they increase abstinence rates in this population.[750,751,763,764]

∎ Future Research

The following topics regarding noncigarette tobacco products require additional research:

- Effectiveness of advice and counseling treatments in promoting abstinence among users of noncigarette tobacco products, especially among users of pipes, cigars, and hookahs

- Effectiveness of medications to promote abstinence among users of noncigarette tobacco products, including users of smokeless tobacco, pipes, cigars, and hookahs

- Effectiveness of combined medications and counseling and behavioral therapies with users of noncigarette tobacco products

- Effectiveness of medication and counseling interventions with individuals who both smoke cigarettes and use noncigarette tobacco products ("dual users")

Pregnant Smokers

Recommendation: Because of the serious risks of smoking to the pregnant smoker and the fetus, whenever possible pregnant smokers should be offered person-to-person psychosocial interventions that exceed minimal advice to quit. (Strength of Evidence = A)

Recommendation: Although abstinence early in pregnancy will produce the greatest benefits to the fetus and expectant mother, quitting at any point in pregnancy can yield benefits. Therefore, clinicians should offer effective tobacco dependence interventions to pregnant smokers at the first prenatal visit as well as throughout the course of pregnancy. (Strength of Evidence = B)

Psychosocial Interventions. The selection criteria for the pregnancy meta-analysis were adjusted to be appropriate for this unique population. Abstinence data were included only if they were biochemically confirmed, due to reports of deception regarding smoking status among pregnant women.[765-769] Two different followup time periods were analyzed: prebirth abstinence (> 24 weeks gestation) and greater than 5 months postpartum abstinence. For the meta-analysis, either minimal interventions (< 3 minutes) or interventions labeled as "usual care" constituted the reference condition. Eight studies met the criteria and were included in the analysis comparing person-to-person psychosocial smoking cessation interventions with usual care in pregnant women. A "usual care" intervention with pregnant smokers typically consists of a recommendation to stop smoking, often supplemented by provision of self-help material or referral to a stop-smoking program or brief counseling. Person-to-person psychosocial interventions typically involved these treatment components as well as more intensive counseling than minimal advice. One study included 12 telephone counseling sessions after an initial in-person counseling session, and the remainder of the studies had at least two in-person counseling sessions. One study used a group intervention, and all of the other studies provided individual counseling. Six of the studies provided counseling only during pregnancy, one provided counseling in the hospital, and one provided counseling postdelivery. As Table 7.5 shows, psychosocial interventions are significantly more effective than usual care in getting pregnant women to quit while they are pregnant. These findings are consistent with other independent reviews.[770] A meta-analysis also was conducted to examine the effects of psychosocial interventions on postpartum abstinence. The odds ratio for psychosocial intervention was consistent with a positive effect of counseling on postpartum abstinence; however, the results were not statistically significant (OR = 1.6, 95 percent C.I. = 0.7–3.5). Studies using telephone counseling as the only format that compared biochemically verified outcomes to a minimal intervention suggest a possible differential effect on light versus heavy smokers and underscore the need for further research about this format.[771,772]

Table 7.5. Meta-analysis (2008): Effectiveness of and estimated preparturition abstinence rates for psychosocial interventions with pregnant smokers (n = 8 studies)[a]

Pregnant smokers	Number of arms	Estimated odds ratio (95% C.I.)	Estimated abstinence rate (95% C.I.)
Usual care	8	1.0	7.6
Psychosocial intervention (abstinence preparturition)	9	1.8 (1.4–2.3)	13.3 (9.0–19.4)

[a] Go to *www.surgeongeneral.gov/tobacco/gdlnrefs.htm* for the articles used in this meta-analysis.

Components of some person-to-person psychosocial interventions are listed in Table 7.6. These interventions were selected from articles included in the Table 7.5 meta-analysis and should guide clinicians when treating pregnant smokers.

Table 7.6. Examples of effective psychosocial interventions with pregnant patients

Physician advice regarding smoking-related risks (2–3 minutes); videotape with information on risks, barriers, and tips for quitting; midwife counseling in one 10-minute session; self-help manual; and followup letters.[773]
Pregnancy-specific self-help materials (*Pregnant Woman's Self-Help Guide To Quit Smoking*) and one 10-minute counseling session with a health educator.[774]
Counselor provided one 90-minute counseling session plus bimonthly telephone followup calls during pregnancy and monthly telephone calls after delivery.[775]

Smoking in pregnancy imparts risks to both the woman and the fetus. Cigarette smoking by pregnant women has been shown to cause adverse fetal outcomes, including stillbirths, spontaneous abortions, decreased fetal growth, premature births, low birth-weight, placental abruption, and sudden infant death syndrome (SIDS); and has been linked to cognitive, emotional, and behavioral problems in children.[776,777] Many women are motivated to quit during pregnancy, and health care professionals can take advantage of this motivation by reinforcing the knowledge that cessation will reduce health risks to the fetus and that there are postpartum benefits for both the mother and child.[778-780]

The first step in intervention is assessment of tobacco use status. This is especially important in a population in which a stronger stigma against smoking increases the potential for deception.[781,782] Research has shown that the use of multiple choice questions (see Table 7.7), as opposed to a simple yes/no question, can increase disclosure among pregnant women by as much as 40 percent.[783,784]

Table 7.7. Clinical practice suggestions for assisting a pregnant patient in stopping smoking

Clinical practice	Rationale
Assess pregnant woman's tobacco use status using a multiple-choice question to improve disclosure.	Many pregnant women deny smoking, and the multiple-choice question format improves disclosure. For example: Which of the following statements best describes your cigarette smoking? • I smoke regularly now; about the same as before finding out I was pregnant. • I smoke regularly now, but I've cut down since I found out I was pregnant. • I smoke every once in a while.

Table 7.7. Clinical practice suggestions for assisting a pregnant patient in stopping smoking (continued)

Clinical practice	Rationale
Assess pregnant woman's tobacco use status using a multiple-choice question to improve disclosure.	• I have quit smoking since finding out I was pregnant. • I wasn't smoking around the time I found out I was pregnant, and I don't currently smoke cigarettes.
Congratulate those smokers who have quit on their own.	To encourage continued abstinence.
Motivate quit attempts by providing educational messages about the impact of smoking on both maternal and fetal health.	These are associated with higher quit rates.
Give clear, strong advice to quit as soon as possible.	Quitting early in pregnancy provides the greatest benefit to the fetus.
Use problemsolving counseling methods and provide social support and pregnancy-specific self-help materials.	Reinforces pregnancy-specific benefits and increases cessation rates.
Arrange for followup assessments throughout pregnancy, including further encouragement of cessation.	The woman and her fetus will benefit even when quitting occurs late in pregnancy.
In the early postpartum period, assess for relapse and be prepared to continue or reapply tobacco cessation interventions, recognizing that patients may minimize or deny smoking.	Postpartum relapse rates are high, even if a woman maintains abstinence throughout pregnancy.

Quitting smoking prior to conception or early in the pregnancy is most beneficial, but health benefits result from abstinence at any time.[742,785-787] It is estimated that 20 percent or more of low birth-weight births could be prevented by eliminating smoking during pregnancy.[592,788] Therefore, a pregnant smoker should receive encouragement and assistance in quitting throughout her pregnancy. Women attending preconception or other medical visits also should be offered tobacco use interventions, as smoking may decrease fertility[789,790] and some adverse effects occur early in the pregnancy.[788] In addition, treating tobacco dependence prior to conception offers more options to the clinician, including medication options, as fetal health concerns are not present.

Even women who have maintained total abstinence from tobacco for 6 or more months during pregnancy have a high rate of relapse in the postpartum period.[787,791,792] Postpartum relapse may be decreased by continued emphasis on the relationship between maternal smoking and poor health outcomes in infants and children (e.g., SIDS, respiratory infections, asthma, and middle ear disease).[793-798] One pilot study found that a relapse prevention intervention was effective;[799] however, two reviews of relapse prevention trials (both pre- and postdelivery) found no significant reduction in relapse.[185,770] There is a great need for research on the prevention of postpartum relapse. Table 7.7 outlines clinical factors to address when counseling pregnant women about smoking.

Meta-analytic results support the effectiveness of self-help materials compared to either basic information sheets or no intervention in assisting women to quit during pregnancy (see Table 7.8). Pamphlets and quitting guides were used as the self-help intervention in both studies analyzed. Other studies document favorable outcomes when self-help materials, with or without brief discussion/counseling, are added to standard advice to quit smoking.[774,800]

Table 7.8. Meta-analysis (2008): Effectiveness of and estimated preparturition abstinence rates for self-help interventions with pregnant smokers (n = 2 studies)[a]

Pregnant smokers	Number of arms	Estimated odds ratio (95% C.I.)	Estimated abstinence rate (95% C.I.)
Usual care	2	1.0	8.6
Self-help materials (preparturition)	2	1.9 (1.2–2.9)	15.0 (10.1–21.6)

[a] Go to *www.surgeongeneral.gov/tobacco/gdlnrefs.htm* for the articles used in this meta-analysis.

Tobacco use medication and pregnant smokers—Effectiveness. The data on the effectiveness of nicotine replacement therapy with pregnant smokers include three randomized, controlled nicotine patch studies. One study randomly assigned 250 pregnant women who still were smoking after the first trimester to either a 15-mg, 16-hour active patch for 8 weeks and a 10-mg, 16-hour patch for 3 additional weeks or to a placebo. No significant differences were seen in smoking abstinence rates, number of cigarettes smoked, birthweight, or number of preterm deliveries.[801] A similar study of the nicotine patch with 30 pregnant women who still were smoking 15 or more cigarettes a day after the first trimester found moderate but nonsignificant differences in abstinence rates (23% in the active patch and counseling condition vs. 0% in the placebo patch and counseling condition).[802] A recent study[803] randomized 181 pregnant women to cognitive behavioral therapy (CBT) and NRT or CBT alone. Women in the CBT plus NRT group were significantly more likely to be abstinent at 7 weeks post-randomization (29% vs. 10%) and at 38 weeks gestation (22% vs. 7%). This study was stopped prior to completion (see safety section below). Based on these data, the Panel did not make a recommendation regarding medication use during pregnancy.

Tobacco use medication and pregnant smokers—Safety. Cigarette smoking during pregnancy is the greatest modifiable risk factor for pregnancy-related morbidity and mortality in the United States.[804] Adverse effects of smoking during and after pregnancy include increased risks of spontaneous abortion,[805] premature labor and delivery,[806] placental abruption,[807] fetal growth retardation,[808-810] SIDS,[811,812] and many health risks for the woman and her child.[794,813]

Cigarette smoke contains thousands of chemicals, many of which may contribute to reproductive toxicity. Of particular concern are carbon monoxide, nicotine, and oxidizing chemicals.[814] High levels of carbon monoxide exert neuroteratogenic effects.[815,816] Oxidizing chemicals are likely to contribute to an increased risk of thrombotic complications and, by reducing nitric oxide availability, contribute to placental vasoconstriction and premature labor.[817,818]

Nicotine may contribute to adverse effects of cigarette smoking during pregnancy and result in injury to the fetus.[819-821] Nicotine has been postulated to cause uteroplacental insufficiency via vasoconstriction, to produce fetal neurotoxicity resulting in delayed or impaired brain development, to inhibit the maturation of pulmonary cells and to increase the risk of SIDS. These concerns are based primarily on animal studies. Relatively little human research with pure nicotine has been done in pregnant smokers.

Several studies of brief exposure to nicotine patches or nicotine gum have demonstrated small hemodynamic effects in the mother and fetus, generally less than those seen with cigarette smoking.[822] The three clinical trials of NRT in pregnant women have yielded information relative to safety. The Wisborg trial of 250 women randomized to nicotine patch (15 mg) or placebo for 11 weeks found no evidence of serious adverse effects of nicotine.[801] To the contrary, birth weight was significantly higher in the NRT group, possibly due to reduced cigarette smoking in the NRT group. The Kapur study included 30 women randomized to nicotine patches (15 mg) or placebo, and reported no serious adverse effects of NRT.[802] One placebo-treated woman experienced extreme nicotine withdrawal, associated with increased fetal movements, prompting discontinuation of the trial. The Pollack study included 181 women, 122 randomized to CBT plus NRT, and 59 to CBT alone.[803] The NRT group could select nicotine patches, gum, or lozenge, or no NRT. More than half the women selected nicotine patches, the dose of which was adjusted according to the number of cigarettes smoked per day on study entry. As described in the "effectiveness" section above, women treated with NRT had significantly higher quit rates during pregnancy than did women receiving CBT alone. However, the study was terminated early by the Data Safety Monitoring Board (DSMB) due to a higher incidence of adverse events. Serious adverse events occurred in 30 percent of the NRT group compared to 17 percent of the CBT-alone group. The most frequent cause of serious adverse events was preterm labor. There was evidence that this difference in preterm labor was due to a difference between groups in history of preterm labor that predated study entry. The DSMB indicated that the study had to be terminated due to *a priori* stopping rules; however, they did not believe that the serious adverse events were related to NRT use. The authors concluded that this study cannot support or negate published literature about the harm of NRT during pregnancy.

Morales-Suarez-Varela et al. reported data from a retrospective cohort study suggesting that the use of NRT in women who quit smoking but who used nicotine substitutes during the first 12 weeks of pregnancy was associated with a small but significant increase in congenital malformations compared to mothers who smoked during the first trimester.[823] This study suffers from multiple, substantial methodological problems, however, making its findings difficult to interpret. Also, the number of malformation cases in the NRT group was quite small, and the relative prevalence rate ratios for malformations in cases compared to controls were of borderline significance. Further, concerns exist about possible undetected spontaneous abortion among continuing smokers. In addition, most women who use NRT do so in the second or third trimester, and no adverse event data were reported in these women.

Safety is not categorical. A designation of "safe" reflects a conclusion that a drug's benefits outweigh its risks. Nicotine most likely does have adverse effects on the fetus during pregnancy. Although the use of NRT exposes pregnant women to nicotine, smoking exposes them to nicotine plus numerous other chemicals that are injurious to the woman and fetus. These concerns must be considered in the context of inconclusive evidence that cessation medications boost abstinence rates in pregnant smokers.

Future Research

The following topics regarding smoking and pregnancy require additional research:

- Relapse prevention with pregnant women and women who have recently given birth

- Effectiveness of psychosocial treatment provided via nonface-to-face modalities, such as quitlines or Web-based programs

- The safety and effectiveness of tobacco dependence medications (bupropion SR, NRTs, and varenicline) during pregnancy for the woman and the fetus, including: the relative risks and benefits of medication use as a function of dependence, and the appropriate formulation and timing of medication use

- Safety and effectiveness of tobacco dependence medications, especially varenicline and bupropion SR as well as various forms of NRT, to the woman and child during nursing

- Effectiveness of economic incentives to promote quitting and sustained abstinence

- Effects of smoking during fertility treatment and the effects and effectiveness of cessation interventions on the infertile population, both men and women

- Effects of reporting smoking status and the provision of cessation interventions as part of the national database for assisted reproductive technology treatments (the Center for Disease Control and Prevention's Assisted Reproductive Technology [ART] database, *www.cdc.gov/art*)

- Effectiveness of relapse prevention programs for spontaneous "self-quitters amongst pregnant women"

- Effectiveness of different types of counseling, behavioral therapies, and motivational interventions (e.g., physiological feedback of adverse impacts, quitting benefits) for pregnant women in general and in high-prevalence populations (e.g., American Indian and Alaska Native women, especially)

- Strategies for linking preconception, pregnancy, and postpartum (including pediatric) interventions

Weight Gain After Stopping Smoking

Recommendation: For smokers who are greatly concerned about weight gain, it may be most appropriate to prescribe or recommend bupropion SR or NRT (in particular, nicotine gum and nicotine lozenge), which have been shown to delay weight gain after quitting. (Strength of Evidence = B)

The majority of smokers who quit smoking gain weight. Most will gain fewer than 10 pounds, but there is a broad range of weight gain, with as many as 10 percent of quitters gaining as much as 30 pounds.[824-827] However, weight gain that follows stopping smoking is a modest health threat compared with the risks of continued smoking.[824]

Women tend to gain slightly more weight than men do.[828] For both sexes, African Americans, people under age 55, and heavy smokers (those smoking more than 25 cigarettes per day) are at elevated risk for major weight gain.[826,829-831]

For some smokers, especially women, concerns about weight or fears about weight gain are motivators to start smoking or continue smoking.[832-836]

Adolescents, even as young as middle-school age, who are concerned about their weight initiate smoking more often than do other adolescents.[683,837-838]

Concern about weight varies substantially by ethnicity. For example, adolescent African-American females are much less likely to report that they smoke to control weight than are white European Americans.[683,839] This is an important area for further study, as little tobacco research focuses on women in racial/ethnic minority groups.[683]

There is no convincing evidence that counseling interventions specifically designed to mitigate weight gain during attempts to stop smoking result in reduced weight gain.[165,499,840] It also is unclear that such interventions affect cessation success; specifically, these interventions do not appear to adversely affect cessation.[499,840-842]

Nicotine replacement—in particular, 4-mg nicotine gum and 4-mg nicotine lozenge—appears to be effective in delaying postcessation weight gain. Moreover, there appears to be a dose-response relation between gum use and weight suppression (i.e., the greater the gum use, the less weight gain occurs). Bupropion SR also appears to be effective in delaying postcessation weight gain.[484,843-845] Once either nicotine gum or bupropion SR therapy is stopped, however, the quitting smoker, on average, gains an amount of weight that is about the same as if she or he had not used these medications.[843,846-848]

Postcessation weight gain appears to be caused both by increased intake (e.g., eating, including high-caloric foods, and alcohol consumption) and by decreased metabolism. The involvement of metabolic mechanisms suggests that even if smokers do not increase their caloric intake upon quitting, they will, on average, gain some weight.[849-852] Once an individual relapses and begins smoking at precessation levels, he or she usually will lose some or all of the weight gained during the quit attempt.

The research evidence reviewed above shows why concerns about weight gain can be barriers to smoking abstinence. Many smokers (especially women) are concerned about their weight and fear that quitting will produce weight gain. Many also believe that they can do little to prevent postcessation weight gain except return to smoking. These beliefs are difficult to address clinically because smoking does appear to affect weight.

Recommendations to Clinicians When Addressing Weight Gain

How should the clinician deal with concerns about weight gain? First, the clinician should neither deny the likelihood of weight gain nor minimize its significance to the patient. Rather, the clinician should inform the patient about the likelihood of weight gain and prepare the patient for its occurrence. The clinician also should counter exaggerated fears about weight gain given the relatively moderate weight gain that typically occurs. Certain types of information may help prepare the patient for postcessation weight gain (see Table 7.9). Clinicians also should inform the patient that smoking presents a much greater health risk than the negligible health risk involved in the modest weight gain associated with smoking abstinence.

Second, during the quit attempt, the clinician should offer to help the patient address weight gain (either personally or via referral) once the patient has successfully quit smoking. The patient should be encouraged to maintain or adopt a healthy lifestyle, including engaging in moderate exercise, eating plenty of fruits and vegetables, and limiting alcohol consumption.[502,853]

Exercise

Available research does not show that interventions to increase exercise reliably boost smoking abstinence rates.[842,854] One recent study, however, showed that an exercise program occurring in three 45-minute sessions per week increases long-term smoking abstinence in women and delays weight gain when it is combined with a cognitive-behavioral smoking cessation program.[853] As was the case for weight loss interventions, there is no evidence that exercise interventions undermine success in stopping smoking. Some evidence suggests that weight gain is reduced if smoking abstinence is accompanied by a moderate increase in physical activity.[855] Vigorous exercise programs should not be implemented without consulting a physician. Although it may be difficult to get smokers to adhere to a vigorous exercise program, smokers should be encouraged to engage in moderate exercise and physical activity as part of a healthy lifestyle.[856]

Table 7.9. Clinician statements to help a patient prepare for and cope with post-cessation weight gain

Clinician statements
The great majority of smokers gain weight once they quit smoking. However, even without special attempts at dieting or exercise, weight gain is usually 10 lbs. or less.
Some medications, including bupropion SR and nicotine replacement medicines, may delay weight gain.
There is evidence that smokers often gain weight once they quit smoking, even if they do not eat more. However, there are medications that will help you quit smoking and limit or delay weight gain. I can recommend one for you.
The amount of weight you will likely gain from quitting will be a minor health risk compared with the risks of continued smoking.
I know that you don't want to gain a lot of weight. However, let's focus on strategies to get you healthy rather than on weight. Think about eating plenty of fruits and vegetables, getting regular exercise, getting enough sleep, and avoiding high-calorie foods and beverages. Right now, this is probably the best thing you can do for both your weight and your health.
Although you may gain some weight after quitting smoking, compare the importance of this with the added years of healthy living you will gain, your better appearance (less wrinkled skin, whiter teeth, fresher breath), and good feelings about quitting.

■ Future Research

The following topics regarding weight gain during tobacco dependence treatment require additional research:

- Effectiveness of weight control measures during quit attempts and their effect on tobacco abstinence and weight, including issues of timing of weight control interventions

- Effectiveness of medications to control weight gain during quit attempts

- Effectiveness of the use of exercise to control weight gain during a quit attempt, including the optimal "dose" of exercise to minimize weight gain and not jeopardize cessation outcome

- Impact of weight gain concerns on specific populations, including adolescents who smoke and ethnic/minority women

- Strategies to increase adherence to exercise protocols as part of cessation interventions that include efforts to decrease weight gain

Glossary

Abstinence percentage. The percentage of smokers who achieve long-term abstinence from smoking. The most frequently used abstinence measure for this Guideline was the percentage of smokers in a group or treatment condition who were abstinent at a followup point that occurred at least 5 months after treatment.

Acupuncture. A treatment involving the placement of needles in specific areas of the body with the intent to promote abstinence from tobacco use. Acupuncture also can be accomplished using electrostimulation or laser.

Addiction. Compulsive drug use, with loss of control, the development of dependence, continued use despite negative consequences, and specific withdrawal symptoms when the drug is removed.

All-comers. Individuals included in a tobacco treatment study regardless of whether they sought to participate. For example, if treatment was delivered to all smokers visiting a primary care clinic, the treatment population would be coded as "all-comers." Presumably, individuals who seek to participate in tobacco treatment studies ("want-to-quit" smokers) likely are more motivated to quit, and studies limited to these individuals may produce higher quit rates. All-comers can be contrasted with "want-to-quit" or self-selected populations.

Agonist. A drug action that generally mimics or enhances the effect of another drug at a neural receptor site. Nicotine is a cholinergic agonist.

Antagonist. A drug action that generally blocks or neutralizes the effect of another drug at a neural receptor site. Naltrexone and mecamylamine are examples of antagonists.

Anxiolytic. A medication used to reduce anxiety symptoms.

Assessment. All tobacco cessation interventions begin with identifying tobacco users and performing an assessment. The assessment is used to identify the most beneficial intervention for each smoker. Assessments may be specialized and may be ongoing throughout a smoking cessation program or occur at followups.

Aversive smoking. Several types of therapeutic techniques that involve smoking in an unpleasant or concentrated manner. These techniques pair smoking with negative associations or responses. Notable examples include rapid smoking, rapid puffing, focused smoking, and satiation smoking.

Behavioral therapy. A psychotherapeutic approach aimed at identifying and modifying the behaviors associated with human problems.

Benzodiazepine. Medication used as an anxiolytic. Benzodiazepines do not have an FDA indication for treating tobacco use and dependence.

Bidis. Small, thin, hand-rolled cigarettes, often consisting of flavored tobacco wrapped in tendu or temburni leaves. Bidis have a higher concentration of nicotine, tar, and carbon monoxide than conventional cigarettes sold in the United States. They are imported to the United States from India and other Southeast Asian countries.

Biochemical confirmation. The use of biological samples (expired air, blood, saliva, or urine) to measure tobacco-related compounds such as thiocyanate, cotinine, nicotine, and carboxyhemoglobin to verify users' reports of abstinence.

Bupropion SR (bupropion sustained-release). A non-nicotine aid for smoking cessation, originally developed and marketed as an antidepressant. It is chemically unrelated to tricyclics, tetracyclics, selective serotonin re-uptake inhibitors, or other known antidepressant medications. Its mechanism of action is presumed to be mediated through its capacity to block the re-uptake of dopamine and norepinephrine centrally.

Buspirone. A nonbenzodiazepine drug with anxiolytic properties. Buspirone does not have an FDA indication for treating tobacco use and dependence.

Coordinated intervention. Tobacco dependence treatment strategy that involves the clinician, health care administrator, insurer, and purchaser to ensure the provision of tobacco dependence treatment as an integral element of health care delivery.

Chronic disease model. Recognizes the long-term nature of tobacco dependence, with an expectation that patients may have periods of relapse and remission. The chronic disease model emphasizes the importance of continued patient education, counseling, and advice over time.

Cigarette fading/smoking reduction prequit. An intervention strategy designed to reduce the number of cigarettes smoked or nicotine intake prior to a patient's quit date. This may be accomplished through advice to cut down or to systematically restrict access to cigarettes. These interventions use computers and/or strategies to accomplish prequitting reductions in cigarette consumption or nicotine intake.

Clinician. A professional directly providing health care services.

Clinic screening system. The strategies used in clinics and medical practices for the delivery of clinical services. Clinic screening system interventions involve changes in protocols designed to enhance the identification of and intervention with patients who smoke. Examples include affixing tobacco use status stickers to patients' charts, expanding the capture of vital signs to include tobacco use, incorporating tobacco use status items into patient questionnaires, and including prompts for tobacco use monitoring in electronic medical records.

Clonidine. An alpha-2-adrenergic agonist typically used as an antihypertensive medication, but also documented in this Guideline as an effective medication for smoking cessation.

Cochrane Review. A service of the Cochrane Collaboration, an international nonprofit and independent organization (*www.cochrane.org/index.htm*) that regularly publishes evidence-based reviews about health care interventions.

Cognitive behavioral therapy (CBT). A psychotherapeutic approach aimed at identifying and modifying faulty or distorted negative thinking styles and the maladaptive behaviors associated with those thinking styles.

Combination medications. Treatment that combines two or more nicotine-containing medications or a nicotine-containing medication with another tobacco treatment medication such as bupropion SR.

Community-level interventions. Interventions for the primary prevention or treatment of tobacco use that usually are not implemented in primary care practice settings. These interventions most often are implemented through mass media campaigns.

Comorbidity. Coexistence of tobacco use with other medical diseases/illnesses, including mental illnesses.

Confidence intervals. Estimated range of values, which is likely to include an unknown population parameter. The estimated range is calculated from a given set of sample data.

Contingency contracting/instrumental contingencies. Interventions that incorporate the use of tangible rewards for cigarette abstinence and/or costs for smoking. For the purposes of analysis, simple agreements about a quit date, or other agreements between treatment providers and patients without specifiable consequences, as well as deposits refunded based on study attendance and/or other incentives that were not contingent on smoking abstinence or relapse were not considered examples of contingency contracting.

Continuous abstinence. A measure of tobacco abstinence based on whether subjects are continuously abstinent from smoking/tobacco use from their quit day to a designated outcome point (e.g., end of treatment, 6 months after the quit day).

Cost effectiveness. Quantified analysis of tobacco dependence program costs relative to tobacco use related costs.

Diazepam. A benzodiazepine medication intended to reduce anxiety.

Discrepancy. A strategy used in motivational interviewing to highlight how a patient's expressed priorities, values, and goals may conflict with the use of tobacco.

Efficacy and effectiveness. *Efficacy* is the outcome achieved from a treatment provided under near-ideal circumstances of control (typically, in a research study). Efficacy studies involve recruitment of motivated participants, random assignment, intensive assessment, and methods designed to keep participants in treatment. *Effectiveness* is the outcome achieved from a treatment provided in a "real-world setting" (in a clinic or community setting). Such studies typically involve participants who do not seek out the study or treatment, and the treatment is delivered in a manner consistent with its likely use in real-world settings. This 2008 clinical update uses the term "effectiveness" exclusively, recognizing that the majority of the studies summarized here reflect efficacy research that requires random assignment and a high degree of experimental control. This was done for purposes of clarity for its intended clinical audience.

Environmental tobacco smoke (ETS). Also known as "secondhand smoke" (SHS). The smoke inhaled by an individual not actively engaged in smoking, but who is exposed to smoke from the lit end of a cigarette and the smoke exhaled by the smoker.

Exercise/fitness component. Refers to an intervention that contains a component related to exercise/fitness. The intensity of interventions falling within this category varies from the mere provision of information/advice about exercise/fitness to exercise classes.

Extratreatment social support component. Interventions or elements of an intervention in which patients are provided with tools or assistance in obtaining social support outside the treatment environment. This category is distinct from intratreatment social support, in which social support is delivered directly by treatment staff.

Fax-to-quit. Patient referral in which the patient and health care provider fill out a form with pertinent patient information, which is faxed to a quit-line for followup.

Food and Drug Administration (FDA). Federal regulatory agency that has control over the safety and release of drugs marketed in the United States.

First-line medications. First-line medications have been found to be safe and effective for tobacco dependence treatment and have been approved by the FDA for this use. First-line medications have an established empirical record of efficacy and should be considered first as part of tobacco dependence treatment, except in cases of contraindications.

Fluoxetine. A selective serotonin re-uptake inhibitor used as a treatment for depression. Fluoxetine does not have an FDA indication for treating tobacco use and dependence.

Formats. Refers to tobacco dependence intervention delivery strategies that include self-help, proactive telephone counseling, computerized or e-health services, individual counseling, and group counseling.

Healthcare Effectiveness Data and Information Set (HEDIS). Serves as a "report card" for providing information on quality, utilization, enrollee access and satisfaction, and finances for managed care organizations and other health care delivery entities.

Higher intensity counseling. Refers to interventions that involve extended contact between clinicians and patients. It is coded based on the length of contact between clinicians and patients (greater than 10 minutes). If that information is unavailable, it is coded based on the content of the contact between clinicians and patients.

Hookah. A smoking pipe designed with a long tube passing through an urn of water that cools the smoke as it is drawn through. Also called "water-pipe," "hubble-bubble," "narghile," "shisha."

Hotline/helpline. A reactive telephone line dedicated to over-the-phone smoking intervention. Hotline/helpline treatment occurs when a hotline/helpline number is provided to a patient, or a referral to a hotline/helpline is made. The key distinction between a hotline/helpline and proactive telephone counseling is that, in the former, the patient must initiate each clinical contact.

Hypnosis. A treatment by which a clinician induces an altered attention state and heightened suggestibility in a tobacco user for the purpose of promoting abstinence from tobacco use. Also referred to as hypnotherapy.

Individualized interventions. Refers to tailoring an intervention to fit the needs of a particular smoker. For example, relapse prevention can be individualized based on information obtained about problems the patient has encountered in maintaining abstinence. See also Tailored Interventions.

Intent-to-treat. Treatment outcome analyses that determine abstinence percentages based on all subjects randomized to treatment conditions, rather than on just those subjects who completed the intervention or those who could be contacted at followup.

Intensive interventions. Comprehensive treatments that may occur over multiple visits for long periods of time and may be provided by more than one clinician.

Internet (Web-based) interventions. Interventions delivered through the use of a computer. The smoker may navigate within a specific Web site to access general treatment and treatment information, or the smoker may interact with a program that delivers a tailored intervention.

Intervention. An action or program that aims to bring about identifiable outcomes. In tobacco dependence treatment, the intervention generally is clinical in nature and may consist of counseling and the use of medications. Also referred to as "treatment."

Intratreatment social support. Refers to an intervention component that is intended to provide encouragement, a sense of concern, and empathic listening as part of the treatment.

Light smoker. The field of tobacco dependence research has not achieved consensus regarding the definition of a light smoker. For this publication, it refers to anyone who smokes between 1 and 10 cigarettes per day.

Literature review. A critical analysis of the research conducted on a particular topic or question in the field of science.

Logistic regression. Statistical technique to determine the statistical association or relation between/among two or more variables, in which the dependent variable is dichotomous (has only two levels of magnitude, e.g., abstinent vs. smoking).

Low-intensity counseling. Low-intensity counseling refers to interventions that involve contact between clinicians and patients that last between 3 and 10 minutes. If the information on length of contact is unavailable, it is coded based on the description of content of the clinical intervention.

Managed care organizations (MCOs). Any group implementing health care using managed care concepts, such as preauthorization of treatment, utilization review, system-wide quality improvement strategies, and a network of providers.

Mecamylamine. A nicotine antagonist used as an antihypertensive agent. Mecamylamine does not have an FDA indication for treating tobacco use and dependence.

Meta-analysis. A statistical technique that estimates the impact of a treatment or variable across a set of related studies, publications, or investigations.

Minimal counseling. Minimal counseling refers to interventions that involve very brief contact between clinicians and patients. It is coded based on the length of contact between clinicians and patients (3 minutes or less). If that information is unavailable, it is coded based on the content of the clinical intervention.

Motivation. Refers to a patient's intent or resolve to quit. Motivation can be bolstered through actions, such as setting a quit date, using a contract with a specified quit date, reinforcing correspondence (letters mailed from clinical/study staff congratulating the patient on his or her decision to quit or on early success), and providing information about the health risks of smoking.

Motivational intervention. An intervention designed to increase the smoker's motivation to quit.

Motivational interviewing (MI). A directive and patient-centered counseling method used to increase motivation and facilitate change.

Naltrexone. An opioid receptor antagonist used in substance abuse treatment. Naltrexone does not have an FDA indication for treating tobacco use and dependence.

National Committee for Quality Assurance (NCQA). Reviews and accredits managed care organizations, develops processes for measuring health plan performance, and disseminates information about quality so consumers can make informed choices (e.g., through "report cards," such as HEDIS).

Negative affect/depression intervention. A type of intervention designed to train patients to cope with negative affect after smoking cessation. The intensity of the interventions in this category may vary from prolonged counseling to the provision of information about coping with negative moods. To receive this code, interventions target depressed mood, not simply stress. Interventions aimed at teaching subjects to cope with stressors are coded as problemsolving. When it is unclear whether an intervention is directed at negative affect/depression or at psychosocial stress, problemsolving is used as the default code.

Neuroteratogenic. The capability of some substances to cause abnormal development of the nervous system in the fetus.

Neurotoxicity. The capablility of some substances to cause damage to the nervous system.

Nicotine gum. Nicotine-containing gum, a smoking cessation aid, that delivers nicotine through the oral mucosa. It is available without a prescription.

Nicotine inhaler. Nicotine-containing inhaler, a smoking cessation aid, that delivers nicotine in a vapor that is absorbed through the oral mucosa. It is available by prescription only.

Nicotine lozenge. Nicotine-containing hard lozenge, a smoking cessation aid, that delivers nicotine through the oral mucosa. It is available without a prescription.

Nicotine nasal spray. Nicotine-containing spray, a smoking cessation aid, that delivers nicotine in a mist that is absorbed in the nasal passages. It is available by prescription only.

Nicotine patch. A nicotine-containing patch, a smoking cessation aid, that delivers nicotine through the skin; available with or without a prescription.

Nicotine replacement therapy (NRT). Refers to medications containing nicotine that are intended to promote smoking cessation. There are five NRT delivery systems currently approved for use in the United States. These include nicotine gum, nicotine inhaler, nicotine lozenge, nicotine nasal spray, and nicotine patch.

Nortriptyline. A tricyclic antidepressant identified by the Guideline Panel as a second-line medication for smoking cessation. Nortriptyline does not have an FDA indication for treating tobacco use and dependence.

Odds ratio. The odds of an outcome on one variable, given the certain status of another variable(s). This ratio expresses the increase in risk of a given outcome if a specific variable is present.

Opioid antagonists. A class of medications that block action at opiate receptor sites. Naltrexone is one type of opioid antagonist. No opioid antagonist has an FDA indication for treating tobacco use and dependence.

Oral mucosa. The mucous membranes that line the mouth.

Over-the-counter (OTC). Drug or medication for which a prescription is not needed.

Pay for performance. An incentive program in which a health care purchaser provides additional payments or other rewards usually to a clinic or provider if a specified goal is met.

Person-to-person intervention. In-person or face-to-face contact between a clinician and a patient for the purpose of tobacco use intervention or assessment.

Physiological monitoring/biological marker feedback. A treatment by which a clinician provides to a tobacco user biological information, such as spirometry readings, carbon monoxide readings, or genetic susceptibility information, for the purpose of increasing abstinence from tobacco use.

Placebo. An inactive, harmless substance with no known direct beneficial effects. Usually used in clinical studies as a comparison to the effectiveness of an experimental drug or regimen.

Point prevalence. A measure of tobacco abstinence based on smoking/tobacco use occurrence within a set period (usually 7 days), prior to a followup assessment.

Potential reduced exposure products (PREP). Products designed to reduce levels of tobacco intoxicants including: (1) modified tobacco products, (2) tobacco products that are heated rather than burned, (3) oral, low-nitrosamine tobacco products, and (4) medicinal nicotine products (e.g., NRTs). With the exception of NRTs, little research has been conducted to evaluate PREPs.

Practical counseling (problemsolving/skills training). Refers to a tobacco use treatment in which tobacco users are trained to identify and cope with events or problems that increase the likelihood of their tobacco use. For example, quitters might be trained to anticipate stressful events and to use coping skills, such as distraction or deep breathing, to cope with an urge to smoke. Related interventions are coping skill training, relapse prevention, and stress management.

Primary care clinician. A clinician (e.g., in medicine; nursing; psychology; pharmacology; dentistry/oral health; physical, occupational, and respiratory therapy) who provides basic health care services for problems other than tobacco use *per se*. Primary care providers are encouraged to identify tobacco users and to intervene, regardless of whether tobacco use is the patient's presenting problem.

Proactive telephone counseling. A quitline that responds to incoming calls and makes outbound followup calls. Following an initial request by the smoker or via a fax-to-quit program, the clinician initiates telephone contact to counsel the patient (see Hotline/Helpline).

Propranolol. A beta-adrenergic blocker often used as an antihypertensive medication. Propranolol does not have an FDA indication for treating tobacco use and dependence.

Psychosocial interventions. Refers to intervention strategies that are designed to increase tobacco abstinence rates due to psychological or social support mechanisms. These interventions comprise counseling, self-help, and behavioral treatment, such as rapid smoking and contingency contracting.

Purchaser. A corporation, company, Government agency, or other consortium that purchases health care benefits for a group of individuals.

Quality-adjusted life years (QALY). Measure of both the quality and the quantity of life lived. Used as a means of quantifying the benefits of a medical intervention.

Quit day. The day of a given cessation attempt during which a patient tries to abstain totally from tobacco use. Also refers to a motivational intervention, whereby a patient commits to quit tobacco use on a specified day.

Quitline. A telephone counseling service that can provide both proactive telephone counseling and reactive telephone counseling (see Proactive Telephone Counseling and Reactive Telephone Counseling).

Randomized controlled trial. A study in which subjects are assigned to conditions on the basis of chance, and where at least one of the conditions is a control or comparison condition.

Random effects modeling. A model in which both study sampling errors (variance) and between-study variation are included in the assessment of the uncertainty (confidence interval) of the results of a meta-analysis. If there is significant heterogeneity among the results of included studies, random effects models will give wider confidence intervals than fixed effect models.

Rapid puffing/smoking. A smoking cessation technique that involves the pairing of concentrated smoking with negative associations or responses (e.g., nausea).

Reactive telephone counseling. Telephone counseling that provides an immediate response to a patient-initiated call for assistance. It is a quitline intended to respond only to incoming calls (see Hotline/Helpline).

Reference group. In meta-analyses, refers to the group against which other groups are compared (i.e., a comparison or control group).

Relapse. Return to regular smoking by someone who has quit. A distinction is sometimes made between "relapse" and a "lapse" (or a "slip"), which is a return to reduced smoking or brief smoking after quitting that falls short of a return to regular smoking (see also Slip).

Relapse prevention. Various intervention strategies intended to prevent a recent quitter from returning to regular smoking.

Relaxation/breathing. An intervention strategy in which patients are trained in relaxation techniques, such as meditation and breathing exercises. This intervention should be distinguished from "problemsolving," which includes a much wider range of stress-reduction/management strategies.

Restricted environmental stimulation therapy (REST). A treatment involving the use of sensory deprivation to promote abstinence from tobacco use.

Return on investment (ROI). Amount of money gained or lost, including money that would have been spent for health care, in relation to the amount of money needed to provide the treatment.

Screening. See Clinic Screening System.

Secondhand smoke. Also known as environmental tobacco smoke (ETS). The smoke inhaled by an individual not actively engaged in smoking, but who is exposed to smoke from the lit end of a cigarette and the smoke exhaled by the smoker.

Second-line medications. Second-line medications are medications for which there is evidence of efficacy for treating tobacco dependence. They have a more limited role than first-line medications because: (1) the FDA has not approved them for a tobacco dependence treatment indication, and (2) there are more concerns about potential side effects than exist with first-line medications. Second-line treatments should be considered for use on a case-by-case basis after first-line treatments have been used or considered.

Selective Serotonin Re-uptake Inhibitors (SSRIs). A class of antidepressant used in the treatment of clinical depression that has been studied for use in tobacco dependence treatment. No SSRI has an FDA indication for treating tobacco use and dependence.

Self-efficacy. One's beliefs about his/her capability to successfully act to achieve specific goals or influence events that affect one's life.

Self-help. An intervention strategy in which the patient uses a nonpharmacologic physical aid to achieve abstinence from tobacco. Self-help strategies typically involve little contact with a clinician, although some strategies (e.g., reactive hotline/helpline) involve patient-initiated contact. Types of self-help materials include: pamphlets/booklets/mailings/manuals; videos; audios; referrals to 12-step programs; mass media, community-level interventions; lists of community programs; reactive telephone hotlines/helplines; and computer programs/Internet.

Self-reported abstinence. Abstinence based on the patient's claim, which may or may not be verified clinically by biochemical confirmation.

Sertraline. A selective serotonin re-uptake inhibitor. Sertraline does not have an FDA indication for treating tobacco use and dependence.

Serum nicotine. Level of nicotine in the blood. This often is used to assess a patient's tobacco/nicotine self-administration prior to quitting, and to confirm abstinence self-reports during followup. Nicotine commonly is measured in urine and saliva.

Serum nicotine/cotinine levels. Level of nicotine/cotinine in the blood. Cotinine is nicotine's major metabolite, which has a significantly longer half-life than nicotine. This often is used to estimate a patient's tobacco/nicotine self-administration prior to quitting, and to confirm abstinence self-reports during followup. Cotinine commonly is measured in urine and saliva.

Side effects. Undesired actions or effects of a drug used in tobacco use treatment, such as insomnia or dry mouth.

Silver acetate. Silver acetate reacts with cigarette smoke to produce an unpleasant taste and has been investigated as a smoking deterrent. It is not approved by the FDA for this use.

Skills training. Refers to a tobacco use treatment in which tobacco users are trained to identify and cope with events or problems that may increase the risk of tobacco use. For example, quitters might be trained to anticipate stressful events and to use coping skills, such as distraction or deep breathing, to cope with an urge to smoke. Related interventions are practical counseling, relapse prevention, and stress management.

Slip. A brief or reduced return to smoking after quitting. Also referred to as a "lapse" (see Relapse).

Smokeless tobacco. Any form of unburned tobacco, including chewing tobacco, snus, and snuff. Use of smokeless tobacco is as addictive as smoking and can cause cancer of the gum, cheek, lip, mouth, tongue, throat, and pancreas.

Social support. Nonmedicinal support for the smoking cessation patient that provides personal encouragement and empathetic listening. Tobacco dependence treatments include two types of social supports: intratreatment social support and extratreatment social support.

Socioeconomic status (SES). Position of an individual or group in a population or society, usually based on income, education, or occupational categories.

Specialized assessments. Refers to assessment of patient characteristics, such as nicotine dependence and motivation for quitting, that may allow clinicians to tailor interventions to the needs of the individual patient.

Stepped-care. The practice of initiating treatment with a low-intensity intervention and then exposing treatment failures to successively more intense interventions.

Sudden Infant Death Syndrome (SIDS). Unexpected and sudden death of an apparently healthy infant during sleep with no autopsic evidence of disease. It is the leading cause of death in infants between 2 weeks and 1 year of age. The cause is unknown, but certain risk factors have been identified, such as prematurity; low birth-weight; birth in winter months; and mothers who are very young, smoke, are addicted to a drug, or have had a recent upper respiratory infection. Also called "cot death" and "crib death."

Tailored interventions. Tailored interventions are based on a dimension or a subset of dimensions of the individual (i.e., weight concerns, dependency, etc.). See also Individualized Interventions.

The Joint Commission (TJC) (formerly Joint Commission on Accreditation of Healthcare Organizations, JCAHO). An independent, not-for-profit organization that evaluates and accredits more than 19,500 health care organizations in the United States, including hospitals, health care networks, managed care organizations, and health care organizations that provide home care, long-term care, behavioral health care, and laboratory and ambulatory care services.

Tobacco dependence. Dependence on any form of tobacco, including, but not exclusive to, cigarettes, pipes, cigars, and chewing tobacco.

Tobacco treatment specialists. These specialists typically provide intensive tobacco interventions. Specialists are not defined by their professional affiliation or by the field in which they trained. Rather, specialists view tobacco dependence treatment as a primary professional role. Specialists possess the skills, knowledge, and training to provide effective interventions across a range of intensities, and often are affiliated with programs offering intensive treatment interventions or services.

Tobacco user. A person addicted to one or more forms of tobacco products.

Transdermal. Refers to delivery of a substance by absorption through the skin. Transdermal nicotine often is used as a synonym for "nicotine patch."

Treatment matching. Differential assignment of a patient to treatment based on the patient's pretreatment characteristics. Treatment matching is based on the notion that particular types of tobacco users are most likely to benefit from particular types of treatments.

Treatment. An action or program that aims to bring about identifiable outcomes. For tobacco dependence, the treatment generally is clinical in nature and may consist of counseling and the use of medications. Also may be referred to as "intervention."

Unaided quit attempts. Quit attempts made by patients, without the assistance of any clinical intervention or medications. Also known as "quitting cold turkey."

Varenicline. FDA-approved, non-nicotine recommended smoking cessation medication. Its mechanism of action is thought to be a function of its ability to serve both as a partial nicotine receptor agonist and a nicotine receptor antagonist. Available by prescription only.

Vital signs. Standard patient measurements to assess the critical body functions, including blood pressure, pulse, weight, temperature, and respiratory rate. The first step (i.e., the first "A") to providing smoking cessation interventions is identifying smokers. Vital signs should be expanded to include tobacco use status (current, former, never) or an alternative universal identification system in patient records.

Web-based interventions. See Internet Interventions.

Weight/diet/nutrition. An intervention strategy designed to address weight gain or concerns about weight gain. Interventions that teach weight/diet/nutrition management strategies, incorporate daily/weekly weight monitoring (for reasons other than routine data collection), require or suggest energy intake maintenance/reduction, and/or convey nutritional information/tips/counseling receive this code.

Withdrawal symptoms. A variety of unpleasant symptoms (e.g., difficulty concentrating, irritability, anxiety, anger, depressed mood, sleep disturbance, and craving) that occur after use of an addictive drug is reduced or stopped. Withdrawal symptoms are thought to increase the risk for relapse.

Contributors

Guideline Panel

Michael C. Fiore, MD, MPH
Panel Chair
Professor, Department of Medicine
Director, Center for Tobacco Research and Intervention
University of Wisconsin School of Medicine and Public Health
Madison, Wisconsin

Dr. Fiore completed medical school at Northwestern University and his internal medicine training at Boston City Hospital. His postgraduate education included a master's degree in public health in epidemiology from Harvard University. Dr. Fiore received additional training in epidemiology as an Epidemic Intelligence Service Officer for the Centers for Disease Control and Prevention, where he completed a preventive medicine residency program. Dr. Fiore worked as a medical epidemiologist at the U.S. Office on Smoking and Health, where he contributed to a wide range of national research, educational, and policy projects to control the epidemic of tobacco-related diseases. He is Director of the Center for Tobacco Research and Intervention and a Professor of Medicine at the University of Wisconsin School of Medicine and Public Health. He served as Chair of the Agency for Healthcare Policy and Research Panel that produced the *Smoking Cessation Clinical Practice Guideline No. 18* (1996) and Chair of the Public Health Service Panel that produced *Treating Tobacco Use and Dependence: A Clinical Practice Guideline* (2000). Dr. Fiore serves as Director (with Dr. Susan Curry) of a Robert Wood Johnson Foundation National Program, Addressing Tobacco in Health Care.

Carlos Roberto Jaén, MD, PhD, FAAFP
Panel Vice Chair
Professor and Chair, Department of Family and Community Medicine
Co-Director, Center for Research in Family Medicine and Primary Care
University of Texas Health Science Center at San Antonio
San Antonio, Texas

Dr. Jaén completed medical school at the State University of New York at Buffalo, and his family medicine residency and primary care research fellowship at Case Western Reserve University in Cleveland, Ohio. His graduate education included a PhD in epidemiology, with a concentration in tobacco control at Roswell Park Cancer Institute. He is Professor and Chair of the Department of Family and Communty Medicine at the University of Texas Health Science Center at San Antonio. He also is Co-Director of the American Academy of Family Physicians-funded Center for Research in Family Medicine and Primary Care. Dr. Jaén, active in primary care and public health research since 1985, has authored more than 70 publications on smoking cessation and related subjects, clinical preventive service delivery in primary care offices, and access to care by the urban poor and Hispanic populations. In 2005, he was appointed to the National Advisory Council to the Agency for Healthcare Research and Quality of the U.S. Public Health Service. He is a practicing family physician in the University of Texas Health Science Center at San Antonio and has been selected to the Best Doctors in America since 2002.

Timothy B. Baker, PhD
Senior Scientist
Professor, Department of Medicine
Associate Director, Center for Tobacco Research and Intervention
University of Wisconsin School of Medicine and Public Health
Madison, Wisconsin

Dr. Baker is a Professor of Medicine at the University of Wisconsin School of Medicine and Public Health. His principal research goals are to increase understanding of the motivational bases of addictive disorders and to develop and evaluate treatments for such disorders. He also is highly interested in developing and using technological advances to deliver effective treatments to ameliorate health problems such as addictive disorders and cancer. Dr. Baker is a long-serving member of the NIDA-E study section, has served as the Editor of the *Journal of Abnormal Psychology*, is the principal investigator of the University of Wisconsin Transdisciplinary Tobacco Use Research Center award (NIDA), and has contributed chapters to multiple Reports of the Surgeon General.

William C. Bailey, MD, FACP, FCCP
Director, Lung Health Center
University of Alabama at Birmingham
Birmingham, Alabama

Dr. Bailey graduated from Tulane University Medical School in 1965. He is a Diplomate of the American Board of Internal Medicine in both Internal Medicine and Pulmonary Disease, having received certified specialty training in these disciplines at Tulane University Medical Center and Charity Hospital of Louisiana. He has been on the faculty of the University of Alabama at Birmingham (UAB) since 1973. He has practiced medicine, taught, performed research, and been involved in administrative endeavors for his entire career. He has served on the Board of Directors of the American Thoracic Society and also has served on the Council of the National Heart, Lung, and Blood Institute. He has been a member of many editorial review boards of peer-reviewed journals and has served as a frequent scientific reviewer of both scientific articles and peer-reviewed research. He currently holds the Eminent Scholar Chair in Pulmonary Diseases and also is the Director of the UAB Lung Health Center, which is devoted to research in the prevention of lung disease.

Neal L. Benowitz, MD
Chief, Division of Clinical Pharmacology and Experimental Therapeutics
University of California-San Francisco
San Francisco, California

Dr. Benowitz is Professor of Medicine, Psychiatry, and Biopharmaceutical Sciences and Chief, Division of Clinical Pharmacology and Experimental Therapeutics, University of California, San Francisco (UCSF). He received his MD from the University of Rochester School of Medicine in 1969, and he served as a resident in internal medicine at the Bronx Municipal Hospital Center from 1969 to 1971. He then completed a postdoctoral fellowship in clinical pharmacology at UCSF and joined the faculty at UCSF in 1974. His research interests have focused primarily on the human pharmacology and toxicology of nicotine, caffeine, and other stimulant drugs. He has published more than 300 research papers. Dr. Benowitz was a scientific editor of the 1988 *United States Surgeon General's Report on Smoking and Health: Nicotine Addiction,* and served as a member of the NIH Pharmacology Study Section. Dr. Benowitz is a member of a number of medical societies, including the American Society for Clinical Investigation and the Association of American Physicians. He has served as President of the American Society for Clinical Pharmacology and Therapeutics and the Society for Research on Nicotine and Tobacco. He has received the Ove Ferno, Alton Ochsner, and Rawls Palmer Progress in Medicine awards and the Oscar B. Hunter Award in Therapeutics for his research on nicotine, tobacco, and health, and was the 2002 UCSF Annual Distinguished Clinical Research Lecturer. Dr. Benowitz is currently Director of the Flight Attendants Medical Research Institute Center of Excellence at UCSF, principal investigator of the Pharmacogenetics of Nicotine Addiction Research Consortium, and Program Leader of the Tobacco Control Program of the UCSF Comprehensive Cancer Center.

Susan J. Curry, PhD
Director, Institute for Health Research and Policy
University of Illinois-Chicago
Chicago, Illinois

Dr. Curry is the Director of the Institute for Health Research and Policy and Professor of Health Policy and Administration at the University of Illinois at Chicago (UIC). Prior to joining UIC in 2001, she was Professor of Health Services in the School of Public Health and Community Medicine at the University of Washington, and Director and Senior Investigator at the Center for Health Studies, Group Health Cooperative. Dr. Curry's research in tobacco includes studies of motivation to quit smoking; randomized trials of promising smoking cessation and prevention interventions; and evaluations of the use and cost-effectiveness of tobacco cessation treatments under different health insurance plans, and health care costs and utilization associated with tobacco cessation. Dr. Curry serves as Director (with Dr. Michael Fiore) of a Robert Wood Johnson Foundation National Program, Addressing Tobacco in Health Care, and heads the Helping Young Smokers Quit national initiative funded by the Robert Wood Johnson Foundation, Centers for Disease Control and Prevention, and the National Cancer Institute (NCI). She currently serves on the Board of Directors for the American Legacy Foundation and is a member of the Board of Scientific Advisors for NCI.

Sally Faith Dorfman, MD, MSHSA
Associate Director, Medical Affairs, Infertility
Ferring Pharmaceuticals, Inc.
Parsippany, New Jersey

Dr. Dorfman holds a degree in economics from Harvard College, a master's degree in health services administration, and an MD from Stanford University. She trained in reproductive health epidemiology as an Epidemic Intelligence Service Officer at the Centers for Disease Control and Prevention. She is board certified both in obstetrics and gynecology and in public health/general preventive medicine, and is an alumna of the Public Health Leadership Institute. Dr. Dorfman has consulted for state, regional, national, and international organizations, and was Commissioner of Health for Orange County, New York, from 1988 to 1994, effectively implementing New York State's then new Clean Indoor Air Act. She has published and presented extensively for professional and lay audiences, co-chaired the American Medical Women's Association (AMWA) Anti-Smoking Task Force, chaired the AMWA Reproductive Health Initiative, and is the recipient of numerous honors and awards. In addition to administrative, research, and editorial responsibilities, Dr. Dorfman remains clinically active as a gynecologist.

Erika S. Froehlicher, PhD, RN, MA, MPH
Professor, Department of Physiological Nursing
Department of Epidemiology & Biostatistics
Schools of Nursing and Medicine
University of California San-Francisco
San Francisco, California

Dr. Froehlicher holds degrees in nursing with a minor in business administration from the University of Washington, Seattle, and an MPH and a PhD from the University of California, Los Angeles. Her areas of research and teaching are in the primary, secondary, and tertiary prevention (rehabilitation) of cardiovascular disease. She served as Co-Chair for the Cardiac Rehabilitation Guideline 1995, and as a reviewer for the Unstable Angina and Congestive Heart Failure Federal Guideline. Her specific research focus is on behavioral interventions to promote physical activity and exercise, women's health issues, and international health. Her focus with respect to smoking is on randomized clinical trials to study the efficacy of nurse-managed smoking cessation in women with cardiovascular disease, the older American smoker, and the African-American population; as well as international initiatives in Korea, Jordan, and Japan.

Michael G. Goldstein, MD
Associate Director, Clinical Education and Research
Institute for Healthcare Communication
New Haven, Connecticut

Dr. Goldstein is board certified in internal medicine and psychiatry and currently serves as an Associate Director for Clinical Education and Research at the Institute for Healthcare Communication (IHC) in New Haven, Connecticut. The IHC is a nonprofit foundation dedicated to improving health care through enhanced clinician-patient communication. Also, he is an investigator at the Centers for Behavioral and Preventive Medicine at the Miriam Hospital in Providence, Rhode Island, and an Adjunct Professor of Psychiatry and Human Behavior at the Warren Alpert Medical School of Brown University. Dr. Goldstein's primary research interests have included developing and testing interventions to enhance the delivery of smoking cessation and other preventive care interventions in primary care settings. Dr. Goldstein has served as a member of the Task Force on Nicotine Dependence of the American Psychiatric Association (APA) and also served on the APA Nicotine Dependence Practice Guideline Panel. He has published extensively in the areas of behavioral medicine, smoking cessation, and health care communication.

Cheryl Healton, DrPH
President and Chief Executive Officer
American Legacy Foundation
Washington, DC

Following the creation of the American Legacy Foundation in 1999, Dr. Healton joined the staff as the first President and Chief Executive Officer of this groundbreaking public health nonprofit, created by the historic Master Settlement Agreement between 46 state attorneys general, five U.S. territories, and the tobacco industry. Dr. Healton was selected for this post following a nationwide search, and she has worked tirelessly to further the foundation's ambitious mission: "To build a world where young people reject tobacco and anyone can quit." During her tenure with the Foundation, she has guided the highly acclaimed, national youth tobacco prevention counter-marketing campaign, *truth,*® which has been credited in part with reducing youth smoking prevalence to its current 28-year low.

Although her current focus is aimed at reducing the deadly toll of tobacco on Americans, Dr. Healton's long and dynamic career in the field of public health has earned her national recognition and praise. She holds a doctorate from Columbia University's School of Public Health and a master's degree in public administration at New York University for health policy and planning. She joined the American Legacy Foundation from Columbia University's Joseph L. Mailman School of Public Health in New York, where she served as Head of the Division of Socio-Medical Sciences and Associate Dean for Program Development.

Patricia Nez Henderson, MD, MPH
Vice President
Black Hills Center for American Indian Health
Rapid City, South Dakota

Dr. Nez Henderson received her bachelor of science degree in biochemistry from the University of Arizona and earned her doctor of medicine and master of public health degrees from Yale University. Upon graduating from medical school, Dr. Nez Henderson joined the Black Hills Center for American Indian Health, an American Indian nonprofit health organization located in Rapid City, South Dakota, where she currently serves as Vice President. In addition, Dr. Nez Henderson is a faculty member at the University of Colorado at Denver Health Sciences Center within the American Indian and Alaska Native Programs. For the past 7 years, her research interest has focused on tobacco-related issues in American Indian communities. Her research findings have been published in peer-reviewed medical journals. Through culturally appropriate and relevant research, she plans to provide Native communities with information that can be used for health planning and policy decisionmaking.

Richard B. Heyman, MD
Former Chair, Committee on Substance Abuse
American Academy of Pediatrics
Cincinnati, Ohio

A graduate of the Columbia University College of Physicians and Surgeons, Dr. Heyman practices pediatric and adolescent medicine in Cincinnati, Ohio, and serves as an Adjunct Professor of Clinical Pediatrics at the University of Cincinnati College of Medicine. He is a consultant to several adolescent chemical dependency programs and lectures widely in the area of substance abuse. As former Chairman of the Committee on Substance Abuse of the American Academy of Pediatrics, he has played a major role in the creation of the Academy's educational programs and materials, as well as the development of policy in the area of alcohol, tobacco, and other drug abuse.

Howard K. Koh, MD, MPH, FACP
Harvey V. Fineberg Professor of the Practice of Public Health
Associate Dean for Public Health Practice
Director of the Division of Public Health Practice
Harvard School of Public Health
Boston, Massachusetts

Dr. Koh graduated from Yale College and Yale University School of Medicine. He completed his postgraduate training at Boston City Hospital and Massachusetts General Hospital, serving as Chief Resident in both institutions. Dr. Koh has earned board certification in four medical fields (internal medicine, hematology, medical oncology, and dermatology) as well as a master of public health degree from Boston University School of Public Health. While serving as Commissioner of Public Health for the Commonwealth of Massachusetts (1997–2003), he oversaw the nationally recognized Massachusetts Tobacco Control Program. During this time, Massachusetts ranked as one of the healthiest states in the country. Dr. Koh is principal investigator of the National Cancer Institute-funded initiative MassCONECT (Massachusetts Community Networks to Eliminate Cancer Disparities through Education, Research, and Training), a project to eliminate cancer disparities in underserved communities. He has published more than 200 scientific articles in the medical and public health literature. President Bill Clinton appointed Dr. Koh to the National Cancer Advisory Board (2000–2002). Dr. Koh also has been elected to the Institute of Medicine (IOM) of the National Academies and is a member of the IOM Roundtable on Racial and Ethnic Health Disparities.

Thomas E. Kottke, MD, MSPH
Senior Clinical Investigator
HealthPartners Research Foundation
Minneapolis, Minnesota
Professor of Medicine
University of Minnesota
Consulting Cardiologist
Regions Hospital
St. Paul, Minnesota

Dr. Kottke is a clinical cardiologist, epidemiologist, and health services researcher whose primary interest is describing, defining, and overcoming the barriers to the delivery of clinical services for the primordial, primary, and secondary prevention of chronic diseases. He has published widely on the evidence that clinical support systems are necessary for physicians and other health care professionals to provide these services to the patients they serve. Dr. Kottke was a member of the first U.S. Preventive Services Task Force.

Harry A. Lando, PhD
Professor, Division of Epidemiology and Community Health
University of Minnesota
Minneapolis, Minesota

Dr. Lando is internationally recognized for his work in smoking cessation. He has been active in this field since 1969 and has published extensively in this area, with a total of more than 170 scientific publications. He was a scientific editor of the *1988 Report of the Surgeon General, The Health Consequences of Smoking: Nicotine Addiction* and a member of the Center for Child Health Research Tobacco Consortium of the American Academy of Pediatrics. He is Deputy Regional Editor for *Addiction*. He has consulted actively with such government and voluntary agencies as the National Heart, Lung, and Blood Institute; the National Cancer Institute; the Centers for Disease Control and Prevention; the National Institute on Drug Abuse; the Agency for Healthcare Research and Quality; the American Cancer Society; the American Lung Association; and the World Health Organization. Dr. Lando is a past president of the Society for Research on Nicotine and Tobacco and currently chairs the SRNT Global Network Committee. He is a 2006 recipient of the University of Minnesota Award for Global Engagement; this award carries with it the title of "Distinguished International Professor." He is serving as Vice President of the 14th World Conference on Tobacco OR Health, to be held in 2009 in Mumbai, India.

Robert E. Mecklenburg, DDS, MPH
Consultant, Tobacco and Public Health
Potomac, Maryland

Dr. Mecklenburg is a Diplomate of the American Board of Dental Public Health and an Assistant Surgeon General (ret. O-8). He organized and managed dental affairs for the National Cancer Institute's (NCI) Tobacco Control Research Branch and was the Tobacco-Related Research and Development Advisor for the National Institute of Dental and Craniofacial Research's Office of Science Policy and Analysis. He chaired the National Dental Tobacco-Free Steering Committee and was Vice-Chairman of the Dentistry Against Tobacco Section/Tobacco and Oral Health Committee of the FDI World Dental Federation. He chaired the committee on noncancer oral effects of tobacco for the first Surgeon General's report on smokeless tobacco. He was the principal author of the NCI publications, *Tobacco Effects in the Mouth* and *How to Help Your Patients Stop Using Tobacco: A Manual for the Oral Health Team.* Dr. Mecklenburg has published and lectured widely in the United States and abroad about dental professionals' involvement in the creation of a tobacco-free society.

Robin Mermelstein, PhD
Deputy Director, Institute for Health Research and Policy
Director, Center for Health Behavior Research
Professor, Department of Psychology
University of Illinois-Chicago
Chicago, Illinois

Dr. Mermelstein is Professor of Psychology, Director of the Center for Health Behavior Research, and Deputy Director of the Institute for Health Research and Policy at the University of Illinois at Chicago. She holds a PhD in clinical and community psychology from the University of Oregon. Her research interests fall broadly in the area of tobacco use, with studies ranging from longitudinal examinations of the etiology of youth smoking and interventions for adolescents to stop smoking to cessation interventions for adult smokers. Dr. Mermelstein has been the principal investigator on several grants from the National Cancer Institute (NCI) investigating trajectories of adolescent smoking, with a focus on social and emotional contextual factors. In addition, she has been funded by the Centers for Disease Control and Prevention to examine factors related to youth smoking, and by the National Heart, Lung, and Blood Institute and NCI for studies of adult smoking cessation. Dr. Mermelstein was the Director of the Robert Wood Johnson Foundation's (RWJF) Program Office, A Partners with Tobacco Use Research Centers: A Transdisciplinary Approach to Advancing Science and Policy Studies. As part of this program, the RWJF collaborated with both NCI and the National Institute on Drug Abuse in funding the Transdisciplinary Tobacco Use Research Centers.

Patricia Dolan Mullen, DrPH
Professor of Health Promotion and Behavioral Sciences
University of Texas School of Public Health
Houston, Texas

Dr. Mullen received her graduate training at the University of California, Berkeley, School of Public Health and has extensive experience in managed care. Her tobacco cessation research has focused on pregnant and postpartum women (non-Hispanic white, African American, and Hispanic) from urban and rural environments, who were both privately insured and covered by Medicaid. She also has collaborated on smoking cessation research with international populations. Dr. Mullen served on the U.S. Expert Panel for the Content of Prenatal Care and on research advisory panels on prenatal smoking cessation for the National Institutes of Health, Centers for Disease Control and Prevention, the American Cancer Society, and the Robert Wood Johnson Foundation Smoke-Free Families Program. She has conducted systematic reviews and meta-analyses of smoking cessation programs for pregnant women and other topics and served as a member and Vice-Chair of the U.S. Community Preventive Services Task Force.

C. Tracy Orleans, PhD
Senior Scientist and Distinguished Fellow
Robert Wood Johnson Foundation
Princeton, New Jersey

Dr. Orleans has led or co-led the Robert Wood Johnson Foundation (RWJF) public policy- and health care system-based grant making in the areas of tobacco control, physical activity promotion, childhood obesity prevention, and chronic disease management. She led the Foundation's Health & Behavior Team and has developed and/or managed numerous RWJF national initiatives, including Addressing Tobacco in Healthcare, Smoke-Free Families, Helping Young Smokers Quit, Bridging the Gap/ Impact Teen, Substance Abuse Policy Research, Improving Chronic Illness Care, Active Living Research, and Healthy Eating Research. An internationally known clinical health psychologist, Dr. Orleans has authored or co-authored more than 200 publications; contributed to several Surgeon General's reports; served on numerous journal editorial boards, national scientific panels, and advisory groups (e.g., U.S. Preventive Services Task Force, Institute of Medicine, National Commission on Prevention Priorities); and as President of the Society of Behavioral Medicine.

Lawrence Robinson, MD, MPH
Deputy Health Commissioner
Philadelphia Department of Public Health
Health Promotion/Disease Prevention
Philadelphia, Pennsylvania

A graduate of Harvard College, Dr. Robinson received his MD from the University of Pennsylvania School of Medicine. He received his MPH and completed a residency in preventive medicine at Johns Hopkins University. He was a resident and faculty member at Rush and Columbia University while performing his internal medicine training. As Deputy Commissioner for Health Promotion/Disease Prevention for the Philadelphia Department of Public Health, Dr. Robinson is responsible for the development, planning, implementation, and evaluation of various programs delivering medical, chronic disease prevention, and health education services. Local antitobacco projects include banning vending machines, assisting the county jail move to a smoke-free environment, Nicotrol Patch replacement, and the American Cancer Society Fresh Start Program. This train-the-trainer program was provided to the mentally ill and other targeted populations. Dr. Robinson also is a board member of the Pennsylvania American Cancer Society and Chairman of the State Tobacco Core Team. He is a member of various groups, organizations, and agencies in the community working on issues such as the State Tobacco Settlement (No Butts/Do the Right Thing) and smoking prevention for youth and specific populations, such as pregnant women.

Maxine L. Stitzer, PhD
Professor, Department of Psychiatry and Behavioral Sciences
Behavioral Biology Research Center
Johns Hopkins/Bayview Medical Center
Baltimore, Maryland

Dr. Stitzer received her PhD in psychology and training in psychopharmacology from the University of Michigan. At Johns Hopkins University, she has developed a varied and extensive grant-supported research program focusing on both pharmacological and behavioral approaches to the treatment of substance abuse. Her many publications reflect active research interests in both illicit drug abuse and tobacco dependence. She has served as President of the Division on Psychopharmacology and Substance Abuse of the American Psychological Association, President of the Society for Research on Nicotine and Tobacco, and as a member of the Board of Directors of the College on Problems of Drug Dependence.

Anthony C. Tommasello, PhD, MS
Director, Office of Substance Abuse Studies
University of Maryland School of Pharmacy
Baltimore, Maryland

Dr. Tommasello, a pharmacist, is an Associate Professor in the Department of Pharmaceutical Health Services Research at the University of Maryland School of Pharmacy and Director, Office of Substance Abuse Studies, which he founded. He received his PhD in policy sciences from the University of Maryland, Baltimore County, and has worked in the addiction field since 1973. He is active in clinical and policy research and in addictions treatment and has created educational programs that have served as national models for pharmacists and other health and human service workers. Dr. Tommasello is President of the Maryland Pharmacists' Education and Advocacy Council, which provides advocacy and treatment referrals for impaired pharmacists. He has published in the areas of general principles of assessment and treatment, methadone maintenance care, and adolescent drug abuse and addiction and the pharmacist's role in substance abuse and addiction management.

Louise Villejo, MPH, CHES
Director, Patient Education Office
Office of Public Affairs
University of Texas M.D. Anderson Cancer Center
Houston, Texas

As Director of the Patient Education Office at the M.D. Anderson Cancer Center, Ms. Villejo is responsible for the design, implementation, evaluation, and management of institution-wide patient and family education programs. She has designed and implemented Patient/Family Learning Centers as well as award-winning, disease-specific patient education programs, and produced more than 100 patient education print materials and videotapes. For the past 10 years, she has served on the National Cancer Institute's Advisory Boards and Patient Education Network's Steering Committee, and on numerous other Federal and private advisory and planning boards and committees. Ms. Villejo's publications include articles on cancer patient education and cultural diversity in health care.

Mary Ellen Wewers, PhD, MPH, RN
Professor, College of Public Health
The Ohio State University
Columbus, Ohio

Dr. Wewers, an Adult Nurse Practitioner, received her PhD in nursing from the University of Maryland and an MPH from Harvard University. She has been funded by the National Institutes of Health (NIH) to investigate reinforcement for nicotine in both human and animal models of dependence. Her current NIH-funded research examines nurse-managed tobacco cessation interventions in underserved groups. Dr. Wewers is past Chair of the Nursing Assembly of the American Thoracic Society and a past member of the Society's Board of Directors. She serves as Co-Program Leader for Cancer Control at The Ohio State University Comprehensive Cancer Center.

Statistical Consultant

Victor Hasselblad, PhD
Statistical Methodologist
Duke Clinical Research Institute
Duke University
Durham, North Carolina

Project Staff

Bruce Christiansen, PhD
Project Director
Center for Tobacco Research and
  Intervention
University of Wisconsin School of
  Medicine and Public Health
Madison, Wisconsin

Megan Piper, PhD
Project Scientist
Center for Tobacco Research and
  Intervention
University of Wisconsin School of
  Medicine and Public Health
Madison, Wisconsin

Doug Jorenby, PhD
Project Scientist
Center for Tobacco Research and
  Intervention
University of Wisconsin School of
  Medicine and Public Health
Madison, Wisconsin

Wendy Theobald, PhD
Senior Research Associate
Center for Tobacco Research and
  Intervention
University of Wisconsin School of
  Medicine and Public Health
Madison, Wisconsin

Cathlyn Leitzke, MSN, RN-C
Senior Research Associate
Center for Tobacco Research and
  Intervention
University of Wisconsin School of
  Medicine and Public Health
Madison, Wisconsin

Michael Connell
Project Database Administrator
Center for Tobacco Research and
  Intervention
University of Wisconsin School of
  Medicine and Public Health
Madison, Wisconsin

Project Administrative Staff

**David Fraser, Assistant Project
  Director**
Barb Bienborn
Carlos Edge
Linda Kurowski
Marie Larson
Margaret Sheldon
Center for Tobacco Research and
  Intervention
University of Wisconsin School of
  Medicine and Public Health
Madison, Wisconsin

Guideline Liaisons

**Ernestine W. Murray, RN, BSN, MAS,
Project Officer**
Agency for Healthcare Research and
  Quality
Rockville, Maryland

Glen Bennett, MPH, CHES
National Heart, Lung, and Blood
  Institute
Bethesda, Maryland

Stephen Heishman, PhD
National Institute on Drug Abuse
Rockville, Maryland

Corinne Husten, MD, MPH*
Now at: Partnership for Prevention
Washington, DC
Formerly at: Centers for Disease
  Control and Prevention
Atlanta, Georgia

Glen Morgan, PhD
National Cancer Institute
Bethesda, Maryland

Christine Williams, MEd
Agency for Healthcare Research and
  Quality
Rockville, Maryland

Guideline Consortium Sponsors

**Agency for Healthcare Research and
  Quality**
Rockville, Maryland

American Legacy Foundation
Washington, DC

**Centers for Disease Control and
  Prevention**
Atlanta, Georgia

National Cancer Institute
Bethesda, Maryland

**National Heart, Lung, and Blood
  Institute**
Bethesda, Maryland

National Institute on Drug Abuse
Rockville, Maryland

**The Robert Wood Johnson
  Foundation**
Princeton, New Jersey

**Center for Tobacco Research and
  Intervention**
**University of Wisconsin School of
  Medicine and Public Health**
Madison, Wisconsin

Contract Support

The Scientific Consulting Group, Inc.
Gaithersburg, Maryland

Marcia Feinleib
Project Director

Joanne Brodsky
Managing Editor

Eric Doty
Art Production Manager

Article Reviewers

Adrian Coon
Scott Hagemann
Christine Harbin
Scott Johnson
Erin Josen
Andrew Kilgust
Shriya Kothur
Sean Ryan
Maurice Shaw
Center for Tobacco Research and
  Intervention
University of Wisconsin School of
  Medicine and Public Health
Madison, Wisconsin

Peer Reviewers

Karen Ahijevych, PhD, RN
Professor and Associate Dean for
  Academic Affairs
The Ohio State University
Columbus, Ohio

Jasjit Ahluwalia, MD, MPH, MS
Executive Director, Office of
  Clinical Research
University of Minnesota Academic
  Health Center
Minneapolis, Minnesota

Debra Annand, BSPH
Project Director
American Lung Association of DC
Representing: DC Tobacco-Free
  Families Campaign
Washington, DC

Linda Bailey, JD, MHS
President and Chief Executive
  Officer
Representing: North American
  Quitline Consortium
Phoenix, Arizona

Dianne Barker, MHS
President and Chief Executive
  Officer
Barker Bi-Coastal Health
  Consultants
Los Angeles, California

Bruce Bender, PhD
Professor, National Jewish Medical
   and Research Center
Representing: American Thoracic
   Society
New York, New York

**Georges G. Benjamin, MD, FACP,
   FACEP(E)**
Executive Director
Representing: American Public
   Health Association
Washington, DC

Stella Bialous, DrPH, RN, MScN
President, Tobacco Policy
   International
Representing: Tobacco Free Nurses
San Francisco, California

Alan Blum, MD, FAAFP
Director
University of Alabama Center for
   the Study of Tobacco and Society
Tuscaloosa, Alabama

Thomas Brandon, PhD
Professor and Director, Tobacco
   Research
Moffitt Cancer Center & Research
   Institute
University of South Florida
Tampa, Florida

David M. Burns, MD
Professor
University of California-San Diego
San Diego, California

Michael Caldwell, MD, MPH
Commissioner of Health
Dutchess County Department of
   Health, New York
Representing: National Associa-
   tion of County and City Health
   Officials
Washington, DC

Doug Campos-Outcalt, MD, MPA
President, Arizona Academy of
   Family Physicians
University of Arizona
Representing: American Academy
   of Family Physicians
Leawood, Kansas

Matthew Carpenter, PhD
Assistant Professor
Medical University of
   South Carolina
Representing: American College of
   Chest Physicians
Northbrook, Illinois

Sally Carter, MSW, LSW
Director of Planning and
   Cessation Services
Oklahoma State Department
   of Health
Oklahoma City, Oklahoma

Moon Chen, Jr., PhD, MPH
Associate Director for Cancer
   Prevention and Control
UC-Davis Cancer Center
Representing: Asian American
   Network for Cancer Awareness,
   Research, and Treatment
Sacramento, California

Paul Cinciripini, PhD
Professor
University of Texas M.D. Anderson
  Cancer Center
Houston, Texas

Nathaniel Cobb, MD
Chief, Chronic Disease Branch,
  Indian Health Service (IHS)
Representing: Indian Health
  Service
Albuquerque, New Mexico

K. Michael Cummings, MD, PhD
Chairman, Department of
  Health Behavior
Roswell Park Cancer Institute
Buffalo, New York

Ronald Davis, MD
President, American Medical
  Association
Director, Center for Health
  Promotion & Disease Prevention
Henry Ford Health System
Detroit, Michigan

Harriet De Wit, PhD
Professor
University of Chicago
Chicago, Illinois

Jacob Delarosa, MD
Chief, Cardiothoracic Surgery
Idaho State University
Pocatello, Idaho

Carlo C. DiClemente, PhD
Lipitz Professor
University of Maryland Baltimore
  Campus
Baltimore, Maryland

Norman Edelman, MD
Chief Medical Officer
Stony Brook University
Representing: American Lung
  Association
New York, New York

Marilyn W. Edmunds, PhD, NP
President, Nurse Practitioner
  Alternatives, Inc.
Representing: American College of
  Nurse Practitioners
Arlington, Virginia

Michael Eriksen, ScD
Professor and Director, Institute of
  Public Health
Georgia State University
Atlanta, Georgia

Linda Hyder Ferry, MD, MPH
Associate Professor
Loma Linda University School of
  Public Health
Representing: American College of
  Preventive Medicine
Washington, DC

Jacquelyn Fried, RDH, MS
Associate Professor and Director
University of Maryland
  Dental School
Baltimore, Maryland

Thomas Frieden, MD, MPH
Commissioner, Department of
    Health and Mental Hygiene
New York, New York

Joseph Giaimo, DO, FCCP, FACOI
Representing: American Osteo-
    pathic Association
Chicago, Illinois

Sam Giordano, MBA, RRT, FAARC
Executive Director and
    Chief Executive Officer
Representing: American Associa-
    tion for Respiratory Care
Irving, Texas

Thomas Glynn, PhD
Director, Cancer Science and
    Trends
Director, International Cancer
    Control
Representing: American Cancer
    Society
Washington, DC

Neil E. Grunberg, PhD
Professor
Uniformed Services University of
    the Health Sciences
Bethesda, Maryland

Sharon Hall, PhD
Professor in Residence
University of California–
    San Francisco
San Francisco, California

Helen Ann Halpin, ScM, PhD
Professor
University of California-Berkeley
Berkeley, California

Kim Hamlett-Berry, PhD
Director, Public Health National
    Prevention Program
Representing: Department of
    Veterans Affairs
Washington, DC

Dorothy K. Hatsukami, PhD
Director, Transdisciplinary Tobacco
    Use Research Center
University of Minnesota
    Cancer Center
Minneapolis, Minnesota

Jack Hollis, PhD
Senior Investigator
Kaiser Permanente Colorado
Denver, Colorado

Kimberly Horn, EdD, MSW
Robert C. Byrd Associate Professor
    of Community Medicine
Associate Director of Population
    Health
Mary Babb Randolph Cancer
    Center
West Virginia University
Morgantown, West Virginia

Thomas Houston, MD
Director, OhioHealth Nicotine
    Dependence Program
Columbus, Ohio

John Hughes, MD
Professor
University of Vermont
Burlington, Vermont

Richard D. Hurt, MD
Director, Nicotine Dependence
  Center
Mayo Clinic
Rochester, Minnesota

Paul Jarris, MD, MBA
Executive Director
Representing: Association of State
  and Territorial Health Officials
Arlington, Virginia

Martin Jarvis, DSc
Professor Emeritus
Department of Epidemiology and
  Public Health
University College London
London, England

Peter Kaufmann, PhD
Leader, Behavioral Medicine and
  Prevention Scientific Research
  Group
National Heart, Lung, and Blood
  Institute
Representing: The Society of
  Behavioral Medicine
Milwaukee, Wisconsin

Jonathan D. Klein, MD, MPH
Acting Chief, Adolescent Medicine
  Division
Department of Pediatrics
AAP Julius B. Richmond Center of
  Excellence for Children
University of Rochester
Representing: American Academy
  of Pediatrics
Elk Grove Village, Illinois

Robert C. Klesges, PhD
Professor
University of Tennessee Health
  Science Center
St. Jude Children's Research
  Hospital
Memphis, Tennessee

Connie Kohler, DrPH
Associate Professor
University of Alabama-Birmingham
Birmingham, Alabama

B. Waine Kong, PhD, JD
Chief Executive Officer
Representing: Association of Black
  Cardiologists
Atlanta, Georgia

Elizabeth Kraft, MD, MHS
Medical Director, Provider
  Education and Resource Tobacco
  Program
Representing: Colorado Clinical
  Guidelines Collaborative
Lakewood, Colorado

Jerry A. Krishnan, MD, PhD
Associate Professor
University of Chicago Medical
 Center
Representing: American Heart
 Association
Dallas, Texas

Scott Leischow, PhD
Professor
University of Arizona
Tucson, Arizona

Caryn Lerman, PhD
Mary W. Calkins Professor
University of Pennsylvania School
 of Medicine
Philadelphia, Pennsylvania

Sandra Zelman Lewis, PhD
Assistant Vice President, Health and
 Science Policy/Quality
American College of Chest
 Physicians
Northbrook, Illinois

Edward Lichtenstein, PhD
Senior Scientist
Oregon Research Institute
Eugene, Oregon

Henri R. Manasse, Jr., PhD, ScD, RPH
Executive Vice President and Chief
 Executive Officer
Representing: American Society of
 Health-System Pharmacists
Bethesda, Maryland

Marc Manley, MD, MPH
Vice President and Medical
 Director
BlueCross BlueShield of Minnesota
St. Paul, Minnesota

James R. Marshall, PhD
Senior Vice President and Chair,
 Department of Cancer Prevention
 and Population Sciences
Roswell Park Cancer Institute
Representing: American Society of
 Preventive Oncology
Madison, Wisconsin

Patrick E. McBride, MD, MPH
Professor
Co-Director, Preventative
 Cardiology Program
University of Wisconsin School of
 Medicine and Public Health
Madison, Wisconsin

**Robert K. McLellan, MD, MPH,
 FACOEM, FAAFP**
Medical Director, Dartmouth-
 Hitchcock Medical Center
 Employee Health System
Representing: American College
 of Occupational and
 Environmental Medicine
Elk Grove Village, Illinois

Cathy Melvin, PhD, MPH
Faculty Director, Lineberger
 Comprehensive Cancer Center
University of North Carolina-
 Chapel Hill
Representing: Smokefree Families
 National Partnership
Chapel Hill, North Carolina

Norman Montalto, DO, FAAFP
Medical Director
Wells Fargo TPA
West Virginia University
Morgantown, West Virginia

Claudia Morrissey, MD, MPH
President Elect
Representing: American Medical
  Women's Association
Philadelphia, Pennsylvania

Mildred Morse, JD, CTAS
President, Morse Enterprises
National Tobacco Independence
  Campaign
Washington, DC

Myra Muramoto, MD, MPH
Associate Professor
Family and Community Medicine,
  Public Health
University of Arizona Colleges of
  Medicine & Public Health
Tucson, Arizona

Matthew L. Myers, JD
President and Chief Executive
  Officer
Representing: Campaign for
  Tobacco-Free Kids
Washington, DC

Raymond Niaura, PhD
Professor
Warren Alpert Medical School of
  Brown University
Representing: Society for Research
  on Nicotine and Tobacco
Madison, Wisconsin

Lloyd F. Novick, MD, MPH
President
Representing: Association for
  Prevention Teaching and Research
Washington, DC

Judy Ockene, PhD, MEd
Professor
University of Massachusetts
  Medical School
Worcester, Massachusetts

Stephanie O'Malley, PhD
Professor
Yale University School of Medicine
New Haven, Connecticut

Deborah Ossip-Klein, PhD
Director, Smoking Research
  Program
University of Rochester Medical
  Center
Rochester, New York

Kenneth Perkins, PhD
Professor
University of Pittsburgh
Pittsburgh, Pennsylvania

Allan Prochazka, MD, MSc
Assistant Chief
Denver VA Medical Center
Representing: Society of General
  Internal Medicine
Washington, DC

Kathleen Rankin, DDS
Baylor College of Dentistry
Texas A&M University Health
  System Science Center
Representing: American Dental
  Association
Chicago, Illinois

Bob Rehm, MBA
Vice President, Public Health and
  Clinical Strategies
Representing: America's Health
  Insurance Plans
Washington, DC

Stephen Rennard, MD
Larson Professor
University of Nebraska Medical
  Center
Omaha, Nebraska

Robert Richards, MA, CADCIII, NCACII
NAADAC Northwest Regional
  Vice President
Representing: The Association for
  Addiction Professionals
Alexandria, Virginia

Nancy Rigotti, MD
Professor of Medicine, Harvard
  Medical School
Representing: American College
  of Physicians
Philadelphia, Pennsylvania

Diane Roberts, DrPH
Associate Professor
Indiana University East
Richmond, Indiana

Gennette Robinson, RDH, MS
Immediate Past President
Representing: National Dental
  Hygienists' Association
Chicago, Illinois

Patricia A. Rowell, PhD, RN, CNP
Representing: American Nurses
  Association
Silver Spring, Maryland

Linda Sarna, DNSc, RN, FAAN
Associate Professor
University of California-
  Los Angeles School of Nursing
Representing: TobaccoFree Nurses
San Francisco, California

Steve A. Schroeder, MD
Distinguished Professor of Health
  and Health Care, Department of
  Medicine
Director, Smoking Cessation
University of California-
  San Francisco
San Francisco, California

Herbert Severson, PhD
Senior Research Scientist
Oregon Research Institute
Eugene, Oregon

Gerard A. Silvestri, MD, MS, FCCP
Professor
Medical University of South
  Carolina
Representing: American College of
  Chest Physicians
Northbrook, Illinois

Carol Southard, RN, MSN
Smoking Cessation Specialist
Northwest Memorial Hospital
Representing: American Dental
  Hygienist Association
Chicago, Illinois

Bonnie Spring, PhD, ABPP
Professor
Northwestern University
Representing: The Society of
  Behavioral Medicine
Milwaukee, Wisconsin

Lindsay Stead, MA, MSc
Review Coordinator
Cochrane Tobacco Addiction
  Group
University of Oxford
Headington, Oxford

Jan Stine, BSEd
Tobacco Program Consultant
Ohio Department of Health
Columbus, Ohio

Steven Sussman, PhD
Professor
University of Southern California
Los Angeles, California

Amber Hardy Thornton, MPH, CHES
Executive Vice President for
  Program Development
American Legacy Foundation
Washington, DC

Olga Tompkins, MPH, RN, COHN-S/SM, FAAOHN
Representing: American Association of Occupational Health Nurses
Atlanta, Georgia

Richard W. Valachovic, DMD, MPH
Executive Director
Representing: American Dental
  Education Association

Rudy Valenzuela, FSP, MSN, RN, FNP-C
President and Chief Executive
  Officer, FSP Health Ministries
Representing: National Association of Hispanic Nurses
Washington, DC

Frank Vitale, MA
Senior Lecturer, Pharmaceutical
  Sciences
University of Pittsburgh
Representing: Pharmacy Partnership for Tobacco Cessation
Bethesda, Maryland

Kenneth E. Warner, PhD
Director
University of Michigan Tobacco
  Research Network
Ann Arbor, Michigan

Larry N. Williams, DDS, MAGD
Captain, Dental Corps
U.S. Navy
Great Lakes, Illinois

David Willoughby, MA
Chief Executive Officer
Clearway Minnesota
Minneapolis, Minnesota

Richard Windsor, PhD, MS, MPH
Professor
George Washington University
School of Public Health and
　Health Services
Washington, DC

Richard A. Yoast, PhD
Director, Reducing Underage
　Drinking Through Coalitions
American Medical Association
Chicago, Illinois

Kathy Zaiken, PharmD
Assistant Professor
Massachusetts College of Pharmacy
　and Health Sciences
Representing: American Association
　of Colleges of Pharmacy
Alexandria, Virginia

Appendixes

Appendix A. Financial Disclosure for Panel Members, Liaisons, and Peer Reviewers

Panel Members

The evaluation of conflict for the 2008 Guideline Update comprised a two-stage procedure designed to obtain increasingly detailed and informative data on potential conflicts over the course of the Guideline development process.

1. In July 2006 and prior to the initial meeting in October 2006, Panel members completed a general screen, reporting any potential conflicts over the previous 5 years. Where potential conflicts existed, Panel members provided a narrative listing of the relevant organizations and types of conflict. Panel members were asked to update this screen as new information or potential conflicts became known.

2. Prior to the second in-person Panel meeting in June 2007, and before any decisions regarding Panel recommendations were made, Panel members were required to complete a more exhaustive disclosure process for calendar years 2005, 2006, and 2007, based on the United States Department of Health and Human Services, PHS Title 42, Chapter 1, Part 50 guidelines for the conduct of research (*ori.hhs.gov/policies/fedreg42cfr50. shtml*). Moreover, Panel members were asked to update this report as new information or potential conflicts became known. In keeping with the PHS-based guidelines, a potential conflict was designated as "significant" if one or more of three criteria were met:

    A. Net reportable compensation in excess of $10,000 in any reporting year to the Panel member, spouse, or dependent child for outside activities from any entity whose interests may be affected by the recommendations in the Guideline (excluding public or nonprofit entities).

    B. Leadership as an officer, director, or trustee in any reporting year by the Panel member, spouse, or dependent child in any entity whose interests may be affected by the recommendations in the Guideline (excluding public or nonprofit entities).

C. Ownership interests either in excess of $10,000 or 5 percent of the business in any reporting year by the Panel member, spouse, or dependent child in any entity whose interests may be affected by the recommendations in the Guideline (excluding public or nonprofit entities).

Panel members were asked to complete this PHS-based report for 3 calendar years (2005, 2006, 2007), that comprised both the 18-month period before the Guideline Panel was constituted, as well as the full period of Guideline development. For any significant conflict that was disclosed, Panel members provided a detailed description of the relevant organizational tie, including categorizing the amount of compensation or financial interests involved. Of the Panel members listed in this document, 21 of 24 had no significant financial interests as defined by the PHS-based criteria. In addition to these mandatory disclosures regarding compensation, leadership, and ownership, members were asked to disclose any other information that might be disclosed in a professional publication.

Three Panel members whose disclosures exceeded the PHS criteria for significant financial interest were recused from Panel deliberations relating to their areas of conflict; one additional Panel member voluntarily recused himself.

The following is a summary listing for any of the years 2005, 2006, and 2007 of all significant financial interests as defined above, as well as any additional disclosures Panel members chose to make.

William C. Bailey reported significant financial interests in the form of compensation from three different pharmaceutical companies in 2006 and two in 2007 for speaking engagements.

Timothy B. Baker reported no significant financial interests. Under additional disclosures, he reported that he has served as a co-investigator on research studies at the University of Wisconsin that were sponsored by four pharmaceutical companies.

Neal L. Benowitz reported significant financial interest in the form of compensation from one pharmaceutical company for each of the years 2005–2007, as well as stock ownership in one pharmaceutical company.

Under additional disclosures, he reported providing expert testimony in lawsuits against tobacco companies.

Susan J. Curry reported no significant financial interests and no additional disclosures.

Sally Faith Dorfman reported no significant financial interests. Under additional disclosures, she reported her employment by Ferring Pharmaceuticals, Inc., a company whose business does not relate to treating tobacco dependence.

Michael C. Fiore reported no significant financial interests. Under additional disclosures, he reported that he served as an investigator on research studies at the University of Wisconsin (UW) that were supported wholly or in part by four pharmaceutical companies, and in 2005 received compensation from one pharmaceutical company. In addition, he reported that, in 1998, the UW appointed him to a named Chair, which was made possible by an unrestricted gift to the UW from GlaxoWellcome.

Erika S. Froehlicher reported no significant financial interests and no additional disclosures.

Michael G. Goldstein reported no significant financial interests. Under additional disclosures, he reported that his employer received support from Bayer Pharmaceutical prior to 2005 and that he was employed by Bayer Pharmaceutical Corporation prior to January 1, 2005. His organization received payments for his professional services from two pharmaceutical companies and one commercial Internet smoking cessation site during the period 2005–2007.

Cheryl Healton reported no significant financial interests and no additional disclosures.

Patricia Nez Henderson reported no significant financial interests and no additional disclosures.

Richard B. Heyman reported no significant financial interests and no additional disclosures.

Carlos Roberto Jaén reported no significant financial interests and no additional disclosures.

Howard K. Koh reported no significant financial interests and no additional disclosures.

Thomas E. Kottke reported no significant financial interests and no additional disclosures.

Harry A. Lando reported no significant financial interests. Under additional disclosures, he reported serving on an advisory panel for a new tobacco use cessation medication and attending 2-day meetings in 2005 and 2006 as a member of this panel.

Robert E. Mecklenburg reported no significant financial interests. Under additional disclosures, he reported assisting Clinical Tools, Inc., through a governmental contract to develop a PHS 2000 Guideline-based Internet continuing education course.

Robin Mermelstein reported no significant financial interests and no additional disclosures.

Patricia Dolan Mullen reported no significant financial interests and no additional disclosures.

C. Tracy Orleans reported significant financial interests in the form of a dependent child who owns pharmaceutical stock, and no additional disclosures.

Lawrence Robinson reported no significant financial interests and no additional disclosures.

Maxine L. Stitzer reported no significant financial interests. Under additional disclosures, she reported participation on a pharmaceutical scientific advisory panel for a new tobacco use cessation medication.

Anthony C. Tommasello reported no significant financial interests and no additional disclosures.

Louise Villejo reported no significant financial interests and no additional disclosures.

Mary Ellen Wewers reported no significant financial interests and no additional disclosures.

Liaisons

Liaisons followed the same process as Panel members in reporting significant financial interests. Their disclosures are summarized below:

Glen Bennett reported no significant financial interests and no additional disclosures.

Stephen Heishman reported no significant financial interests and no additional disclosures.

Corinne Husten reported no significant financial interests and no additional disclosures.

Glen Morgan reported no significant financial interests and no additional disclosures.

Ernestine W. Murray reported no significant financial interests and no additional disclosures.

Christine Williams reported no significant financial interests and no additional disclosures.

Peer Reviewers

Peer reviewers were required to report significant financial interests at the time they submitted their peer reviews. The interests were reviewed prior to the adjudication of each reviewer's comments. Any significant financial interests are noted below their listing in the Contributors Section of this Guideline.

Outside Comments

The availability of the draft Guideline report for review was announced in the *Federal Register* on September 28, 2007 (Volume 72, Number 188). Individuals who had informed Panel members or staff that they wished the opportunity to review the document were provided with an opportunity to do so. All those submitting comments were asked to disclose significant financial interests at the time their comments were submitted. Prior to each set of comments being considered and adjudicated, the disclosure information (or lack of disclosure) was noted and taken into consideration.

Appendix B. Helpful Web Site Addresses

The inclusion of Web sites in this appendix is intended to assist readers in finding additional information regarding the treatment of tobacco use and dependence and related topics and does not constitute endorsement of the contents of any particular site. All Web sites listed are either Government-sponsored organizations or nonprofit foundations.

Addressing Tobacco in Healthcare (formerly Addressing Tobacco in Managed Care): *www.atmc.wisc.edu*

Agency for Healthcare Research and Quality: *www.ahrq.gov*

American Academy of Family Physicians: *www.aafp.org*

American Cancer Society: *www.cancer.org*

American College of Chest Physicians: *www.chestnet.org*

American Legacy Foundation: *www.americanlegacy.org*

American Lung Association: (maintains profiles of state tobacco control activities): *www.lungusa.org*

American Psychological Association: *www.apa.org*

Association for the Treatment of Tobacco Use and Dependence: *www.attud.org*

Campaign for Tobacco-Free Kids: *www.tobaccofreekids.org*

Chest Foundation: *www.chestfoundation.org/tobaccoPrevention/index.php*

Kaiser Family State Health Facts: *www.statehealthfacts.org*

Medicare and Medicaid: *www.cms.hhs.gov/mcd/viewdecisionmemo. asp?id=130* and *www.cms.hhs.gov/Smoking Cessation*

North American Quitline Consortium (NAQC): *www.Naquitline.org*

National Cancer Institute: *www.nci.nih.gov*

National Guideline Clearinghouse: *www.guideline.gov*

National Heart, Lung, and Blood Institute: *www.nhlbi.nih.gov*

National Institute on Drug Abuse: *www.nida.nih.gov*

Office on Smoking and Health at the Centers for Disease Control and Prevention: *www.cdc.gov/tobacco*

Robert Wood Johnson Foundation: *www.rwjf.org*

Society for Research on Nicotine and Tobacco: *www.srnt.org*

TobaccoFree Nurses: *www.tobaccofreenurses.org*

Tobacco Technical Assistance Consortium: *www.ttac.org*

University of Wisconsin Center for Tobacco Research and Intervention: *www.ctri.wisc.edu*

World Health Organization: *www.who.int*

World Health Organization – Tobacco Atlas: *www.who.int/tobacco/statistics/tobacco_atlas/en*

Appendix C. Coding Information Regarding the Diagnosis of and Billing for Tobacco Dependence Treatment

Coding for the Treatment of Tobacco Use

Clinicians, clinic administrators, and health care delivery systems require appropriate diagnostic and billing codes for the documentation and reimbursement of tobacco dependence treatment. Information on such codes may help address a common clinical concern regarding the treatment of tobacco-dependent patients: it is difficult to accurately document and obtain reimbursement for this treatment. Although examples of such codes are provided below, clinicians and billing coders may use other diagnostic and reimbursement codes to document and obtain payment for this medical treatment. Additionally, it is incumbent on the clinician to ensure that appropriate billing guidelines are followed and to recognize that reimbursement of these codes may vary by payor or benefits package. For example, although psychiatric therapeutic codes appropriate for treating tobacco dependence exist, some payors or benefits packages have restrictions on mental health benefits. Similarly, reimbursement for preventive visits varies greatly among payors and benefits packages.

A systems-based approach will facilitate the understanding and use of such codes by clinicians. For example, various clinic or hospital meetings (e.g., business sessions, grand rounds, seminars, and coding in-service sessions) can explain and highlight the use of tobacco dependence codes for diagnosis and reimbursement. Additionally, these diagnostic codes can be preprinted on the billing and diagnostic coding sheets as a "check-off" so that clinicians are not required to recall and manually document such treatment. Finally, clinicians can be reminded that counseling by itself is a reimbursable activity and can be billed-for based on the number of minutes of counseling.

1. Diagnostic Codes (ICD-9-CM)

When clinicians provide treatment to patients dependent on tobacco, the following diagnostic codes can be used. They can be found in the ICD-9-CM (*International Classification of Diseases, 9th Revision, Clinical Modification*) coding manual under several sections:

Mental Disorders (290-319)

305.1 Tobacco Use Disorder (Tobacco Dependence). Cases in which tobacco is used to the detriment of a person's health or social functioning or in which there is tobacco dependence. Tobacco dependence is included here rather than under drug dependence because tobacco differs from other drugs of dependence in its psychotropic effect. This excludes: History of tobacco use (V15.82).

V Codes

V15.82 History of Tobacco Use. This excludes: Tobacco dependence (305.1).

Diseases of Oral Cavity, Salivary Glands, and Jaws

523.6 Accretions on teeth
Supragingival: Deposits on teeth: tobacco.

Accidental Poisoning by Other Solid and Liquid Substances, Gases, and Vapors

E869.4 Secondhand tobacco smoke.

Complications Mainly Related To Pregnancy

649.0 Tobacco use disorder complicating pregnancy, childbirth, or the puerperium.

2. Billing Codes (Current Procedural Terminology [CPT] Codes)

A number of billing codes may be used for reimbursement of the provision of tobacco dependence treatment. The examples provided fall under the general categories of preventive medicine services, psychiatric therapeutic procedures, and dental codes.

A. Preventive Medicine Services

The following codes are used to report the preventive medicine evaluation and management of infants, children, adolescents, and adults.

The "comprehensive" nature of the Preventive Medicine Services codes 99383–99397 reflects an age- and gender-appropriate history/exam and is NOT synonymous with the "comprehensive" examination required in Evaluation and Management codes 99201–99350.

Codes 99383–99397 include counseling/anticipatory guidance/risk factor reduction interventions, which are provided at the time of the initial or periodic comprehensive preventive medicine examination. (Refer to codes 99401–99412 for reporting those counseling/anticipatory guidance/risk factor reduction interventions that are provided at an encounter separate from the preventive medicine examination.)

A1. Initial or Periodic Comprehensive Preventive Medicine Examination

New Patient

99383 Initial comprehensive preventive medicine.

Initial comprehensive preventive medicine evaluation and management of an individual, including an age and gender-appropriate history, examination, counseling/anticipatory guidance/risk factor reduction interventions, and the ordering of appropriate immunization(s), laboratory/diagnostic procedures, new patient; late childhood (age 5 through 11 years).

99384 Adolescent (age 12–17 years).

99385 Adult (age 18–39 years).

99386 Adult (age 40–64 years).

99387 Adult (age 65 years and older).

Established Patient

99393 Periodic comprehensive preventive medicine.

Reevaluation and management of an individual, including an age- and gender-appropriate history, examination, counseling/anticipatory guidance/risk factor reduction interventions, and the ordering of appropriate immunization(s), laboratory/diagnostic procedures, established patient; late childhood (age 5 through 11 years).

99394 Adolescent (age 12–17 years).

99395 Adult (age 18–39 years).

99396 Adult (age 40–64 years).

99397 Adult (age 65 years and older).

A2. Counseling and/or Risk Factor Reduction Intervention.

These codes are used to report services provided to individuals at a separate encounter for the purpose of promoting health and preventing illness or injury. As such, they are appropriate for the specific treatment of tobacco use and dependence. They are appropriate for initial or followup tobacco dependence treatments (new or established patient). For the specific preventive medicine counseling codes, the number of minutes counseled determines the level of billing (codes **99400–99404** for 15 to 60 minutes of counseling).

Preventive Medicine, Individual Counseling

99401 Preventive medicine counseling and/or risk factor reduction intervention(s) provided to an individual (separate procedure); approximately 15 minutes.

99402 Approximately 30 minutes.

99403 Approximately 45 minutes.

99404 Approximately 60 minutes.

Smoking Cessation Counseling

These codes are for face-to-face counseling by a physician or other qualified health care professional, using "standardized, evidence-based screening instruments and tools with reliable documentation and appropriate sensitivity."

99406 For intermediate visit of between 3 and 10 minutes.

99407 For an intensive visit lasting longer than 30 minutes.

Preventive Medicine, Group Counseling

99411 Preventive medicine counseling and/or intervention to treat the risk factor of tobacco use provided to an individual (separate procedure); approximately 30 minutes.

99412 Approximately 60 minutes.

B. Psychiatric Therapeutic Procedures/Codes for Billing

The psychiatric therapeutic procedure billing codes are typically used for insight-oriented, behavior modifying, and/or supported psychotherapy. This refers to the development of insight of affective understanding, the use of behavior modification techniques, the use of supportive interactions, the use of cognitive discussion of reality, or any combination of the above to provide therapeutic change. All of the counseling interventions for tobacco dependence demonstrated to be effective in this Guideline fall under these headings.

It should be noted that these billing codes can be modified for those patients receiving only counseling (psychotherapy) and for others that receive counseling (psychotherapy), medical evaluation, and management services. These evaluation and management services involve a variety of responsibilities unique to the medical management of psychiatric patients, such as medical diagnostic evaluation (e.g., evaluation of comorbid medical conditions, drug interactions, and physical examinations); drug management when indicated; physician orders; and interpretation of laboratory or other medical diagnostic studies and observations. Thus, the use of a psychiatric therapeutic billing code with medical evaluation and management services would be appropriate for the clinician who provides both of the key tobacco dependence interventions documented as effective in the Guideline: counseling and medications.

In documenting treatment for tobacco dependence using the psychiatric therapeutic procedure codes, the appropriate code is chosen on the basis of the type of psychotherapy (e.g., insight-oriented, behavior modifying, and/or supportive using verbal techniques); the place of service (office vs. inpatient); the face-to-face time spent with the patient during the treatment (both for psychotherapy and medication management); and whether evaluation and management services are furnished on the same date of service as psychotherapy.

B1. Office or Other Outpatient Facility

Insight-oriented, behavior modifying, and/or supportive psychotherapy.

90804 Individual psychotherapy, insight oriented, behavior modifying and/or supportive, in an office or outpatient facility, approximately 20 to 30 minutes face-to-face with the patient.

90805 With medical evaluation and management services.

90806 Individual psychotherapy, insight-oriented, behavior modifying, and/or supportive, in an office or outpatient facility, approximately 45 to 50 minutes face-to-face with the patient.

90807 With medical evaluation and management services.

90808 Individual psychotherapy, insight-oriented, behavior modifying, and/or supportive, in an office or outpatient facility, approximately 75 to 80 minutes face-to-face with the patient.

90809 With medical evaluation and management services.

B2. Inpatient Hospital, Partial Hospital, or Residential Care Facility

Insight-oriented, behavior modifying, and/or supportive psychotherapy.

90816 Individual psychotherapy, insight-oriented, behavior modifying, and/or supportive, in an inpatient hospital, partial hospital, or residential care setting, approximately 20 to 30 minutes face-to-face with the patient.

90817 With medical evaluation and management services.

90818 Individual psychotherapy, insight-oriented, behavior modifying, and/or supportive, in an inpatient hospital, partial hospital or residential care setting, approximately 45 to 50 minutes face-to-face with the patient.

90819 With medical evaluation and management services.

90821 Individual psychotherapy, insight-oriented, behavior modifying, and/or supportive, in an inpatient hospital, partial hospital or residential care setting, approximately 75 to 80 minutes face-to-face with the patient.

90822 With medical evaluation and management services.

B3. Other Psychotherapy

90853 Group psychotherapy (other than a multiple-family group).

C. Dental Code –CDT Codes

D1320 Tobacco counseling for the control and prevention of oral disease.

Please Note: The following section is included for informational purposes only.

The National Center for Health Statistics (NCHS), the Federal agency responsible for use of the International Statistical Classification of Diseases and Related Health Problems, 10th revision (ICD-10) in the United States, has developed a clinical modification of the classification for morbidity purposes. The **ICD-10** is used to code and classify mortality data from death certificates, having replaced ICD-9 for this purpose as of January 1, 1999. ICD-10-CM is planned as the replacement for ICD-9-CM, volumes 1 and 2.

An updated July 2007 release **of ICD-10-CM** is available for public viewing. **However, at the time of this printing, the codes in ICD-10-CM are not currently valid for any purpose or use other than mortality coding. Once implemented, this information must be validated as current before use.**

F17 Nicotine dependence

Excludes1: history of tobacco dependence (Z87.82) tobacco use NOS (Z72.0) Excludes2: tobacco use (smoking) during pregnancy, childbirth, and the puerperium (O99.33-) toxic effect of nicotine (T65.2-).

F17.2 Nicotine dependence

F17.20	Nicotine dependence, unspecified
F17.200	Nicotine dependence, unspecified, uncomplicated
F17.201	Nicotine dependence, unspecified, in remission
F17.203	Nicotine dependence, unspecified, with withdrawal nicotine-induced disorders
F17.209	Nicotine dependence, unspecified, with unspecified nicotinc-induced disorders

F17.21 Nicotine dependence, cigarettes
F17.210 Nicotine dependence, cigarettes, uncomplicated
F17.211 Nicotine dependence, cigarettes, in remission
F17.213 Nicotine dependence, cigarettes, with withdrawal
F17.218 Nicotine dependence, cigarettes, with other nicotine-induced disorders
F17.219 Nicotine dependence, cigarettes, with unspecified nicotine-induced disorders

F17.22 Nicotine dependence, chewing tobacco
F17.220 Nicotine dependence, chewing tobacco, uncomplicated
F17.221 Nicotine dependence, chewing tobacco, in remission
F17.223 Nicotine dependence, chewing tobacco, with withdrawal
F17.228 Nicotine dependence, chewing tobacco, with other nicotine-induced disorders
F17.229 Nicotine dependence, chewing tobacco, with unspecified nicotine-induced disorders

F17.29 Nicotine dependence, other tobacco product
F17.290 Nicotine dependence, other tobacco product, uncomplicated
F17.291 Nicotine dependence, other tobacco product, in remission
F17.293 Nicotine dependence, other tobacco product, withwithdrawal
F17.298 Nicotine dependence, other tobacco product, with other nicotine-induced disorders
F17.299 Nicotine dependence, other tobacco product, with unspecified nicotine-induced disorders

O99.3 Mental disorders and diseases of the nervous system complicating pregnancy, childbirth, and the puerperium

O99.33 Smoking (tobacco) complicating pregnancy, childbirth, and the puerperium
Use additional code from F17 to identify type of tobacco.
O99.330 Smoking (tobacco) complicating pregnancy, unspecified trimester
O99.331 Smoking (tobacco) complicating pregnancy, first trimester

O99.332   Smoking (tobacco) complicating pregnancy, second trimester

O99.333   Smoking (tobacco) complicating pregnancy, third trimester

O99.334   Smoking (tobacco) complicating childbirth

O99.335   Smoking (tobacco) complicating the puerperium

T65   Toxic effect of other and unspecified substances

T65.2   Toxic effect of tobacco and nicotine

Excludes2: nicotine dependence (F17.-).

T65.21   Toxic effect of chewing tobacco

T65.211   Toxic effect of chewing tobacco, accidental (unintentional)
Toxic effect of chewing tobacco NOS

T65.212   Toxic effect of chewing tobacco, intentional self-harm

T65.213   Toxic effect of chewing tobacco, assault

T65.214   Toxic effect of chewing tobacco, undetermined

T65.22   Toxic effect of tobacco cigarettes
Toxic effect of tobacco smoke
Use additional code for exposure to secondhand tobacco smoke (Z57.31, Z58.7).

T65.221   Toxic effect of tobacco cigarettes, accidental (unintentional)
Toxic effect of tobacco cigarettes NOS

T65.222   Toxic effect of tobacco cigarettes, intentional self-harm

T65.223   Toxic effect of tobacco cigarettes, assault

T65.224   Toxic effect of tobacco cigarettes, undetermined

T65.29   Toxic effect of other tobacco and nicotine

T65.291   Toxic effect of other tobacco and nicotine, accidental (unintentional)
Toxic effect of other tobacco and nicotine NOS

T65.292   Toxic effect of other tobacco and nicotine, intentional self-harm

T65.293   Toxic effect of other tobacco and nicotine, assault

T65.294   Toxic effect of other tobacco and nicotine, undetermined

Z71   Persons encountering health services for other counseling and medical advice, not elsewhere classified

    Z71.6   **Tobacco abuse counseling**
            Use additional code for nicotine dependence (F17.-).

Z72   Problems related to lifestyle

    Z72.0   **Tobacco use**
            Tobacco use NOS
                Excludes1: history of tobacco dependence (Z87.82), nicotine dependence (F17.2-), tobacco dependence (F17.2-), tobacco use during pregnancy (O99.33-).

Z87   Personal history of other diseases and conditions

    Z87.8   Personal history of other specified conditions
    Z87.82   Personal history of nicotine dependence
                Excludes1: current nicotine dependence (F17.2-).

Appendix D. Key Recommendation Changes From the 2000 PHS-Sponsored Clinical Practice Guideline: Treating Tobacco Use and Dependence

Below is a summary of the substantive changes in recommendations from the 2000 Guideline to the 2008 Guideline Update. These changes include new 2008 update recommendations as well as recommendations that were deleted or changed substantially from the 2000 Guideline.

NEW RECOMMENDATIONS IN THE 2008 UPDATE

Most, but not all, of the new recommendations appearing in the 2008 Treating Tobacco Use and Dependence Update resulted from new meta-analyses of the topics chosen by the Guideline Panel.

1. Formats of Psychosocial Treatments

Recommendation: Tailored materials, both print and Web-based, appear to be effective in helping people quit. Therefore, clinicians may choose to provide tailored self-help materials to their patients who want to quit. (Strength of Evidence = B)

2. Combining Counseling and Medication

Recommendation: The combination of counseling and medication is more effective for smoking cessation than either medication or counseling alone. Therefore, whenever feasible and appropriate, both counseling and medication should be provided to patients trying to quit smoking. (Strength of Evidence = A)

Recommendation: There is a strong relation between the number of sessions of counseling when it is combined with medication, and the likelihood of successful smoking abstinence. Therefore, to the extent possible, clinicians should provide multiple counseling sessions, in addition to medication, to their patients who are trying to quit smoking. (Strength of Evidence = A)

3. For Smokers Not Willing To Make a Quit Attempt at This Time

Recommendation: Motivational intervention techniques appear to be effective in increasing a patient's likelihood of making a future quit attempt. Therefore, clinicians should use motivational techniques to encourage smokers who currently are not willing to quit to consider making a quit attempt in the future. (Strength of Evidence = B)

4. Nicotine Lozenge

Recommendation: The nicotine lozenge is an effective smoking cessation treatment that patients should be encouraged to use. (Strength of Evidence = B)

5. Varenicline

Recommendation: Varenicline is an effective smoking cessation treatment that patients should be encouraged to use. (Strength of Evidence = A)

6. Specific Populations

Recommendation: The interventions found to be effective in this Guideline have been shown to be effective in a variety of populations. In addition, many of the studies supporting these interventions comprised diverse samples of tobacco users. Therefore, interventions identified as effective in this Guideline are recommended for all individuals who use tobacco, except when medically contraindicated or with specific populations in which medication has not been shown to be effective (pregnant women, smokeless tobacco users, light smokers, and adolescents). (Strength of Evidence = B)

7. Light Smokers

Recommendation: Light smokers should be identified, strongly urged to quit, and provided counseling cessation interventions. (Strength of Evidence = B)

RECOMMENDATIONS FROM THE 2000 GUIDELINE THAT WERE DELETED FROM THE 2008 UPDATE

All "C" level recommendations were reconsidered by the Panel, with the goal of limiting those that are based, in part, on Panel opinion. The 2008 Guideline Update has 8 "C" recommendations; the 2000 Guideline had 18. There were additional deletions of recommendations from the 2000 Guideline. Some of these other deletions reflect addressing specific populations differently in the 2008 Guideline update.

1. Advice To Quit Smoking

Recommendation: All clinicians should strongly advise their patients who use tobacco to quit. Although studies independently have not addressed the impact of advice to quit by all types of nonphysician clinicians, it is reasonable to believe that such advice is effective in increasing their patients' long-term quit rates. (Strength of Evidence = B)

2. Types of Counseling and Behavioral Therapies

Recommendation: Aversive smoking interventions (rapid smoking, rapid puffing, other aversive smoking techniques) increase abstinence rates and may be used with smokers who desire such treatment or who have been unsuccessful using other interventions. (Strength of Evidence = B)

3. Medications

Recommendation: Long-term smoking cessation medications should be considered as a strategy to reduce the likelihood of relapse. (Strength of Evidence = C)

4. Gender

Recommendation: The same smoking cessation treatments are effective for both men and women. Therefore, except in the case of the pregnant smoker, the same interventions can be used with both men and women. (Strength of Evidence = B)

5. Pregnancy

Recommendation: Medications should be considered when a pregnant woman otherwise is unable to quit, and when the likelihood of quitting, with its potential benefits, outweighs the risks of the medications and potential continued smoking. (Strength of Evidence = C)

6. Racial and Ethnic Minority Populations

Recommendation: Smoking cessation treatments have been shown to be effective across different racial and ethnic minorities. Therefore, members of racial and ethnic minorities should be provided treatments shown to be effective in this Guideline. (Strength of Evidence = A)

Recommendation: Whenever possible, tobacco dependence treatments should be modified or tailored to be appropriate for the ethnic or racial populations with which they are used. (Strength of Evidence = C)

7. Hospitalized Smokers

Recommendation: Smoking cessation treatments have been shown to be effective for hospitalized patients. Therefore, hospitalized patients should be provided smoking cessation treatments shown to be effective in this Guideline. (Strength of Evidence = B)

8. Psychiatric Illness and/or Nontobacco Chemical Dependency

Recommendation: Smokers with comorbid psychiatric conditions should be provided smoking cessation treatments identified as effective in this Guideline. (Strength of Evidence = C)

Recommendation: Bupropion SR and nortriptyline, efficacious treatments for smoking cessation in the general population, also are effective in treating depression. Therefore, bupropion SR and nortriptyline especially should be considered for the treatment of tobacco dependence in smokers with current or past history of depression. (Strength of Evidence = C)

Recommendation: Evidence indicates that smoking cessation interventions do not interfere with recovery from chemical dependency. Therefore, smokers receiving treatment for chemical dependency should be provided smoking cessation treatments shown to be effective in this Guideline, including both counseling and medications. (Strength of Evidence = C)

9. Children and Adolescents

Recommendation: When treating adolescents, clinicians may consider prescriptions for bupropion SR or NRT when there is evidence of nicotine dependence and desire to quit tobacco use. (Strength of Evidence = C)

10. Older Smokers

Recommendation: Smoking cessation treatments have been shown to be effective for older adults. Therefore, older smokers should be provided smoking cessation treatments shown to be effective in this Guideline. (Strength of Evidence = A)

11. Weight Gain After Stopping Smoking

Recommendation: The clinician should acknowledge that quitting smoking is often followed by weight gain. Additionally, the clinician should: (1) note that the health risks of weight gain are small when compared to the risks of continued smoking; (2) recommend physical activities and a healthy diet to control weight; and (3) recommend that patients concentrate primarily on smoking cessation, not weight control, until exsmokers are confident that they will not return to smoking. (Strength of Evidence = C)

12. Cost-Effectiveness of Tobacco Interventions

Recommendation: Intensive smoking cessation interventions are especially efficacious and cost-effective, and smokers should have ready access to these services as well as to less intensive interventions. (Strength of Evidence = B)

Note: The tobacco dependence treatments shown to be effective in this Guideline still are recommended as highly cost-effective with Strength of Evidence = A. The above recommendation, number 12, was deleted because it refers only to "intensive" smoking cessation interventions.

RECOMMENDATIONS FROM THE 2000 GUIDELINE THAT WERE SUBSTANTIALLY CHANGED IN THE 2008 UPDATE:

The results of meta-analyses or consideration of literature not available for the 2000 Guideline led to substantive changes in some of the 2000 Guideline recommendations. Minor changes in wording are not listed here.

1. Screening and Assessment

2000 Guideline. Recommendation #1: All patients should be asked if they use tobacco and should have their tobacco-use status documented on a regular basis. Evidence has shown that this significantly increases rates of clinician intervention. (Strength of Evidence = A)

2000 Guideline. Recommendation #2: Clinic screening systems, such as expanding the vital signs to include tobacco use status, or the use of other reminder systems, such as chart stickers or computer prompts, are essential for the consistent assessment, documentation, and intervention with tobacco use. (Strength of Evidence = B)

2008 Guideline Update. Recommendation: All patients should be asked if they use tobacco and should have their tobacco use status documented on a regular basis. Evidence has shown that clinic screening systems, such as expanding the vital signs to include tobacco use status, or the use of other reminder systems, such as chart stickers or computer prompts, significantly increase rates of clinician intervention. (Strength of Evidence = A)

2. Types of Counseling and Behavioral Therapies

2000 Guideline. Recommendation: Three types of counseling and behavioral therapies result in higher abstinence rates: (1) providing smokers with practical counseling (problemsolving skills/skills training); (2) providing social support as part of treatment; and (3) helping smokers obtain social support outside the treatment environment. These types of counseling and behavioral therapies should be included in smoking cessation interventions. (Strength of Evidence = B)

2008 Guideline Update. Recommendation: Two types of counseling and behavioral therapies result in higher abstinence rates: (1) providing smokers with practical counseling (problemsolving skills/skills training); and

(2) providing support and encouragement as part of treatment. These types of counseling elements should be included in smoking cessation interventions. (Strength of Evidence = B)

3. Medications

2000 Guideline. Recommendation: All patients attempting to quit should be encouraged to use effective medications for smoking cessation, except in the presence of special circumstances. (Strength of Evidence = A)

2008 Guideline Update. Recommendation: Clinicians should encourage all patients attempting to quit to use effective medications for tobacco dependence treatment, except where contraindicated or for specific populations for which there is insufficient evidence of effectiveness (i.e., pregnant women, smokeless tobacco users, light smokers, and adolescents). (Strength of Evidence = A)

4. Combination Medications

2000 Guideline. Recommendation: Combining the nicotine patch with a self-administered form of nicotine replacement therapy (either the nicotine gum or nicotine nasal spray) is more efficacious than a single form of nicotine replacement, and patients should be encouraged to use such combined treatments if they are unable to quit using a single type of first-line medication. (Strength of Evidence = B)

2008 Guideline Update. Recommendation: Certain combinations of first-line medications have been shown to be effective smoking cessation treatments. Therefore, clinicians should consider using these combinations of medications with their patients who are willing to quit. Effective combination medications are long-term (> 14 weeks) nicotine patch + other NRT (gum and spray), the nicotine patch + the nicotine inhaler, and the nicotine patch + bupropion SR. (Strength of Evidence = A)

5. Children and Adolescents

2000 Guideline. Recommendation #1: Counseling and behavioral interventions shown to be effective with adults should be considered for use with children and adolescents. The content of these interventions should be modified to be developmentally appropriate. (Strength of Evidence = C)

2008 Guideline Update. Recommendation #1: Counseling has been shown to be effective in treatment of adolescent smokers. Therefore, adolescent smokers should be provided with counseling interventions to aid them in quitting smoking. (Strength of Evidence = B)

2000 Guideline. Recommendation #2: Clinicians in a pediatric setting should offer smoking cessation advice and interventions to parents to limit children's exposure to secondhand smoke. (Strength of Evidence = B)

2008 Guideline Update. Recommendation #2: Secondhand smoke is harmful to children. Cessation counseling delivered in pediatric settings has been shown to be effective in increasing cessation among parents who smoke. Therefore, to protect children from secondhand smoke, clinicians should ask parents about tobacco use and offer them cessation advice and assistance. (Strength of Evidence = B)

6. Noncigarette Tobacco Users

2000 Guideline. Recommendation: Smokeless/spit tobacco users should be identified, strongly urged to quit, and treated with the same counseling cessation interventions recommended for smokers. (Strength of Evidence = B)

2008 Guideline Update. Recommendation: Smokeless tobacco users should be identified, strongly urged to quit, and provided counseling cessation interventions. (Strength of Evidence = A)

7. Cost-Effectiveness of Tobacco Dependence Interventions

2000 Guideline. Recommendation: Sufficient resources should be allocated for clinician reimbursement and systems support to ensure the delivery of efficacious tobacco use treatments. (Strength of Evidence = C)

2008 Guideline Update. Recommendation: Sufficient resources should be allocated for systems support to ensure the delivery of effective tobacco use treatments. (Strength of Evidence = C)

8. Tobacco Dependence Treatment as a Part of Assessing Health Care Quality

2000 Guideline. Recommendation: Provision of Guideline-based interventions to treat tobacco use and addiction should be included in standard ratings and measures of overall health care quality (e.g., NCQA HEDIS, the Foundation for Accountability [FACCT]). (Strength of Evidence = C)

2008 Guideline Update. Recommendation: Provision of Guideline-based interventions to treat tobacco use and dependence should remain in standard ratings and measures of overall health care quality (e.g., NCQA, HEDIS). These standard measures also should include measures of outcomes (e.g., use of cessation treatment, short- and long-term abstinence rates) that result from providing tobacco dependence interventions. (Strength of Evidence = C)

9. Providing Smoking Cessation Treatments as a Covered Benefit

2000 Guideline. Recommendation: Smoking cessation treatments (both medication and counseling) should be included as a paid or covered benefit by health benefit plans, because doing so improves utilization and overall abstinence rates. (Strength of Evidence = B)

2008 Guideline Update. Recommendation: Providing tobacco dependence treatments (both medication and counseling) as a paid or covered benefit by health insurance plans has been shown to increase the proportion of smokers who use cessation treatment, attempt to quit, and successfully quit. Therefore, treatments shown to be effective in the Guideline should be included as covered services in public and private health benefit plans. (Strength of Evidence = A)

Index

Silver acetate, 125-126
Skills training, 7, 65-66, 96-99
Skin reactions, nicotine patch, 52
Smokefree policies, 101
Smokeless tobacco. *See* Noncigarette
tobacco use
Smoker identification. *See* Tobacco user
identification
Smoking
cessation, 2. *See also* Tobacco cessation
perspective, 1-2
Smoking Cessation Clinical Practice Guideline
(1996), 1, 12-13
Smoking-related disease, 1
Social economic status smokers, low, 6-7, 33,
151-152
effective treatments for, 145
Social support, 7, 43, 65-66, 76, 96-98,
149, 168
Specialized assessment, research, 81-82
Specific populations, 6, 33, 143. *See also*
specific types
clinical issues for, 148
effective treatments for, 143-147
Staff performance evaluations, 69, 71
State of Health Care Quality Report, 35
Stepped-care interventions, 92
Strength-of-evidence rating, 29-30
Stroke, 11
Substance use disorders, 6, 33, 104, 153-155
effective treatments for, 146-147
Supplementary materials, 43
Surgeon General reports, 18-19
Systems evidence, 33, 130-134
Systems interventions, 5, 32, 67-72

T
Tailored intervention, 80, 93, 149, 151,
153, 155
Telephone quitline, 2, 64, 91-92
counseling, 8, 28, 88-92
Telephone quitline counseling, 8
Theophylline, 115
Tobacco cessation
rates, 6
tobacco user identification, 78-79
Tobacco dependence, 4
brief treatment, 7
as chronic disease, 15-16
Tobacco dependence treatment/intervention,
2, 7, 8, 79-80
cost-effectiveness of, 134-138
coverage, 2
five A's model, 38, 39

Tobacco research, 8-9
Tobacco screening, 77-79
Tobacco tax increases, 16
Tobacco use
in adults, 1
algorithm, 36
assessment, 5, 32, 35-36
cost of, 11
decrease in, 10
dependence, treatment model, 34
morbidity, mortality, 11
screening for, 36
status, 7, 11
Tobacco user, 4, 14
number of, 11
special populations, 6
Tobacco user identification, 40, 69, 70, 78-79
specialized assessment, 79-81
Transgender smokers. *See* Lesbian/gay/
bisexual/transgender smokers
Treating Tobacco Use and Dependence, 13-14
Treatment. *See also* Counseling, Intervention
model, 34
strategies, 17
Tricyclic antidepressants, 116

U-V
Unaided quit attempts, 9-10, 19
Valproate, 116
Varenicline, 8, 42, 44, 45
clinical use of, 53-54
coding rules for, 108
drug interactions, 116
effectiveness of, 113-115
for intensive interventions, 66
Venlafaxine, 119
Veteran's Health Administration, 2
Vital signs, 40, 70, 77

W-Y
Weight gain, 6, 33, 46, 62, 173-176
Withdrawal, 60
Women smokers, 6, 33, 156-157
effective treatments for, 147
Young adults/youth
counseling, 3
tobacco users, 11

Guideline Availability

This Guideline is available in several formats suitable for health care practitioners, the scientific community, educators, and consumers.

The *Clinical Practice Guideline* presents recommendations for health care providers, with brief supporting information, tables and figures, and pertinent references.

The *Quick Reference Guide* is a distilled version of the clinical practice Guideline, with summary points for ready reference on a day-to-day basis.

The *Consumer Version* is an information booklet for the general public to increase consumer knowledge and involvement in health care decisionmaking.

The full text of the Guideline, with and without the text references and the meta-analyses references (listed by evidence table), is available by visiting the Surgeon General's Web site at: *www.ahrq.gov/path/tobacco.htm#Clinic*.

Single copies of these Guideline products and further information on the availability of other derivative products can be obtained by calling any of the following Public Health Service organizations' toll-free numbers:

Agency for Healthcare Research and Quality (AHRQ)
800-358-9295

Centers for Disease Control and Prevention (CDC)
800-311-3435

National Cancer Institute (NCI)
800-4-CANCER